Lambton Central Collegiate V. I.

LAMBTON COUNTY BOARD OF EDUCATION

This book, the property of the Lambton County Board of Education,
is on loan to the pupil and must be returned in good condition.

YEAR	PUPIL	FORM
78	Mark Lemaud	1 H
78-9	Scott Huggett	I J
79	Larry Core	1 N
79	Carl Brooks	2 A.

Automotive Fundamentals

Fourth Edition

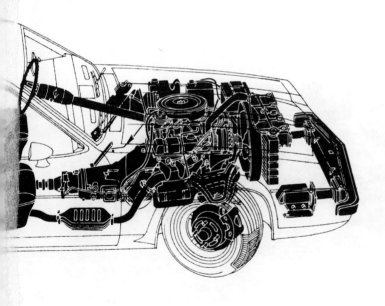

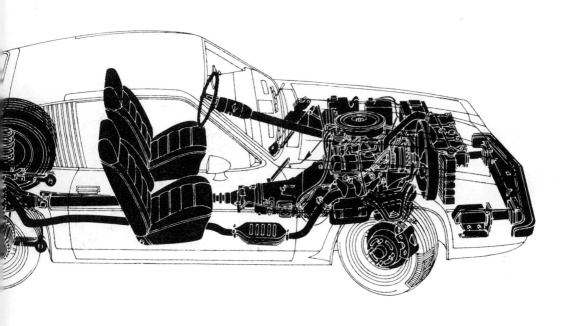

Automotive Fundamentals
Fourth Edition

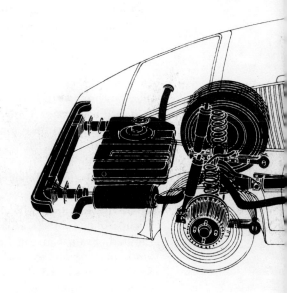

FREDERICK C. NASH

Head, Automotive Mechanics
R. S. McLaughlin Collegiate & Vocational Institute
Oshawa, Ontario

McGRAW-HILL RYERSON LIMITED

Toronto   Montreal   New York   London   Sydney   Auckland
Johannesburg   Mexico   Panama   Düsseldorf   Singapore
Madrid   New Delhi   São Paulo   Paris   Bogotá

PREFACE

This text has been compiled for the beginning student and presents information with respect to the essential features of the principles, construction, and mechanical operation of the modern automobile.

The review questions after each chapter are intended for homework assignments, which the student must complete before attempting the suggested practical assignments. The latter range from the simple, for the beginning student, to the complex, for the more advanced student, and can be completed for the most part on shop units. However, automobiles in service may be used. At crucial points in each assignment, the instructor should inspect the work. The equipment and tools used are basic and should be available in any junior automotive mechanics shop.

The fourth edition makes use of the SI system throughout and also incorporates new information on car maintenance, pollution control, ignition systems, and metrication in the automotive industry. Many new illustrations and drawings highlight the text.

ACKNOWLEDGEMENTS

The author wishes to express his sincere thanks to General Motors Products of Canada, Limited, Imperial Oil Limited, Ford Motor Company of Canada Limited, Snap-on Tools of Canada Limited, the L. S. Starrett Company, Canadian Curtiss-Wright, Limited, Hein-Werner Corporation, Canadian SKF Company Limited, Orange Roller Bearing Company, Incorporated, The Weatherhead Company of Canada, Limited, H. Paulin and Company Limited 1963, Chrysler Canada Limited, Atlas Supply Company of Canada, Champion Spark Plug Company of Canada Limited, Fram Canada Limited, Shell Canada Limited, for their kind permission to use illustrations from their publications. Special thanks are due to Mr. C. H. Jensen for the fine line drawings contained in the text.

ISBN   0-07-082367-7
 234567890   D   654321098
Printed and bound in Canada

CONTENTS

INTRODUCTION
METRICATION IN THE
AUTOMOTIVE INDUSTRY

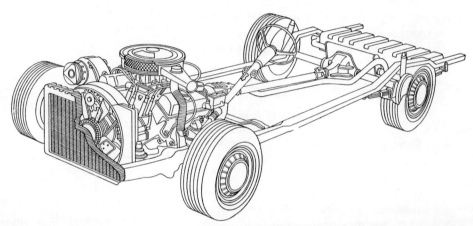

THE NEED TO STANDARDIZE MEASUREMENT

The nations of our planet are becoming more and more dependent on one another. Goods and services are exchanged and traded between countries quickly and easily. World exchange has brought about the necessity for a common system of measurement.

Throughout previous centuries, several measurement systems developed. Most of these systems lacked rational structure. The *inch-pound* (Imperial, United States, Canadian) system using the inch, pint, and pound is one such conglomeration of poorly related units. In this system, each measurement is subdivided into smaller units by a variety of divisor numbers such as 2, 4, 12, 16, 5280, etc.

In contrast to the inch-pound systems, there have been several metric systems, in which units are related to each other by a power of 10. Although metric systems are basically clear and logical, each country added more metric units to suit its particular needs, causing unnecessary complication and confusion. A simple, universal metric system was needed.

THE SI METRIC SYSTEM

In 1960, a new metric system was unveiled. Called SI, from its French name, Système International d'Unités, this system is now replacing all older systems of measurement. Being a metric system, SI is based on the convenience of the decimal number system. Units are related by decimal factors such as 10, 100, and 1000, and a great deal of arithmetic involving SI units can be done by merely shifting the decimal point. For example, in finding the total length in millimetres of three parts which measure 2.4 m, 27 cm, and 42 mm respectively, the conversion of each measurement to millimetres is easily done.

$$
\begin{array}{r}
2.4 \text{ m} \times 1000 = 2400 \\
27 \text{ cm} \times 10 \quad = \quad 270 \\
42 \text{ mm} \qquad\qquad \underline{42} \\
2712 \text{ mm}
\end{array}
$$

SI uses standard prefixes for most units of measurements. For example, the prefix "kilo," meaning 1000, is used for:

  length measurements: one kilometre (1 km) = 1000 metres

  mass measurements: one kilogram (1 kg) = 1000 grams

  volume measurements: one kilolitre (1 kℓ) = 1000 litres

Similarly, the prefix "centi," meaning 1/100, is used with metre, gram, litre, and other SI units. Thus, one centimetre = 0.01 metre, one centigram = 0.01 gram, and so on.

  SI has seven base units:

  metre (m), for measurement of length

  kilogram (kg), for measurement of mass

  second (s), for measurement of time

  ampere (A), for measurement of electric current

  kelvin (K), for measurement of temperature (in everyday use, the degree Celsius (°C) is used instead of kelvin)

  mole (mol), for measurement of amount of substance

  candela (cd), for measurement of luminous intensity

Units for measuring energy, power, force, electrical resistance, etc. are derived from these seven base units.

METRIC CONVERSION IN THE AUTOMOTIVE INDUSTRY

Automotive manufacturers in Canada and the United States are now designing engines and other automotive components in metric units or are planning to do so in the near future. The General Motors Chevette is completely designed and manufactured to metric sizes. Variations of this vehicle are also manufactured in Europe, South America, and Australia, where SI is used; thus, many of the components of the Chevette are now interchangeable throughout the world.

Most of the metric changes occurring in automobiles produced in North America will not be noticed by the average driver, as they will be changes to the sizes of the parts and components that make up the automobile. However, some equipment, such as the speedometer, will be noticeably changed. Speedometers will show both kilometres per hour (km/h) and miles per hour (mph) until all highway mileage and speed signs have been changed. After that, speedometers on new cars will show only kilometres per hour (km/h). Speed limits will be rounded out to the nearest equivalent SI units. For example, 50 km/h instead of 30 mph for cities and towns, and 100 km/h instead of 60 mph for highways, will probably be the new limits.

Soon, all automobile specifications and dimensions will be shown in SI units. Fuel tank, lubrication, and cooling system capacities will be shown in litres; wheel base and tread measurements will be given in millimetres; vehicle mass will be listed in kilograms; tire pressures will be expressed in kilopascals; engine power will be stated in kilowatts; and so on.

One of the changes most noticeable to motorists will be the measurement of gasoline in litres instead of gallons. However, the common practice of buying gasoline by the dollar's worth instead of by units of volume will probably continue.

USING SI

In SI, a unit can be divided into 10 parts, or 100, or 1000, for more accurate measurements; or it can be multiplied by 10 or 100 or 1000 for longer measurements. To simplify the process, all of these divisions and multiples have prefixes which indicate what the factors are. The following prefixes are most commonly used:

micro = 1/1 000 000 (μ)
milli = 1/1000 (m)
centi = 1/100 (c)
deci = 1/10 (d)
deca = 10 (da)
hecto = 100 (h)
kilo = 1000 (k)
mega = 1 000 000 (M)

The most commonly used prefixes for use with all types of measurement in *auto mechanics* are micro, milli, kilo, and mega.

All SI units besides the seven base units are derived from them. Some of these derived units, such as the newton, the joule, and the watt, are used in auto mechanics. Many other units are of interest only to scientists and engineers, and need not concern us here. The units most often used in auto mechanics are covered in the following sections.

Length   The base unit of length is the metre. Like other SI units, the metre can be multiplied and divided by factors of ten by employing the prefixes listed above. Mechanics talk of millimetres of wheel base, or of kilometres travelled per hour.

To visualize a millimetre, think of the thickness of a dime. A micrometre is one thousand times smaller. A metre is one thousand times as long as a millimetre and is about half the height of an average household door. A kilometre equals a thousand metres, or about the length of thirty-three football fields laid end to end.

Area   An area is the surface surrounded by a line or a group of lines. Area is measured in square units of length. The most commonly employed units of area in auto mechanics are the square millimetre (mm²), square centimetre (cm²), and square metre (m²). A square millimetre (mm²) is about the size of the head of a pin. A square centimetre (cm²) is about the size of a sugar cube face. A square metre

is about half the area of the average household door.

Mass   The term *mass* is used to refer to the quantity of material making up an object. This material is composed of particles, atoms, and molecules, which may be densely packed and thus occupy a small volume, or loosely packed and thus occupy a larger volume. For example, a quantity of water might be boiled and transformed into steam; the steam would have the same mass as the water, although it would occupy a much larger volume than the water. Similarly, a kilogram of feathers and a kilogram of lead have exactly the same mass. The kilogram of feathers would occupy a much greater volume than the more densely packed kilogram of lead, however. A dense "heavy" object always has more mass per unit volume than a less dense "light" object. *Relative density* is a term used to describe the density of one object in comparison to the density of some standard object, usually water.

Weight   is a term that is misused every day. Actually, weight means the force of gravity acting on a mass. Thus, mass has weight on earth, but in space, the same mass would have no weight! Weight cannot exist outside of the force of gravity. Gravity's force can vary even on the surface of the earth. It can also be modified by such devices as springs used to partially support a mass, or by immersion of a mass in a liquid of similar density. (Divers often experience a sense of weightlessness, since the human body has a density similar to that of water. You should think twice, therefore, before using the word *weight*. Is weight what you really mean, or is *mass* the accurate word?

The terms are used correctly in the following examples.

1. The **mass** of an automobile is supported by the springs, which offset its **weight**.
2. On the moon, the **weight** of a **mass** is far less than it is on earth.

3. A litre of water has a greater **mass** than a litre of gasoline. This is because water has a greater density than gasoline.
4. Volume unit for volume unit, iron has a greater **mass** than aluminum.
5. The **mass** of the steel ball was not influenced when it was immersed in heavy oil. The effect of the force of gravity, however, was influenced, affecting the **weight** of the steel ball.

Although the old units of measurement, pounds and ounces, referred to both mass and weight very loosely, the SI units refer only to mass. There is no SI unit for weight, as weight is totally dependent on varying gravitational force which can be influenced by various factors (such as springs, etc.). Forces, such as gravity, are measured in newtons (N).

The base unit for mass in SI is the kilogram (kg), and this is the unit most commonly used to measure mass in auto mechanics. A thousandth of a kilogram is a gram. A gram is very small, smaller than the mass of two standard paper clips. Grams (g) are occasionally used in auto mechanics. Smaller units, such as the centigram (cg) and milligram (mg) are used only by engineers and scientists. Vehicle mass and freight mass are measured in tonnes. The metric tonne is equal to 1000 kilograms.

Volume and Capacity   The volume of an object is the amount of three-dimensional space it occupies. Capacity is the amount of three-dimensional space enclosed by a container, such as a box, bottle, tank, etc.

In SI, both volume and capacity may be measured either in cubic units (the cubic centimetre (cm³) is the most commonly used cubic unit) or in litres (ℓ) and millilitres (mℓ). A cubic centimetre is equal to a millilitre.

Sometimes litres and millilitres are called "capacity units" or "fluid units of volume." However, cubic units also are frequently used to measure fluids and the capacity of containers. For example, engine piston displacement in automobiles is measured in litres, but in lawn mowers and motorcycles it is usually measured in cubic centimetres (cm³). Fuel tank capacity is measured in litres, but trunk and truck body capacities are measured in cubic metres (m³).

Temperature   Temperature is measured in degrees Celsius (C°). On the Celsius scale, 0°C (zero) indicates the freezing point of water and 100°C indicates the boiling point of water. No prefixes are used in temperature measurement. 20°C is about room temperature. 30°C is a very warm day. Normal body temperature is 37°C, −20°C is nippy cold, and at −30°C automobiles often have trouble getting started.

Force   Force is defined as that agent which causes a change in the speed of movement of some body or object. Think of a ball hurtling through space. Assuming that the ball was once at rest, some force had to be applied to the ball to put it in motion. Also, if the ball has been travelling through space at a constant rate of speed and the rate suddenly changes, either increasing or decreasing, we must assume that a force was applied to the ball to change the rate of speed.

Force is very common right here on earth. Every time you push, pull, squeeze, or stop something, you are exerting force. Winds and waves exert force, as can machines and tools. When a hammer strikes a nail, force is exerted on the nail, driving it into something else, like a wood board. The most noticeable force on earth is, of course, the force of gravity. Its effect is to pull toward the centre of the earth everything that is on or near the earth's surface. Thus, if you let go of a hammer, it falls—that is, it is pulled toward the earth's centre by the force of gravity.

The SI unit for measuring force is the newton (N). The newton is a *derived unit*. A derived unit is based on a particular relationship between two or more of the base units. A newton is defined as the force required to accelerate a mass of one kilogram one metre per second squared.

In more practical terms, one newton is about the amount of force you must exert with your hand to support one "D" cell flashlight battery against the force of gravity. About one kilonewton (kN) must be applied to lift a mass of 100 kilograms off the ground.

Forces in addition to the force of gravity are exerted on many of the moving and stationary parts in an automobile. The driver, for example, exerts force on the steering wheel, the brake and accelerator pedals, and the seat he or she sits in. For the most part the forces involved in auto mechanics can be expressed in newtons without the use of prefixes. The kilonewton may be used for certain applications, however.

Energy & Work   Energy is the ability to perform work. Work is energy channelled to some purpose. Moving water is possessed of energy. If the energy of moving water is harnessed to some machine, such as a generator, which will provide us with a useful product like electrical power, we can say that the water has been put to work.

Energy which is in motion is called *kinetic energy*. Think of the moving water again. If a dam were put in front of the moving water, the water would stop moving past the point of the dam. Water would collect behind the dam in a resevoir. This water would still have energy as long as we could put it to work, but the energy would no longer be active. This type of energy is called *potential energy*. A truck in motion has kinetic energy. A truck at rest facing down a hill would be said to have potential energy.

In SI, energy and work are measured in joules (J). One joule equals one newton metre

(1J = 1N·m). If the flashlight battery used to describe a force of one newton is to be lifted a height of 1 m, 1 J of work must be done. The potential energy in an average piece of apple pie is about 1200 J. If you ate the piece of pie and wanted to "burn up" all of its potential energy, you would have to lift the flashlight battery one metre about 1200 times!

Joules, kilojoules (kJ), and megajoules (MJ) are most commonly used for measuring energy and work in auto mechanics.

Power   Power is the rate (speed) at which work is done. If one engine can do more work in the same period of time than another engine, the first engine is said to be more powerful than the second engine.

In SI, power is measured in watts (W). One watt is defined as one joule of work or energy released in one second (1 W = 1 J/s). The greater the number of joules produced in one second, the greater the power.

Watts and kilowatts (kW) are used to rate the power capacity of engines, motors, and electrical devices, as well as for other measurements of power.

New North American automobile engines will be rated in kilowatts. Older car engines were rated in horsepower units. It should not be necessary for you to work in horsepower units. However, should it prove absolutely necessary at some time to convert from horsepower to kilowatts, you will find a definition of horsepower and the necessary conversion factors in the conversion chart section at the end of this book. Do not convert from SI to the older system or vice versa unless you absolutely must!

Pressure   Pressure is force applied over a surface area. If you push on a table top with your hand, you are applying pressure to that area of the table top which your hand is touching. If you squeeze a balloon full of air with both hands you are exerting pressure on both the walls of the balloon and the air inside it. If you squeeze too hard, the pressure on the air inside the balloon will be great enough to make the air burst the walls of the balloon, letting the air escape and leaving you short one balloon.

In SI, pressure is measured in pascals (Pa). A pascal is defined as the pressure caused by a force of one newton acting uniformly over an area of one square metre ($1 \ Pa = 1 \ N/m^2$). A single pascal is therefore a very small amount of pressure. Kilopascals (kPa) and megapascals (MPa) are commonly used prefix applications.

Air pressure and *atmospheric pressure* are important concepts for the auto mechanics student to master. As you know, the force of gravity pulls the air towards the earth. The effect of all this air being pulled downwards creates a pressure called atmospheric pressure. Atmospheric pressure is relatively constant at sea level and has been measured at 101.325 kPa. Usually we do not need this degree of accuracy and can talk of standard atmospheric pressure as 100 kPa. All things on earth are under the influence of atmospheric pressure, including our own bodies. Normally we do not notice this pressure, as we are constantly under its influence.

Pressure of less than 100 kPa in a container at or near sea level indicates that a partial vacuum exists in the container. Pressure greater than 100 kPa in a container indicates that the gases inside the container are compressed and are exerting greater pressure against the inside walls of the container than the atmospheric pressure is exerting against the outside walls. Pressure greater than atmospheric pressure is known as air pressure. The walls of the container holding a vacuum or air pressure must be strong. If they are not, the side against which the greater pressure is being applied may burst, much as the walls of our balloon burst from too much pressure.

Tires are inflated; that is, the air inside of a tire is compressed. Air pressure is present in an inflated tire, but is not present in a totally flat tire. What is present both inside and outside of a flat tire is atmospheric pressure. Atmospheric pressure is often referred to as zero air pressure. Tire pressures are given in air pressure above atmospheric pressure. Vacuums occur at times within the parts of the working engine. The presence of a vacuum in the cylinder helps move the fuel-air mixture into the cylinder.

Torque Torque is a twisting or turning force. In SI, torque is measured in newton metres (N•m). If a force of 1 N is applied perpendicular to one end of an arm which is one metre long in such a way that the arm tends to turn about its axis, a torque force of one newton metre (N•m) will be produced in the axis.

Torque is an important concept in discussions of gears, drive shafts, and other parts which experience this force.

Speed/Velocity Speed, or velocity, is distance travelled per unit of time. In SI, speed is expressed in either metres per second (m/s) or kilometres per hour (km/h). In auto mechanics most discussions of speed will use kilometres per hour.

Electrical Current, Resistance, and Pressure Electrical current is the movement of electricity from one point to another. The ampere (A), an SI base unit, is used to measure electrical current.

Electrical resistance is the resistance of a conductor to the passage of electrical current. Resistance is measured in ohms (Ω).

Electrical pressure (potential) has been defined as the amount of power required to cause a constant current of 1 A to flow through a conductor. Electrical pressure is usually expressed in volts (V).

COMMON AUTOMOTIVE APPLICATIONS

Some common automotive specifications are given in SI units in the chart below. Although they do not refer to any particular vehicle or operating condition, they should serve to familiarize you with the type of SI specifications you will see in the near future. Naturally many cars still on the road were built to inch-pound specifications with inch-pound tools and materials. When dealing with such vehicles you may have to convert some inch-pound specifications to SI units. It is likely, also, that you may have to use inch-pound tools if work is to be performed on such vehicles. When this happens, be careful not to confuse SI units, measurements, and tools with inch-pound ones.

TYPICAL METRIC SPECIFICATIONS	
Engine power	110 kW
Engine torque	345 N.m
Bore of cylinder	100 mm
Stroke of cylinder	100 mm
Displacement (engine)	5.7 ℓ
Oil pressure	345 kPa
Manifold vacuum	40 kPa
Coolant pressure	200 kPa
Fuel pump pressure	115 kPa
Fuel tank capacity	75 ℓ
Cooling system capacity	20.5 ℓ
Crankcase capacity	5.7 ℓ
Transmission capacity	4.5 ℓ
Thermostat opens at	82°C
Tire pressure	295 kPa
Speed	km/h
Fuel consumption	ℓ/100 km
Oil consumption	ℓ/1000 km

TYPICAL INCH-POUND SPECIFICATIONS	
Engine power	145 HP
Engine torque	250 lb. ft.
Bore of cylinder	4 in.
Stroke of cylinder	4 in.
Displacement (engine)	350 cu. in.
Oil pressure	35 psi
Manifold vacuum	15 in. of vacuum
Coolant pressure	14 psi
Fuel pump pressure	2 psi
Fuel tank capacity	20 gal.
Cooling system capacity	18 qt.
Crankcase capacity	5 qt.
Transmission capacity	5 qt.
Thermostat opens at	180°F
Tire pressure	28 psi
Speed	mph
Fuel consumption	mpg
Oil consumption	qts. per 1000 mi.

THE AUTOMOBILE 1

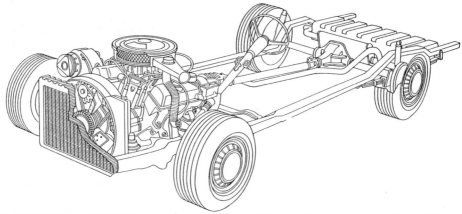

HISTORY OF THE AUTOMOBILE INDUSTRY

The progress of transportation has always been closely related to the progress of civilization. Transportation on water has evolved from the simple raft to the modern ocean liner; in the air, from the first balloon to the supersonic aircraft; and on land, from the unhurried oxcart to the high-speed automobile.

The evolution of the automobile has met with many obstacles including severe legal action and disapproval from the general public. For example, in Great Britain, laws were passed in 1865 which required that at least three people should be in charge of the motor vehicle while it was moving. One person carrying a red flag was to precede the vehicle on foot by at least sixty yards (55 m), to warn drivers and riders of horses of the approaching danger. A speed limit was enforced of two miles per hour (3 km/h) in the city and four miles per hour (6 km/h) in the country. This act was enforced until 1896.

In 1885, Carl Benz of Germany introduced the first road vehicle powered by an internal combustion engine. In 1891, C. E. Duryea produced the first American made gasoline-powered automobiles, and in 1896 Henry Ford built his first car.

Around the turn of the century, gasoline-powered vehicles had stiff competition from steam and electric automobiles. The steam and electrically powered vehicles had the advantage of an abundance of power at low speed, making a transmission unnecessary. The danger of high-pressure steam boilers and the inconvenience of recharging the electric car's batteries reduced their popularity.

The gasoline-powered vehicle, despite the necessity of the transmission, had many advantages:

(a) Producing a large amount of power from a small quantity of fuel

(A) 1896 FORD'S FIRST CAR

(B) 1903 MODEL "A" FORD

(C) 1915 MODEL "T"

(D) 1928 MODEL "A" FORDOR

(E) 1932 V8 TUDOR

(F) 1938 FORDOR

(G) 1949 CUSTOM FORDOR

(H) 1955 MERCURY HARDTOP

(I) 1968 HARDTOP FASTBACK

(J) 1975 ELITE

Fig. 1-1   Evolution of the Automobile   Ford Motor Company of Canada Limited

(A) A typical service station in 1916

(B) A typical service station of today

Fig. 1-2 Automotive Service Stations

Imperial Oil Limited

(b) The ability to travel farther than the steam-powered or electric units without stopping for fuel or water or recharging of the batteries

(c) The fuel required could be replenished easily and quickly.

AUTOMOBILES OF TODAY

The modern automobile is the result of the accumulation of many years of pioneering, research and development. The result is seen in the manufacturing of an efficient, dependable low-cost means of mass transportation. Today's automobile is a highly complicated machine involving numerous mechanical and electrical devices employing many scientific principles.

The servicing of the automobile has also changed greatly to keep in step with the engineering advances of the industry. The early automobile repairer was usually the local blacksmith, since he was frequently the only person in the community who had any experience or the facilities to make repairs to the running gear of the early vehicles. However, the blacksmith lacked the knowledge and experience required to make repairs to the engine or drive line. When these units required repair, the vehicle could not be used until a factory-employed mechanic arrived to service the vehicle.

From 1910 to 1930, the people who called themselves mechanics were self-trained. They gained their knowledge from books and trial-and-error experiences while on the job. Their place of employment was usually some small, dirty dark converted building, located in an off-street lane. By the late 1920s the first specially designed repair garages were constructed.

The tools and equipment which the early mechanic used were poor compared to today's standard, and in many cases were made by the mechanic.

In 1935, the Ontario Government instituted a policy of voluntary Automotive Mechanic Certification and Apprenticeship. In order to be certified, the mechanic had to prove at least five years in the trade, or serve a five-year apprenticeship period, and pass the certification examination. Compulsory certification became law in 1944.

Today's automotive mechanic is well trained and works in a clean, bright, well-ventilated, specially designed automotive service centre.

Automotive service work falls into two categories; preventive service, and breakdown or repair service. The trend today is to prevent breakdowns rather than to repair them.

A thorough knowledge of the parts, and an understanding of the mechanisms are essential in order that faulty conditions in any part

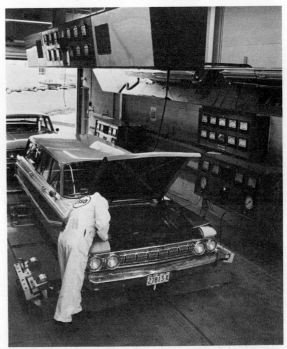

Imperial Oil Limited

Fig. 1-3   Equipment Required for the Modern Automobile

of the automotive mechanism may be detected and corrected. As a result, the mechanic must possess the knowledge, skill, and experience in this field to be successful.

You can only gain experience over a period of time, by putting your best effort into every possible situation that may arise. Experience consists of practising the different small operations over and over again, and mastering the difficulties and problems as they arise. A fully trained mechanic can tackle with confidence what appears to be a new mechanical problem. After an inspection and analysis of the job to be done, the mechanic may discover that the job simply involves a series of small operations which are already familiar. Here again, knowledge is important in order to determine the sequence of the known operations in dealing with the new problem.

One of the most important habits to form, in order to become a thorough mechanic, is to make a final inspection of every job. Cotter pins, patent locking devices, lock washers, loose screws, spacers, small defects, the lubrication of parts, the proper assembly of parts in new positions, and the proper marking of parts are a few of the many small details that are easily overlooked or forgotten. Any one of these may be important in doing a good job. Returned work quickly pulls down a mechanic's reputation, and care should be taken to prevent it.

AUTOMOBILE DIVISIONS

The modern automobile can be divided into two distinct sections known as the *body* and the *chassis*.

THE BODY

The body gives the vehicle its lines and finished appearance. Its chief purpose is to provide comfort and protection for the passengers.

The body section includes the passenger compartment, trunk, bumpers, fenders, radiator grille, hood, interior trim, glass, and paint. A wide variety of body styles, such as two-door and four-door sedans or hard tops, convertibles and station wagons, are available for each chassis model. Various types of interior and exterior trim packages are also available to transform any body style from a plain austerity model to a glamorous show-piece of luxury and splendour. Automobile manufacturers offer a greater selection of models by offering at least three types of trim packages with each model.

The interior of the body is covered with various types of upholstering materials such as cloth, vinyl, and leatherette. Protective padding, placed under the upholstery of the dashboard and roof, and on the seat springs, adds to the comfort and safety of the passengers and driver.

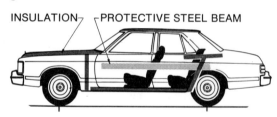

INSULATION⌐   ⌐PROTECTIVE STEEL BEAM

Fig. 1-4   Body Protection and Insulation

Safety glass must be used for all windshields and windows of the vehicle. Safety glass, when broken, does not shatter into sharp splinters. Instead, it has a tendency to crumble into small rectangular shapes. Windshields are extremely strong when struck from the outside of the vehicle, but will crumble when hit by a moderate blow from the inside. This feature helps reduce injury to the passengers should they be thrown against the windshield by a sudden stop.

Many passenger safety devices are now incorporated in body construction. Seat belts, break-away ash trays, concealed interior door

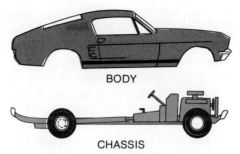

BODY

CHASSIS

Fig. 1-5   Sections of the Automobile

and window handles, padded dash and sun visors, and concealed control knobs are now required by law.

The exterior of the body is protected from rusting and weathering by being either dipped or sprayed with rust inhibitors, then sprayed with several coats of enamel or acrilic paint. Bright metal parts are protected by chromium plating or anodizing.

Repairs to the body of a vehicle are the job of the *Automobile Body Repair Mechanic*.

THE CHASSIS

The chassis is a complete operating unit which can be driven under its own power. It does not include the body parts.

The right and left sides and the front and rear of the chassis are determined from the driver's seat. The right front wheel, for example, is in front of and to the right of the driver.

The chassis can be divided into four sections as illustrated in Figure 1-6.

Repairs to the mechanical parts of the chassis are performed by the *Motor Mechanic,* who will also be called upon to do minor repairs to the body. The modern motor mechanic may specialize in any one of the subsections of the chassis.

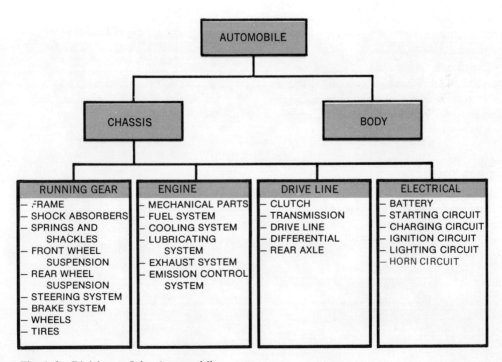

Fig. 1-6   Divisions of the Automobile

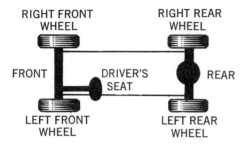

Fig. 1-7   Chassis and Wheel Location

BODY AND CHASSIS CONSTRUCTION

There are two methods of body and chassis construction; the separate body and chassis method, and unibody construction.

In the separate body and chassis construction, the body is held to the frame of the chassis by means of a number of body bolts, passing through the sill or base of the body and the upper part of the frame. To prevent squeaks and rattles, pads of anti-squeak or vibration materials, such as rubber, are placed between the body and the frame where each body bolt is located.

In the unibody construction, the body and the frame of the chassis are combined, thus eliminating the mounting squeaks and rattles.

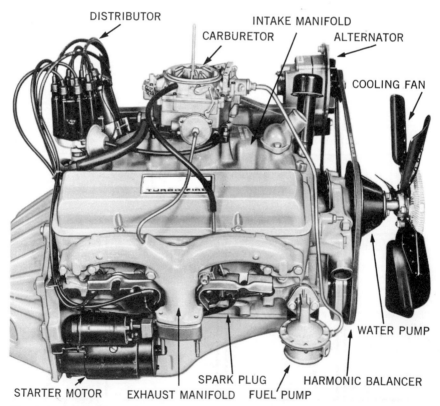

Fig. 1-8   Automobile Engine   General Motors Products of Canada, Limited

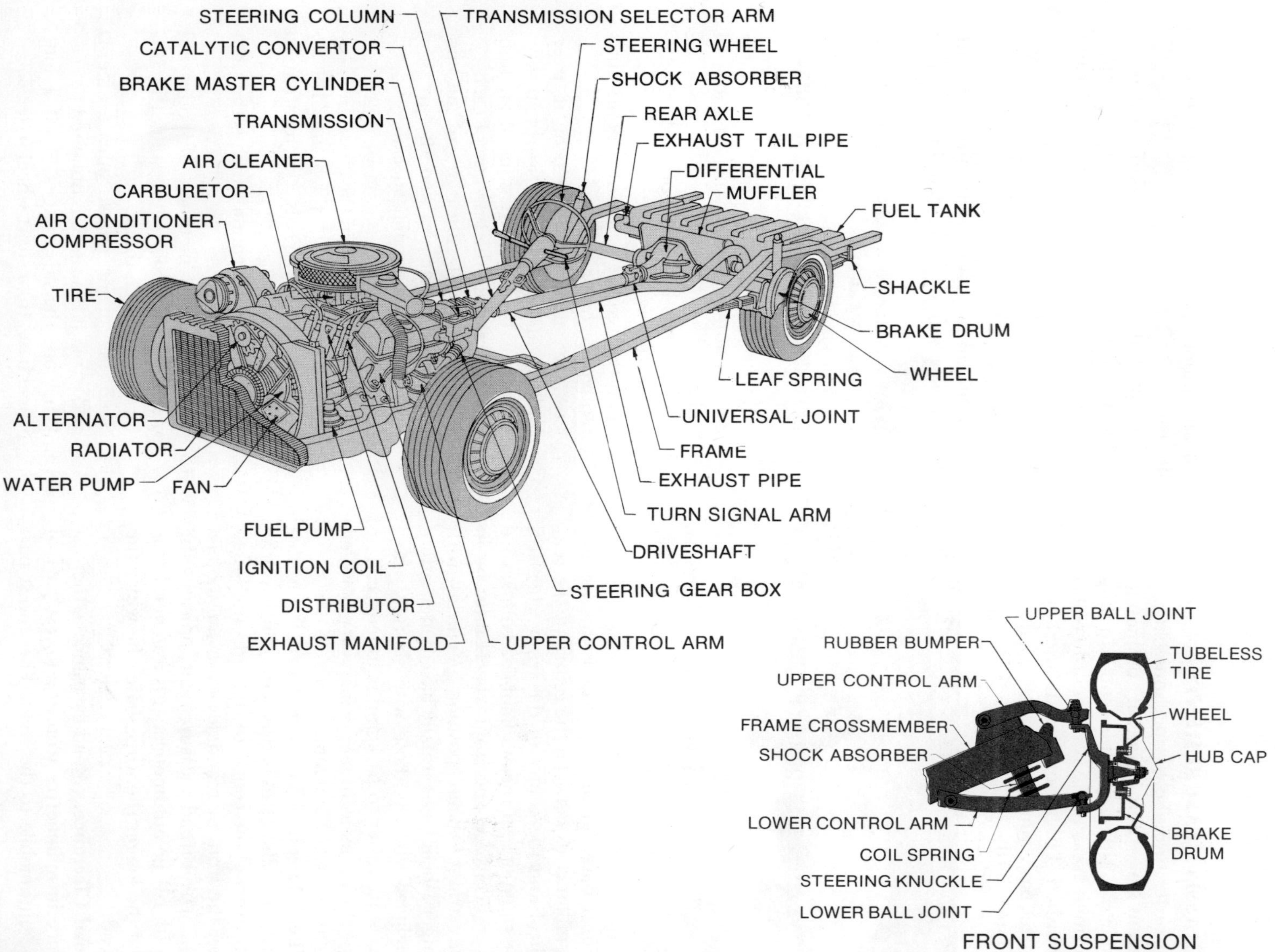

STEERING COLUMN

CATALYTIC CONVERTOR

BRAKE MASTER CYLINDER

TRANSMISSION

AIR CLEANER

CARBURETOR

AIR CONDITIONER
COMPRESSOR

TIRE

ALTERNATOR

RADIATOR

WATER PUMP — FAN

FUEL PUMP

IGNITION COIL

DISTRIBUTOR

EXHAUST MANIFOLD — UPPER CONTROL ARM

TRANSMISSION SELECTOR ARM

STEERING WHEEL

SHOCK ABSORBER

REAR AXLE

EXHAUST TAIL PIPE

DIFFERENTIAL

MUFFLER

FUEL TANK

SHACKLE

BRAKE DRUM

WHEEL

LEAF SPRING

UNIVERSAL JOINT

FRAME

EXHAUST PIPE

TURN SIGNAL ARM

DRIVESHAFT

STEERING GEAR BOX

UPPER BALL JOINT

TUBELESS
TIRE

WHEEL

HUB CAP

BRAKE
DRUM

RUBBER BUMPER

UPPER CONTROL ARM

FRAME CROSSMEMBER

SHOCK ABSORBER

LOWER CONTROL ARM

COIL SPRING

STEERING KNUCKLE

LOWER BALL JOINT

FRONT SUSPENSION

Fig. 1-9   Automobile Chassis

Shell Canada Limited

CHASSIS MEASUREMENTS

In order to make comparisons between different makes and models of automobiles as to their size, riding qualities, and handling ease, definite areas of measurement have been established. The measurements used are called wheel base, wheel tread, and road clearance (Figure 1-10).

General Motors Products of Canada, Limited

Fig. 1-10   Chassis Measurements

Wheel Base.   The wheel base is the distance in millimetres between the centre of the rear wheel and the centre of the front wheel on the same side of the automobile. To measure the wheel base, the front wheels must be in the straight-ahead position. Vehicles with longer wheel bases usually have better riding qualities, whereas those with shorter wheel bases are easier to park and manoeuvre. The wheel base measurements may vary between 2000 mm and 3300 mm.

Wheel Tread.   The wheel tread is the distance in millimetres between the centre of the left tire and the centre of the right tire on either the front or rear axle of the automobile. The wheel tread measurement indicates the width of the automobile. It is a general rule that the longer the wheel base, the wider the tread.

Road Clearance.   Road clearance is the distance in millimetres from the lowest part of the automobile to the road. The lowest part of an automobile is usually the differential housing.

The overall length and width of a motor vehicle is governed by the body design rather than wheel base and wheel tread measurements.

REVIEW QUESTIONS

1. Name three early manufacturers of automobiles and state the date of their first vehicle.
2. Why was the local blacksmith also the local auto repairer?
3. How were mechanics trained in the period (a) 1910-1930, (b) 1935 to today?
4. Compare the working conditions of the early automotive mechanic to those of today's.
5. State the two basic categories of automotive service work.
6. State the requirements of a good automotive mechanic.
7. List the small details which, if overlooked, can result in poor workmanship.
8. Name the two basic divisions of an automobile and state the purpose of each.
9. Name the two classifications of automotive repair mechanics and the areas in which one of these may specialize.
10. What is a chassis?
11. List all of the parts on the chassis and engine diagrams Figures 1-8 and 1-9 according to the chassis classification in which they belong.
12. How do you determine which is the right front wheel?
13. Name the two methods of body and chassis construction and state the difference between them.
14. State the major chassis measurements and explain how each is obtained.
15. What are the advantages of (a) a long wheel base, (b) a short wheel base?

SHOP PRACTICE 2

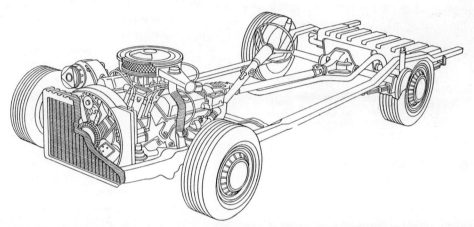

This chapter describes the common hand tools, fastenings, bearings, gaskets, and safety practices that are used in the servicing and repair of the modern automobile.

USE OF TOOLS

Many kinds, types, and sizes of tools are used in automobile work. The progressive and efficient mechanic and engineer learns to use them intelligently. Using the proper tool in the correct way is the first and most important step towards doing successful work. Use each tool for the job for which it is intended. Select the right kind and size of tool for each operation. Do not abuse tools.

HAND TOOLS

Hand tools are the tools owned by the mechanic. They include wrenches of various types and assorted pliers, screwdrivers, punches, chisels, files, gauges, and hammers.

WRENCHES AND ACCESSORIES

There are many types of wrenches available, such as sockets and handles, open end, combination, and tappet. Each type has a special use. The mechanic should always make sure that the wrench fits the bolt head or nut exactly, thereby preventing damage to the nut or bolt head, or personal injury.

A pull on a wrench is preferable to a push, as pulling lessens the possibility of a wrench slipping and causing injury.

The pressure applied to a wrench used to tighten a nut or bolt increases in direct proportion as the diameter of the bolt increases. Learn to judge the amount of pressure required for each size of bolt. The leverage between wrench-handle and socket size is generally between 10 and 12 to 1.

Socket Wrench. The socket and handle wrench is the most efficient type and should be used in preference to other wrenches

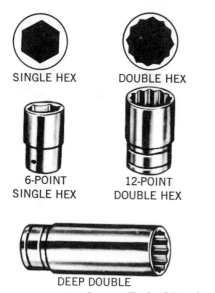

SINGLE HEX   DOUBLE HEX

6-POINT   12-POINT
SINGLE HEX   DOUBLE HEX

DEEP DOUBLE

Snap-on Tools of Canada, Ltd.

Fig. 2-1 Sockets

wherever possible. *Sockets* are cylindrical in shape and have a square opening at one end for the driving handles and either a single or double hexagonal opening at the other end. Sockets are made with either single or double hexagonal positions, are available in standard or deep lengths, and can be used interchangeably with a variety of handles. The opening in a socket is designed to fit snugly over the hexagonal shape of a bolt head or nut. The possibility of the socket slipping off the bolt head or nut is very small and injury to the mechanic is, therefore, unlikely.

For the present, tool manufacturers are providing metric size sockets of all types to fit the socket handles, extensions, and accessories in the size drives that mechanics presently own. There is no indication that the tool manufacturers are intending to change the sizes of these socket drives.

Sockets and handles are available in four different sizes of drives:

(a) The ¼-inch drive or Midget drive for small light work

(b) The ⅜-inch drive or Ferret drive for loosening and tightening nuts, bolts or cap screws up to 10 mm diameter
(c) The ½-inch drive or Standard drive for loosening and tightening nuts, bolts or cap screws 10 mm to 16 mm diameter
(d) The ¾-inch drive or Heavy-Duty drive for nuts, bolts or cap screws larger than 16 mm diameter

Socket-Wrench Handles. Sockets are provided with various types of handles which serve different purposes.

The *speed handle* is in the shape of a crank or a carpenter's brace. It is a fast handle but has not sufficient leverage for large nuts and bolts. The speed handle is recommended, therefore, for use on sockets 16 mm or smaller.

The *T-handle* is also a fast handle, but it too has little leverage. It is also used on sockets 16 mm and smaller.

The *L-handle, flex handle* or *nut spinner* is

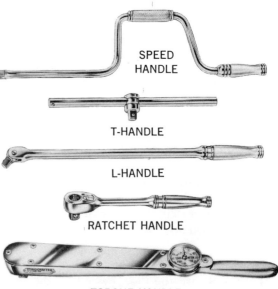

SPEED HANDLE

T-HANDLE

L-HANDLE

RATCHET HANDLE

TORQUE HANDLE

Snap-on Tools of Canada, Ltd.

Fig. 2-2 Socket-wrench Handles

used to tighten bolts or nuts when the socket is larger than 16 mm. It has greater leverage than the above two, but its operation is very slow.

The *ratchet handle* is the same as the *L-handle,* except that it has a built-in ratchet, a device that permits the socket to rotate in one direction only, yet allows the handle to turn in the opposite direction. As a result, it is much faster than the L-handle.

The *torque handle* is also similar to the L-handle. It has a measuring device that indicates, in newton metres (N·m) the amount of torque (twist) put on the fastening. A newton metre is a force of one newton applied to the wrench handle one metre from the socket.

At the present time some torque wrench scales are being manufactured using kilogram per metre or kilogram per centimetre readings. These units are derived units which are not part of the SI system. They are of smaller value than the newton metre.

Socket Accessories. *Extensions* are placed between the socket and the handle to facilitate more convenient operation of the handle when the socket is in a confined area. Rigid extensions are available in various lengths from 50 mm to 600 mm in all four sizes of

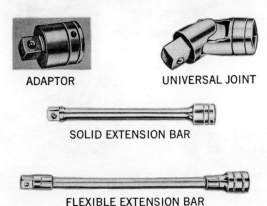

ADAPTOR   UNIVERSAL JOINT

SOLID EXTENSION BAR

FLEXIBLE EXTENSION BAR

Snap-on Tools of Canada, Ltd.

Fig. 2-3   Socket-wrench Accessories

drivers. Flexible extensions are available in ¼-inch and ⅜-inch drivers to assist in reaching awkwardly placed nuts or cap screws. They are not intended for breaking loose or final tightening of nuts, bolts or cap screws.

Universal joints are placed between the socket and the handle when the handle must be used at an angle to the socket. Flex sockets, a combination of a socket and universal joint, are also available for this purpose.

Adaptors are used when it is necessary to join a socket of one size drive with a handle of a different size drive.

Open-End Wrench.   An open-end wrench is not as convenient to use as a socket wrench and is used when a socket wrench cannot be placed over the bolt or nut. The open-end wrench has a U-shaped opening at each end. This opening is machined to specific size to fit a bolt head or nut and the opening is usually at an angle of 15° to the body of the wrench. This angle assists the working of the wrench in close quarters. Turning the wrench over so that the other face is down will enable the wrench to fit the next two flats of the hexagon-shaped nut, bolt or cap screw head, even though the swing of the wrench may be limited to 30°.

Be sure to select the proper size of wrench in order to avoid spreading the wrench sides or damaging the bolt, cap screw or nut.

Tappet Wrench.   A tappet wrench is similar in appearance to an open-end wrench, except that it is longer and thinner. It is used for adjusting valve tappets and must not be used for any other purpose.

Box Socket Wrench.   The box socket wrench has a socket on each end and is used under similar conditions to the open-end wrench. It is safer than the open-end wrench and is used in places where a socket wrench cannot be used easily.

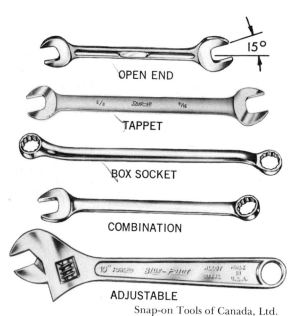

Fig. 2-4 Wrenches

Combination Wrench. This is a combination of two types of wrenches. It has an open-end wrench on one end and a box socket wrench of the same size on the other end.

Adjustable Wrench. Adjustable wrenches are equipped with movable, smooth jaws. They should be used only when no other wrench will fit, because the jaws do not form as snug a fit as those of other wrenches.

PLIERS

Side-cutting or **diagonal pliers** have hardened steel cutting jaws set at an angle and are used for cutting electrical wire and sheet metal, and for pulling out cotter pins.

Combination or **slip-joint pliers** are made with a slip joint at the hinge pin. This permits the jaws to close tightly in one position or to open wider in the other. The pliers are used for gripping round stock, but in so doing, they leave teeth marks. Therefore, they

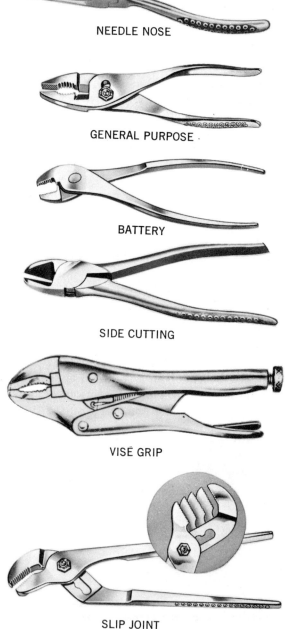

Snap-on Tools of Canada, Ltd.

Fig. 2-5 Pliers

should not be used on finished surfaces, which may be spoiled by such marks. Never use pliers on nut or bolt heads.

Needle-nose pliers are used for fine work on instruments, radio, and other electrical equipment.

Vise-grip pliers are special lever-action, adjustable pliers that can be clamped tightly onto an unfinished surface. Vise-grip pliers may be substituted for other pliers, a vise clamp or a pipe wrench, but should not be used to loosen or tighten nuts, bolts or cap screws.

Battery pliers have specially shaped jaws designed to loosen or tighten battery terminal nuts that have been corroded by acid action.

SCREWDRIVERS

A screwdriver is designed to turn screws. I: the blade is used for prying or chiseling, the stem will bend or the blade will be damaged.

Screwdrivers are available in various sizes and lengths. The blade width and thickness are proportional; the wider the blade the thicker the blade. When a standard type screwdriver is required, the blade width should be approximately the same as the diameter of the screw head. When a Phillips screwdriver is required, the cross should be the size of the slot in the screw head. The length chosen should be sufficient to enable the screwdriver to be turned conveniently on the centre line of the screw.

To prevent damage to screw heads, always choose the proper size screwdriver, maintain proper alignment between the screwdriver and the screw, and be sure the end of a standard screwdriver blade sits flat and square in the screw slot.

Standard screwdrivers have flat blades that fit into the slots in the screw head. The shank may be round or square and the handle be made of wood or plastic. The square-shank

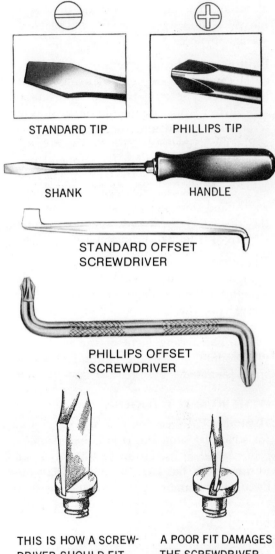

STANDARD TIP   PHILLIPS TIP

SHANK   HANDLE

STANDARD OFFSET SCREWDRIVER

PHILLIPS OFFSET SCREWDRIVER

THIS IS HOW A SCREW-DRIVER SHOULD FIT THE SCREW SLOT.   A POOR FIT DAMAGES THE SCREWDRIVER AND SCREW SLOT.

Snap-on Tools of Canada, Ltd.

Fig. 2-6 Screwdrivers

type is designed so that a wrench may be used to assist in turning the screwdriver.

The width of the blade and the shank length are usually given when specifying the screwdriver size. Generally speaking, the longer the shank length, the wider the blade, although many special long- or short-shank narrow-bladed screwdrivers are available for special purposes.

Phillips screw heads have two slots that cross at the centre and are used to attach body and trim parts. The cross-type slots prevent the screwdriver from slipping out of the slots and scratching or damaging the finished surface.

Phillips screwdrivers are available in four sizes numbered from 1 to 4, number 1 being the smallest, number 4 the largest. The diameter of the screw determines the depth, width, and thickness of the cross; the larger the diameter, the larger the cross. Shank lengths of from 2 to 12 inches are available.

Offset screwdrivers are designed for use in limited space. They are available with either straight or Phillips-shaped ends. In an offset screwdriver the blades are at right angles to the shank and are set 90 degrees from each other. The arrangement of the blades permits continuous turning of the screw when space is limited.

OTHER USEFUL TOOLS

Hammers. A steel *ball peen hammer* is used for striking a punch or cold chisel. A *lead* or *plastic hammer* is used to strike soft metal parts of finished surfaces which would be damaged by a steel hammer. A *rubber-tipped hammer* is frequently used in tire work and for replacing hub caps. (See Figure 2-7).

Always grip any hammer handle near the end.

Punches. Three punches are commonly used in the automotive trade. (See Figure 2-8).

The *starter* punch is tapered and is used to free a pin or shaft.

The *drift* or *pin* punch is used to drive out a shaft or pin. Drift punches come in various sizes, such as 1/4, 5/16, and 3/8 inch. Metric punches and chisels are not yet available.

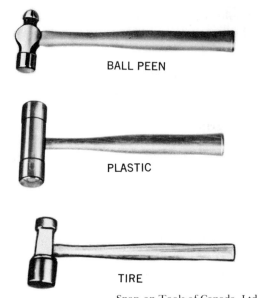

BALL PEEN

PLASTIC

TIRE

Snap-on Tools of Canada, Ltd.

Fig. 2-7   Hammers

The *centre* punch is a sharp steel punch used for marking or making holes to start drills.

Cold Chisels.   The cold chisel is used to cut rivets and bolts or sheet metal. It should never be used in place of a drift punch. Cold

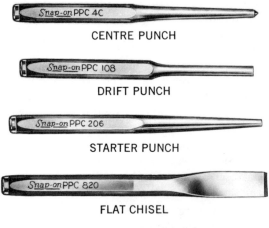

CENTRE PUNCH

DRIFT PUNCH

STARTER PUNCH

FLAT CHISEL

Snap-on Tools of Canada, Ltd.

Fig. 2-8   Punches and Chisels

chisels are available in various shapes and sizes to suit specific jobs.

Files. Files are available in various types of cut, degrees of coarseness, shapes, and sizes.

The degree of cut and coarseness is determined by the number of rows of teeth angled across the face of the file. They may have single rows (single cut) or two rows crisscrossed (double cut). The spacing and size of the teeth determines the coarseness of the file; the larger the teeth and the greater the spacing, the coarser the file. Four degrees of coarseness are available; coarse, bastard, second cut, and fine.

Files are available in *flat, round, half-round, square,* and *three-cornered* shapes. A file should be fitted with a tight-fitting handle to prevent injury to the user and should be cleaned frequently with a file card to preserve the life of the file and prevent scratching of the work.

Coarse files are used when a considerable

amount of metal is to be removed. A fine file is used to smooth a surface.

Hacksaws. A hacksaw consists of a frame and a blade which is placed in the frame with the teeth pointing forward. See Figure 2-10. A thumbscrew is tightened sufficiently to keep tension on the blade. When using the hacksaw, take great care not to twist the blade, as this would cause it to break. A slight

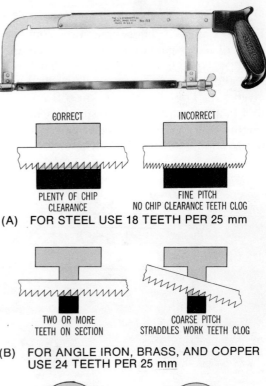

(A) FOR STEEL USE 18 TEETH PER 25 mm

(B) FOR ANGLE IRON, BRASS, AND COPPER USE 24 TEETH PER 25 mm

(C) FOR CONDUIT AND OTHER THIN WORK USE FINE, 32 TEETH PER 25 mm

The L. S. Starrett Company

Fig. 2-10   Hacksaw and Blades

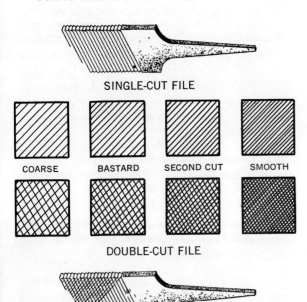

General Motors Products of Canada, Limited

Fig. 2-9   Files

pressure should be applied on the forward stroke, and released with the return stroke. Operate with a slow, steady motion, passing the entire length of the blade over the work.

Blades with 14, 18, 24 and 32 teeth per 25 mm are available. The selection of the right type of blade depends upon the type and shape of the material to be cut. The 18-tooth blade is used by automotive mechanics to cut most materials. The 32-tooth blade is used to cut thin metal and tubing.

Feeler Gauges. There are two common types of feeler gauges, the *flat-strip* type and the *wire* type. Both are made of hardened steel and are accurately ground or rolled to a given size. They vary in thickness from 0.05 to 1.0 mm and are usually supplied in sets (Figure 2-11). Older inch feeler gauges range in size from 0.001 to 0.050 inches.

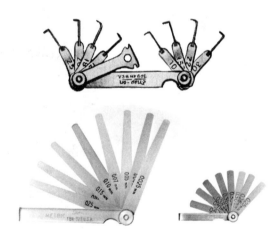

Snap-on Tools of Canada, Ltd.

Fig. 2-11   Feeler Gauges

SPECIAL TOOLS AND POWER TOOLS

Some of the special tools used in the automotive trade are valve-spring compressors, piston-ring compressors, micrometers, dial indicators, taps and dies, pullers, and pipe flaring tools. The special tools are frequently sup-

plied by the shop owner, not by the individual mechanic (Figure 2-12).

Since most special tools are delicate and require special care in use, the beginner must receive complete instruction regarding the tool before using it.

Valve-Spring Compressors. Valve-spring compressors or lifters are used to compress the valve spring to facilitate the removal of the valve retainer lock or keeper from the valve stem. A C-type valve-spring compressor is used when the valves are located in the cylinder head. A standard expansion-type compressor is used when the valves are in the block.

Piston-Ring Compressors. Piston-ring compressors are placed around the piston, covering the rings. As the compressor is tightened, it compresses the piston rings into their grooves on the piston. Then the piston and rod assembly is installed into the cylinder.

Micrometers. Micrometers are precision measuring instruments. Metric micrometers are graduated in steps of 0.01 mm. The older inch micrometers are graduated in steps of 0.001 inches. Both are used to measure the wear on automotive parts and the thickness of adjusting shims.

Dial Indicators. Dial indicators are also accurate precision instruments measuring in steps of either 0.01 mm or 0.001 inches, depending on whether they are metric or inch tools. They are used to measure gear lash, the amount of run out or wobble of a gear, and the trueness of a shaft.

Taps and Dies. Taps and dies are used for cutting threads. Taps are used to cut inside threads, such as in a hole in a casting, whereas dies are used to cut outside threads on pieces of round stock. Taps are available in various types: the *taper tap* for starting a thread, the

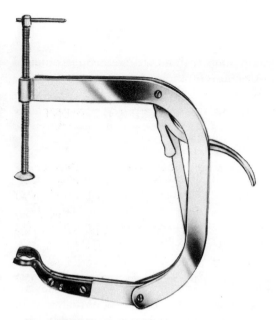

"C" TYPE VALVE-SPRING COMPRESSOR

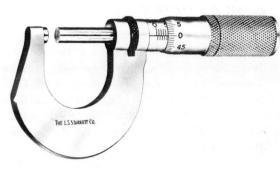

MICROMETER

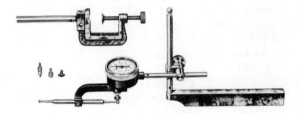

DIAL TEST INDICATOR

EXPANSION TYPE VALVE-SPRING COMPRESSOR

PULLER

Snap-on Tools of Canada, Ltd.
The L. S. Starrett Company

SLIDE HAMMER PULLERS

PISTON-RING COMPRESSOR

TAPS

DIE

Fig. 2-12 Special Tools

plug tap for threading near the bottom of a hole after a taper tap has been used, and the *bottoming tap* to thread to the bottom of a blind hole. Taps and dies are available in many thread types and sizes. Special handles are used to hold both taps and dies during the threading operation.

Pullers.   Pullers come in a variety of types and sizes and are used to remove wheels, gears, and bearings from shafts, or to remove shafts from housings. Each pulling operation differs from the other, and care must be exercised to prevent damage to the parts during pulling.

Power Tools.   These are tools such as valve-refacing machines, valve-seat refacing machines, honing machines, electric drills, hydraulic jacks, and hoisting equipment (Figure 2-13). Since most of this equipment is highly specialized, students should not operate any power tools without first receiving complete instructions on their operation.

CARE OF TOOLS AND EQUIPMENT

HAND TOOLS

Hand tools should be clean, because greasy or oily tools are difficult to hold and use. They should be wiped clean and returned to their proper storage place immediately after use. Adoption of this policy will speed up work.

Good mechanics keep their tools in good repair. Punches and chisels should have mushroom ends removed as soon as they appear; chisels and drills should always be sharp; screwdrivers correctly ground; hammers inspected before use to ensure that the head is not loose nor the handle cracked. Worn or loose ratchets should not be used, as personal injury could result.

(A) 2-POST HOIST	(B) HYDRAULIC JACK	(C) VALVE REFACER
Canadian Curtiss-Wright, Limited	Hein-Werner Corporation	Snap-on Tools of Canada, Ltd.

Fig. 2-13   Power Tools

GROUND RIGHT GROUND WRONG

(A) SCREWDRIVERS

HAMMER HEAD
IS WEDGED ON
HANDLE IN BOTH
DIRECTIONS

(B) HAMMERS

BEFORE AND AFTER DRESSING

(C) CHISELS

Fig. 2-14 Care of Hand Tools

SHOP EQUIPMENT

Shop equipment and special tools should be cleaned and returned to their proper storage place immediately after use, as other mechanics may require them. Power equipment should be lubricated and serviced as required, and electrical cords and plugs should be inspected and serviced frequently.

As mechanics are judged by their tools, a repair shop is judged by its cleanliness and equipment. A cluttered, dirty shop is neither a pleasant nor a safe place to work, nor does it appeal to clients. Customers prefer to do business with an organization that has a clean, neat appearance and employs mechanics who show proper respect and care for tools and shop equipment.

Develop a sense of responsibility toward the tools and equipment that you own or use. This is one of the important steps in becoming a successful mechanic.

AUTOMOTIVE FASTENINGS

An automobile is made up of a number of units and parts, securely fastened together in such a manner that each unit or part may be removed for repairs or inspection.

Threads. Most automotive fasteners that join together the mechanical parts of an automobile are threaded. Threads are classified by the diameter of the fastener and the thread pitch (the distance between corre-

sponding points on one thread and the next) for metric sizes, or, by the number of threads per inch for the inch sizes. Class (quality of finish or fit) may also be added to the thread designation when required.

The automotive industry uses three types of threads: coarse pitch, fine pitch, and extra fine pitch. The *coarse pitch* which, because of the depth of its thread, is not easily stripped or cross-threaded, is used in aluminum and cast-iron where a deep thread is necessary to take hold, and is the most common type used in the automotive industry. The *fine pitch* has more threads making contact per given length and therefore has less tendency than the coarse pitch to work loose with vibration. It is most commonly used in nuts and bolts. The *extra fine pitch* is used for special applications such as thin-walled tubing.

Metric Threads. Metric threads are grouped into diameter-pitch combinations distinguished from each other by the pitch applied to a specific diameter. The diameter of the fastener and its length are given in millimetres. In accordance with ISO standards, metric threads are defined on drawings in the following manner: an "M" specifying a metric thread precedes the diameter size; "×" separates the size from the pitch. If the thread length is given, another "×" separates this measurement from the pitch. When coarse threads are required the pitch is not usually

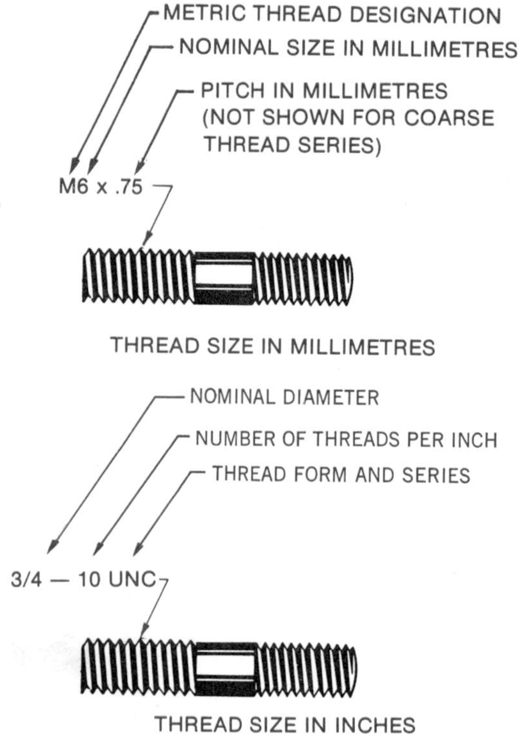

METRIC THREAD DESIGNATION
NOMINAL SIZE IN MILLIMETRES
PITCH IN MILLIMETRES
(NOT SHOWN FOR COARSE
THREAD SERIES)

M6 x .75

THREAD SIZE IN MILLIMETRES

NOMINAL DIAMETER
NUMBER OF THREADS PER INCH
THREAD FORM AND SERIES

3/4 — 10 UNC

THREAD SIZE IN INCHES

Fig. 2-15　Thread Specifications

given, but for fine and constant pitch series threads it is always given.

The *Metric coarse thread pitch* is between the pitches of the old Unified National Coarse and Unified National Fine threads, and it is the most commonly used type in the automotive industry. For this type of fastener, the industry uses a slightly different method of identification. The "M" indicates the standard coarse metric thread and precedes the fastener diameter size which is separated from the fastener length by "×". (e.g., M8 × 20; "M" indicates a metric coarse thread, 8 indicates the diameter size, and 20 is the nominal length of the fastener.)

Inch Threads. Inch threads are available in three types, Unified National Coarse (UNC),

Unified National Fine (UNF), and small machine screw threads. Inch threads are classified as follows: diameter size in inches is given first, followed by the number of threads per inch (pitch) or the thread series (which indicates the shape and number of threads per inch). An "×" separates the thread series from the fastener length. Class (quality of finish and fit) may be added to the thread classification when required. A Unified National Coarse fastener would be identified as follows: 5/16 UNC × 1-1/2. The 5/16 indicates the diameter size, the UNC the thread series, and the 1-1/2 represents the length. For a Unified National Fine fastener the identity would be as follows: 5/16 UNF × 1-1/2. The 5/16 and the 1-1/2 represent diameter size and fastener length respectively, and the UNF the thread series.

Small machine screws (below 1/4") are identified by using number sizes for diameter, with pitch and length in inches. E.g., #10-32 × 1 means the diameter is #10 (.194 inches), the number of threads per inch is 32, and the nominal fastener length is 1 inch.

For nuts and threaded holes in castings the same type of thread information is required as for bolts, cap screws or studs, except for the length, which is proportional to the diameter. This applies to both metric and inch type threads.

SCREWS

Cap Screws. The cap screw is similar to a bolt, but it does not require a nut. It is screwed into a threaded hole. Either coarse or fine thread is used, depending on the type of material into which it is to be screwed.

Machine Screws. Machine screws come in a variety of screw slot and head designs and are available in sizes ranging up to 5 mm in diameter. In the inch system, when the thread di-

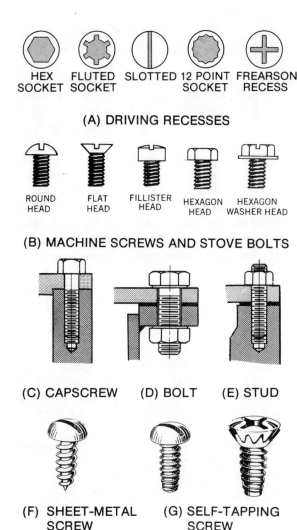

HEX SOCKET FLUTED SOCKET SLOTTED 12 POINT SOCKET FREARSON RECESS

(A) DRIVING RECESSES

ROUND HEAD FLAT HEAD FILLISTER HEAD HEXAGON HEAD HEXAGON WASHER HEAD

(B) MACHINE SCREWS AND STOVE BOLTS

(C) CAPSCREW (D) BOLT (E) STUD

(F) SHEET-METAL SCREW (G) SELF-TAPPING SCREW

Fig. 2-16   Common Automotive Threaded Fasteners

ameter is less than 1/4 inch, it is designated by the number sizes 2, 4, 6, 8, 10, and 12. Machine screws are available in either coarse or fine threads. Identity is by number, e.g. 10-32 (10 is the size, 32 is the number of threads per inch). Machine screws may be threaded into a threaded hole or used with a nut.

Sheet Metal and Self-Tapping Screws. These screws are case-hardened screws that cut or form a thread in metal, plastic, and other materials without pre-tapped holes. They permit rapid installation, since nuts are not required and access is required from only one side of the joint. Various head and screw-slot designs are available.

BOLTS

Several types of bolts with either square, round or hexagonal heads are used as fasteners. The hexagon head type is the one most commonly used in automotive work. The stem of the bolt is threaded to a sufficient length to enable a nut to tighten the parts sufficiently and complete the fastening.

Stove Bolts.   Stove bolts are presently available only in inch sizes and have round heads with screwdriver slots. They are threaded the entire length of the stem, and are available only in the coarse thread series and in sizes of 3/16 inch, 1/4 inch, 5/16 inch, and 3/8 inch. The fastening is completed with a square or hexagon nut.

Studs.   Studs are steel rods with threads at each end, usually a fine thread at one end and a coarse thread at the other. The coarse end is screwed into a threaded hole in a casting, because the coarse thread holds better in cast iron; the other end passes through a hole in the part to be attached. A nut on the outside end completes the fastening.

Nuts.   Several types of nuts are used in the automotive industry. The majority are hexagonal in shape. Some of the common types are plain, castle (castellated), slotted, and self-locking. Slotted and castle nuts have slotted tops, so that a cotter pin may be installed for locking purposes. There are several types of self-locking nuts. One type has the upper threads slightly distorted. When this nut is tightened, the sections are drawn together,

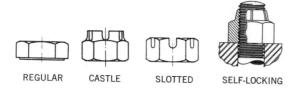

REGULAR   CASTLE   SLOTTED   SELF-LOCKING

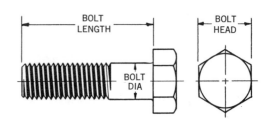

Fig. 2-18   Bolt Measurements

creating friction and locking the nut in position. Another type of self-locking nut is called the interference type, which uses a fibre or soft metal insert near the top; as the nut is tightened new threads are cut in the insert, creating friction which holds the nut in place. A third type (which is illustrated) has thin vertical slots cut in the upper portion of the nut. This upper portion of the nut is smaller in diameter than the bolt. As a result the slotted portion presses tightly against the bolt, holding the nut in place.
NOTE: Self-locking nuts are not reusable.

Flat Washers.   This type of washer is used under the head of a bolt, cap screw or nut, to protect the surface of the parts being joined. The flat washer also helps to distribute the pressure of the fastening over a larger area.

CAP SCREW, BOLT, NUT, AND WRENCH SIZES

Bolt and cap screw sizes are calculated by measuring the diameter of the stem and the length from under the head to the end of the stem (Figure 2-17). The nut size is the largest diameter of the thread. The thread in a nut of specific size will fit the thread on a bolt of the same size and thread. For example, a 12 mm bolt will measure 12 mm in diameter over the thread, and a 12 mm nut will have a 12 mm threaded hole. A knowledge of the standard bolt head and nut sizes will greatly help the student in selecting the proper wrench. The nut sizes are the same as the bolt head sizes. The table below for nut, bolt, and wrench sizes should be memorized.

BOLT AND NUT THREAD SIZE		WRENCH SIZE (BOLT HEAD SIZE)	
METRIC SYSTEM MILLIMETRES AND INCH EQUIVALENTS			
6	(.236)	10	(.394)
8	(.315)	13	(.510)
10	(.394)	17	(.670)
12	(.472)	19	(.750)
INCH SYSTEM FRACTION AND DECIMAL			
1/4	(.250)	7/16	(.438)
5/16	(.312)	1/2	(.500)
3/8	(.375)	9/16	(.562)
7/16	(.438)	5/8	(.625)
1/2"	(.500)	3/4	(.750)

Fig. 2-19   Bolt and Nut Data

LOCKING DEVICES

Locking devices are used to prevent bolts and nuts from working loose with vibration. Every bolt or nut should have a locking device on it to prevent possible accident. It has been said that the locking device is the most imporant device in the automobile. (See Figure 2-18).

The most commonly used locking devices are:

Cotter Pins.   These are long, slender, split metal pins with rounded heads. They are placed through the slots in castellated nuts and through holes in bolts; the split ends are

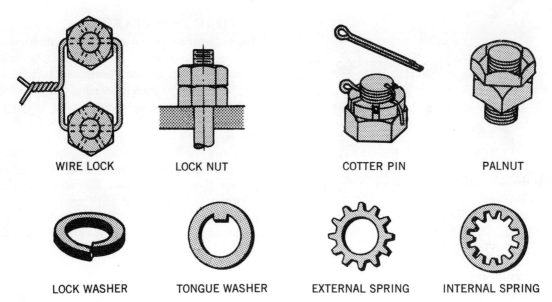

WIRE LOCK   LOCK NUT   COTTER PIN   PALNUT

LOCK WASHER   TONGUE WASHER   EXTERNAL SPRING   INTERNAL SPRING

Fig. 2-20   Locking Devices

then bent apart. This type of lock is one of the best.

Lock Washers and Shakeproof Washers.   Both types are of spring steel and have one or more offset ends. When the nut is tightened, the offset ends are drawn together, creating a great pressure under the nut and forming a tight lock.

Lock Nuts and Palnuts.   When two nuts are drawn tightly against each other, a great pressure is exerted on the threads. This pressure prevents their loosening. The lock nut is a plain nut that is tightened against the nut already in place.

A palnut is a thin, steel, one-thread nut that is frequently used instead of a second plain nut. To lock properly, the palnut should be tightened until the flat side just touches the first nut, then tightened a half-turn more. Palnuts should not be reused.

Tongue Washers.   These are flat washers with a small tongue-like projection on the inner edge. The tongue fits into a groove in the bolt or shaft and prevents the washer from turning. This lock is used in places where the turning motion of a bearing might loosen the nut. For example, the front-wheel spindle has a tongue washer between the outer wheel bearing and the spindle nut.

Wire.   Sometimes wire is placed through a bolt head when space does not permit the use of other locking devices. Wire may be placed through holes in two or more bolt heads, binding them together and making an adequate locking device.

BEARINGS

Every part of an automobile that moves with a rotary or sliding motion is supported in bearings, which reduce friction and wear, if lubricated properly.

Bearings are called upon to do three kinds of work: to take a *radial load,* a *thrust load,* or a *combination* of both. A radial load exerts pressure at right angles to a shaft. A thrust load exerts pressure parallel to or in the direction of the shaft (Figure 2-21).

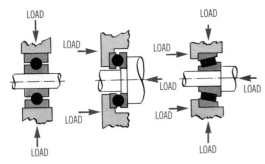

(A) RADIAL   (B) THRUST   (C) COMBINATION
                                       RADIAL AND
                                       THRUST

Fig. 2-21   Bearing Loads

PLAIN BEARINGS

A plain bearing is a bearing with no moving parts. It acts as a lining between a housing and a shaft and is made of metal which is softer than the shaft it supports. Alloys of lead and tin, called *babbitt,* or copper and tin, called *bronze,* are the two most common types of bearing materials. Since most bearing metal is soft and weak, it must be fused to a steel backing for strength. Plain bearings can be either made in one piece or split in two pieces for convenience of assembly. *Piston-pin bushings* and *camshaft bearings* are examples of one-piece plain bearings; *crankshaft main bearings* and *connecting-rod bearings* are examples of the split type. Plain bearings can be designed with flanges that will enable them to support a combination of both radial and thrust loads (Figure 2-22). At least one crankshaft main bearing is designed to support a combination of the radial load and the end thrust load of the crankshaft.

RADIAL   THRUST   COMBINATION   BUSHING

Fig. 2-22   Plain Bearings

ANTIFRICTION BEARINGS

There are five popular types of antifriction bearings: the annular ball bearing, the ball-thrust bearing, the cup-and-cone ball bearing, the straight roller bearing, the tapered roller bearing, and the needle roller bearing.

Antifriction bearings consist of four principal parts; the *cone,* or inner race, which fits over the shaft or spindle; the *cup,* or outer race, which fits inside the wheel hub or other carrier; a series of *balls* or *rollers* which revolve between the cone and cup; and a *cage* or other device to keep the balls or rollers in position between the cup and cone (Figure 2-23).

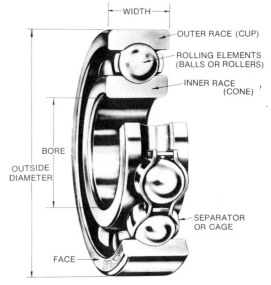

WIDTH

OUTER RACE (CUP)

ROLLING ELEMENTS
(BALLS OR ROLLERS)

INNER RACE
(CONE)

BORE

OUTSIDE
DIAMETER

SEPARATOR
OR CAGE

FACE

Canadian SKF Company Limited

Fig. 2-23   Bearing Nomenclature

When *needle roller bearings* are used, the rollers may or may not be held by a cage, the bore in the housing serves as the cup, and the hardened shaft serves as the cone (Figure 2-24).

Orange Roller Bearing Co., Inc.

Fig. 2-24   Needle Bearings

ANNULAR
BALLBEARING

CUP-AND-CONE
BALLBEARING

CYLINDRICAL
ROLLER
BEARING

TAPERED
ROLLER BEARING

BALL THRUST
BEARING

Canadian SKF Company Limited

Fig. 2-25   Antifriction Bearings

In bearing design, several different methods are used to take care of the different kinds of load. One method uses a separate bearing for each; a second method uses annular ball bearings or straight roller bearings, equipping them with plain thrust washers to carry the thrust load; a third method uses tapered roller bearings or cup-and-cone bearings. The third type is most suitable and most efficient because it supports both kinds of load, takes up less room, and is adjustable.

There are three types of adjustable bearings: the split type of plain bearing, the cup-and-cone ball bearing, and the tapered roller bearing.

GENERAL TYPES		INDIVIDUAL TYPE	TYPE OF LOAD	ADJUSTABLE
Plain		Babbit Bearings Bronze Bushings	Radial, Thrust & Combination Radial, Thrust & Combination	Yes Yes
Ball		Annular Ball Ball Thrust Cup and Cone	Radial Thrust Combination	No No Yes
Roller	Standard	Straight Tapered	Radial Combination	No Yes
	Needle	Straight	Radial	No

Fig. 2-26   Bearing Data

GASKETS

Gaskets are used on many parts of the automobile, such as the engine, transmission, and differential. The purpose of a gasket is to provide a seal between two connecting metal surfaces. To make a metal-to-metal sealed joint without gaskets would require expensive grinding and lapping, in order to make both surfaces smooth enough to resist the leaking of either air or oil pressure. It is for this reason that some sort of soft or flexible material is placed between the surfaces. (See Figure 2-27.)

There are many types of gasket materials used for different purposes. Gaskets are made of special paper, fibre, cork, neoprene, asbestos, copper, copper lined with asbestos, or steel lined with asbestos. Special gasket papers are known by various trade names such as *Vellumoid*. They are paper or cardboard-like materials treated with oil to make them soft and flexible. Gasket pastes are sometimes used, either in place of gaskets or in addition to gaskets to improve their sealing ability.

Oil and Grease Seals. Oil and grease seals are used to prevent leaks between stationary and moving parts and to exclude foreign matter. The seal most commonly used in the automotive industry is the radial seal, which is often referred to as a shaft seal. This type of seal applies a sealing pressure to a rotating shaft to retain the fluid. The sealing insert, made of materials such as leather, neoprene or felt, is held in a metal retainer.

O-Rings. Static O-ring seals are classified as gasket-type seals. When an O-ring is used, a groove is machined in one or both surfaces to be sealed. The O-ring fits into the groove and is compressed, which provides the seal when the parts are tightened together.

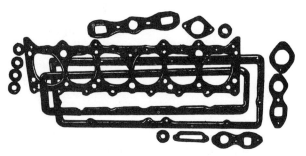

Fig. 2-27   Automotive Gaskets

TYPE OF MATERIAL	AMOUNT OF HEAT	LOCATION OR USE
Asbestos Copper Asbestos Steel Asbestos	Large Amount	cylinder head, manifold, exhaust pipe
Cork Neoprene (Synthetic Rubber)	No Heat	rocker cover, tappet cover, oil pan, fuel-pump cover, timing-gear cover, transmission cover, and differential cover
Velumoid	No Heat	carburetor, fuel pump, transmission, water pump, oil pan, differential, and rear-axle flange
Fibre	Some Heat	where a sealing washer is required

Fig. 2-28   Gasket Data

(A) O-RING SEAL

RADIAL SEAL
APPLICATION

NOMENCLATURE
(B) RADIAL SEAL

Fig. 2-29   Oil and Grease Seals

(A) FLEXIBLE RUBBER TUBING

(B) CONNECTORS

The Weatherhead Company of Canada Ltd.

Fig. 2-30   Flexible Rubber Tubing and
Connections

O-rings are also used to provide a seal between a stationary and a moving part. In this case the groove is cut in one surface only.

TUBING, CONNECTORS, AND FITTINGS

Various types of leakproof tubing are needed in automobiles, for purposes such as:
1. To transfer fuel from the gasoline tank to the fuel pump, then to the carburetor
2. To transmit hydraulic pressure from the master cylinder to the wheel cylinder of the hydraulic brake system

These lines are connected to the units by a variety of connectors and fittings, which eliminate the soldering of connections. Three types of tubing materials are used in the automotive service industry: steel, copper, and flexible hoses.

TUBING

Steel Tubing.   Steel tubing is used by all automotive manufacturers as original equipment for fuel, oil, brake, and vacuum lines. It is formed to the assorted shapes required to join the various units. Steel tubing is difficult to rework or to bend to a different shape.

Copper Tubing.   Copper tubing is soft and pliable when new and can be formed into any desired shape. Copper tubing work hardens (becomes less flareable and more brittle, due to the vibration of the automobile), and a used piece must be annealed before it can be reworked.

Flexible Rubber Tubing.   Flexible tubing consists of three separate layers: a neoprene (synthetic rubber) inner layer, a fabric reinforcement layer, and an outer cover of neoprene. The number of reinforcement layers or plies varies from one to six, depending upon the pressure requirements. The necessary fittings or couplings are permanently attached to the hose. Flexible lines are used where the movement or vibration of the line would cause a rigid line to break. For example, a flexible hose is always used between the frame and the wheel cylinder of the braking system.

Tubing Sizes. The outside diameter of a tube indicates the size. Copper and steel tubing are made in various wall thicknesses, to withstand various amounts of pressure.

Tubing Flares.   In order to use certain types of connectors, it is necessary to flare or spread the end of the tubing. Two methods of flaring are used: the single flare and the double flare (Figure 2-31). The flare is the

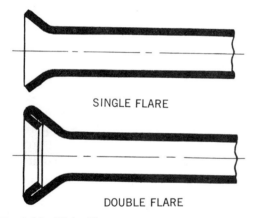

SINGLE FLARE

DOUBLE FLARE

Fig. 2-31   Tube Flares

part of the tubing that is squeezed between the fitting and the nut to form the seal. The single flare is usually used with copper tubing; the double flare is used with steel tubing, because single-flared steel tubing has a tendency to split at the end of the flare.

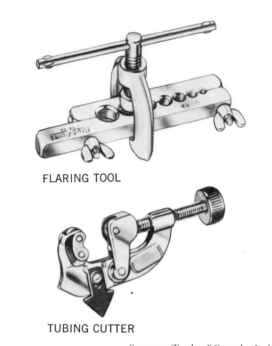

FLARING TOOL

TUBING CUTTER

Snap-on Tools of Canada, Ltd.

Fig. 2-32   Flaring Tool and Tubing Cutter

CONNECTORS AND FITTINGS

To connect the lines to their units, connectors or fittings of various types are used: SAE 45-degree Flared, Inverted Flared, Compression, and Double Compression. There are also a number of shapes used, such as straight, 45° and 90° elbows, and tees (Figure 2-33).

Each of these types consists of a male fitting, a seal, and a female nut. The male fitting is usually threaded on both ends, one end having a pipe thread that is threaded into the unit, the other end having a special fitting thread. Each type of fitting has its own unique thread, which prevents mismating of the connectors.

To prevent damage to the seal when tightening or loosening a connection, hold the fitting with one wrench while turning the nut with another.

To prevent damage to the fittings, a special flare nut wrench is used (Figure 2-34). This wrench eliminates the possibility of rounding the corners or collapsing the centre of the fitting.

SAE 45° Flared Fitting. The male portion of this fitting is threaded tightly into the unit, whereas the female or nut portion is placed on the tubing before flaring takes place. The seal is obtained by compressing the flare on the tubing between the tapered faces of the male and female connectors.

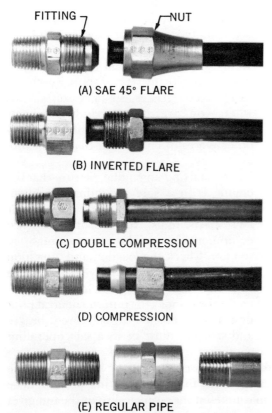

FITTING ⌐   ⌐NUT

(A) SAE 45° FLARE

(B) INVERTED FLARE

(C) DOUBLE COMPRESSION

(D) COMPRESSION

(E) REGULAR PIPE

The Weatherhead Company of Canada Ltd.

Fig. 2-33   Tube Fittings

Inverted Flared Fitting. In this type of fitting, the female connector has an external pipe thread, which is threaded into the unit; the male portion is placed on the tubing before flaring takes place. The seal is produced by compressing the flare on the tubing in the same manner as for the SAE 45° fitting. This type of connector provides the best seal and is used on brakeline connections.

SAE Compression Fitting. This type of fitting does not require a flared tubing, but uses instead a compression sleeve or olive. The sleeve is placed on the tubing between the nut and the fitting, and the seal is produced by compressing the sleeve tightly onto the tubing as the connection is tightened.

Snap-on Tools of Canada, Ltd.

Fig. 2-34   Flare Nut Wrench

SAE Double Compression Fitting. This connection requires neither flared tubing nor compression sleeves. The seal is produced when the tubing is crimped by the male fitting as it is forced against the female nut.

Hose Clamps. Some low-pressure neoprene or rubber hoses, such as gasoline lines or radiator hoses, do not have permanently attached end-fittings. Instead, the end of the hose is placed over the plain neck of the fitting, and held in place and prevented from leaking by a hose clamp. Hose clamps are tightened by stove bolts, worm screws, or the spring tension of the clamp (Figure 2-35).

SINGLE WIRE   STRAP AND BOLT

WORM GEAR

H. Paulin & Co. Limited 1963

Fig. 2-35   Hose Clamps

SAFETY PRACTICES

Safety is everyone's business, and safe work habits are another important step towards becoming a successful automotive mechanic. Listed below are a few important safety habits for the beginning student. Study the list and add any other rules that will apply to your particular situation.

1. Fire is a constant threat in any automotive shop. Therefore, use gasoline only as a fuel. Do not, under any circumstances, use it as a cleaning agent. If gasoline is spilled, wipe it up immediately, and place the wiping cloths outside or in a safe place to dry.

    Oily rags and waste are other potential fire hazards and *must* be kept in covered metal containers.

    Fire extinguishers are available for use on various classes of fires. The most com-

mon type of extinguisher for gasoline or oil fires is CO_2 (carbon dioxide). Know the location of the fire extinguishers in your shop and how to operate them.

2. Exhaust fumes from internal-combustion engines contain carbon monoxide fumes. These fumes are poisonous and can cause asphyxiation and death. Do not run an engine in a shop or garage unless a suitable pipe is connected to the exhaust system to conduct the fumes out of the building, or unless at least three large windows, or two windows and one door, are wide open while the engine is running and for some time after the engine has stopped.

3. If it is necessary to work under a car, make certain that the jack is properly in place. Solid safety stands must always be placed under the car in case the jack should slip.

4. Wear safety glasses at all times when you are working in any type of shop. Be sure to wear safety glasses, goggles, or shields when you are using grinding wheels (bench, valve or disc machines) and any other pieces of equipment that may cause eye injury.

5. Before starting an engine, be sure that the engine is in a safe operating condition. Check the oil and coolant levels. Check for loose parts, tools, trouble lights, and test equipment that might become caught in the fan. Check the location and operation of the controls, particularly to make sure that the gear-shift lever or automatic transmission selector is in the neutral position. If the vehicle is to be moved, brakes and steering must be in a safe operating condition.

6. When loosening nuts or bolts, make sure that your fingers are not in a position to be jammed if the wrench slips or the nut gives suddenly. A pull on the wrench is always preferred to a push as it lessens the possibility of the wrench's slipping and causing injury.

7. When a hoist is to be used, be sure that the support plates between the hoist and the vehicle are so placed as to support the vehicle safely, but not damage any of the vehicle's parts. If the vehicle is to be left up on the hoist for a long period of time, special safety stands should be placed under the vehicle.

PRACTICAL ASSIGNMENTS

a. Tools. Go to the tool board and locate all the tools described in this chapter.

b. Fastenings. Obtain from the instructor some sample fastenings. Study these and be prepared to identify them according to their type, size, and type of thread.

c. Bearings. Study some sample bearings and be prepared to identify them according to their type, the type of load they support, and whether they are adjustable.

d. Cut a Gasket. Use a sheet of paper that can simulate gasket material and a suitable part which requires a gasket.

1. Place the paper on the part to be fitted.
2. Hold the material on the part and, with the peen of a ball peen hammer, tap lightly around the bolt holes. This operation produces holes in the gasket material of the same size and location as those on the part. Place bolts through the holes of the gasket material and the part. This will

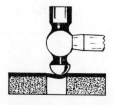

Fig. 2-36 Cutting a Gasket

hold the gasket material in position while you finish cutting the gasket to the shape of the object.

Your skill in cutting gaskets will be due partly to the lightness with which you tap the paper. Remember that the blow should be heavy enough only to cut the paper and not to damage the object under the gasket material. (See Figure 2-36.)

3. In some cases it is not practical to cut all parts of the gasket with a hammer. If necessary, the gasket may be finished by trimming with scissors.
4. When a gasket is to be made for a part where the hammer method cannot be used, because of the danger of breaking the part, cover the surface of the part with a light coating of grease and place the gasket material on top. Press your hand around the edges of the part; an imprint of the part will be formed on the gasket material. Cut out the imprint with scissors.
5. Show your finished gasket to the instructor.

e. Fittings. Obtain from the instructor sample tubing fittings. Study them and be prepared to identify them as to type and size.

f. Tubing. Obtain from the instructor copper tubing, tubing cutters, and tube flaring tools. Using the tubing cutters, cut off a piece of tubing 50 mm in length. Place the tubing in the proper size hole in the flaring clamp bar and tighten the clamp bar, making sure that the tube is flush with the top of the bar on the tapered side of the hole. Place the flaring point in the centre of the tubing; tighten the screw to form the flare on the tubing. When the screw has been tightened sufficiently to form the flare, remove the flare attachment and clamp bar (Figure 2-37). Have the instructor inspect your work.

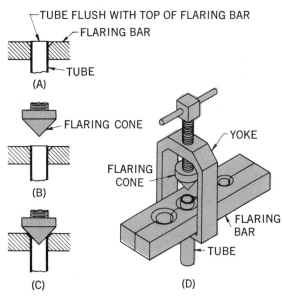

Fig. 2-37   Tube Flaring

g. Jack Up a Vehicle. After suitable instruction is given by the instructor as to the operation of hydraulic jacks and the proper placing of safety stands under a vehicle, jack up the front end of the vehicle and place safety stands in a position suitable for the removal of the front wheels. Jack up the rear of the vehicle, and place the safety stands in a suitable place for the removal of the rear axle assembly. Have the instructor inspect your work; then reverse the above procedure and remove the jacks properly.

REVIEW QUESTIONS

1. Name four ways in which the progressive and efficient mechanic uses tools intelligently.
2. State a good safety rule to apply when using any type of wrench. Why?

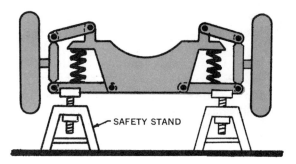

(A) FLOOR STANDS

(B) HOIST STANDS

Fig. 2-38   The Use of Safety Stands

3. Describe a socket.
4. State the name, size and uses of the four common types of socket drives.
5. Name and describe four types of socket handles.
6. Name and state the purposes of four socket accessories.
7. Sketch and identify (a) an open-end wrench, (b) a tappet wrench, (c) a box-socket wrench, (d) a combination wrench, (e) an adjustable wrench.
8. Name four types of pliers and state where each should be used.
9. Name three ways in which a screwdriver blade may be damaged by improper use.
10. State how the proper blade or point size, and handle length should be selected for (a) a standard, (b) a Phillips screwdriver.

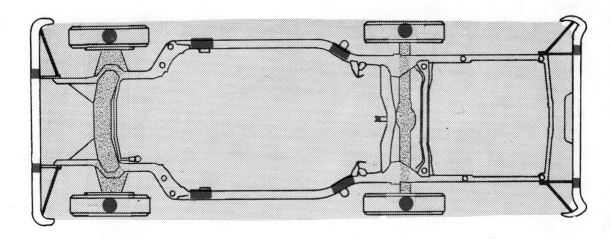

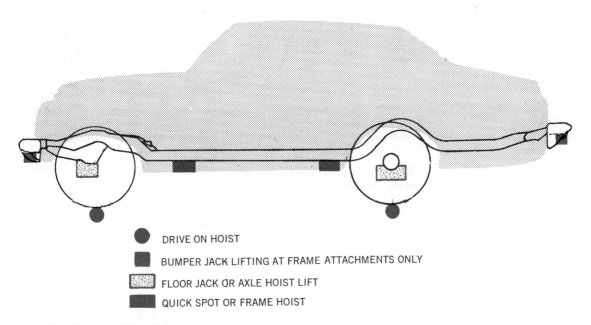

● DRIVE ON HOIST

■ BUMPER JACK LIFTING AT FRAME ATTACHMENTS ONLY

▦ FLOOR JACK OR AXLE HOIST LIFT

■ QUICK SPOT OR FRAME HOIST

Fig. 2-39 Vehicle Lifting Points

11. State how damage to screwheads may be prevented.
12. Where should a hammer handle be held?
13. State the difference in appearance between a starter and a drift punch.

14. Give two precautions which are required when using a file.
15. When should a 32 teeth per 25 mm hacksaw blade be used?
16. Explain the use of (a) valve-spring compressors, (b) piston-ring compressors.

17. Why must micrometers and dial indicators be handled with care?
18. What is used to cut threads (a) on a piece of round stock, (b) in a drilled hole?
19. Name three types of taps and state when each should be used.
20. Give three reasons why a mechanic takes good care of hand tools.
21. Name three ways by which a garage can be made more appealing to customers.
22. Name the two types of thread commonly used on motor vehicles, and state the difference in appearance between the two threads.
23. What type of thread is always found in cast iron? Why?
24. What advantages has the fine thread?
25. Explain in detail the following thread classifications: (a) M8 × 1.25, (b) ¼" − 28 UNF.
26. What is the difference between a bolt and a cap screw?
27. How are machine screws identified?
28. What is a self-tapping screw?
29. Explain why self-locking nuts do not loosen.
30. List the proper wrench size for the following nuts and bolts: (a) 1/2" bolt (b) 5/16" nut, (c) 10 mm cap screw, (d) 8 mm nut.
31. How is the size of a bolt or cap screw determined?
32. Name four types of locking devices, and explain how each one accomplishes its purpose.
33. By means of a sketch, show the proper method of installing a cotter pin.
34. Explain why bearings are used.
35. Describe the following types of bearing loads: (a) radial load, (b) thrust load, (c) combination load.
36. Name the four major parts of a ball or roller antifriction bearing.
37. Name the types of bearings that are adjustable.
38. What are the advantages of combination bearings?
39. Make a chart showing the following information: (a) three general types of bearings, (b) individual types of bearings, (c) the type of load each bearing can carry, (d) whether or not the bearing is adjustable.
40. What is the purpose of a gasket?
41. Name three places where Vellumoid gaskets may be used.
42. How may a gasket be made for a part which would be damaged by a hammer blow?
43. What is the difference between an oil seal and a gasket?
44. What are the advantages of tube fittings?
45. What is meant by work hardening?
46. Why must steel tubing be double flared?
47. Name the type of tube fitting that requires (a) a flared tube, (b) a compression sleeve.
48. How is the mismating of tube fittings prevented?
49. What type of fire extinguisher is used on gasoline fires? Where is that type of extinguisher located in your auto shop?
50. When must safety glasses be worn?
51. How might asphyxiation occur in a shop? How can it be prevented?
52. Name three items to be checked, for safety reasons, before an engine is started.
53. What are safety stands? Why are they used?

THE RUNNING GEAR 3

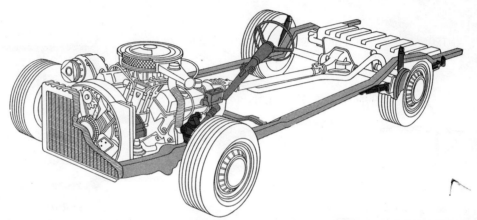

The Running Gear consists of the frame, suspension systems, steering gear and linkage, wheels, tires, and braking system.

THE FRAME

The frame is used to support all of the various units of the chassis and body, and to keep these units in correct alignment with one another. It usually extends the entire length of the automobile. The frame must be strong enough to withstand the many twists, shocks, vibrations and distortions which occur when the car is standing or running on uneven roads.

Maximum strength and minimum mass are the essential characteristics of an automobile frame. An exceptionally strong frame could be made if solid steel beams were used, but such a frame would be far too heavy to be practical. To make the strong, light frame needed for an automobile, *channel section* is used. It is a specially constructed U-shaped beam made of light but tough steel alloy.

The frame consists of two long pieces of channel section called *side-members,* connected near each end by *cross-members.* At the rear, the side-members are arched upwards over the rear axle to provide clearance for the vertical movement of the axle, and to keep the frame in a low-slung position. On older automobiles, in addition to the two cross-members, diagonal cross-members are often used to provide extra bracing. These diagonal members are located about midway along the frame and form an X- or K-pattern.

Small triangular plates or brackets, known as *gussets,* are welded at points where cross-members and side-members intersect. Gussets serve as additional braces and help keep the frame in correct alignment.

In some late-model automobiles, the manufacturers have completely eliminated the frame side-members from the passenger

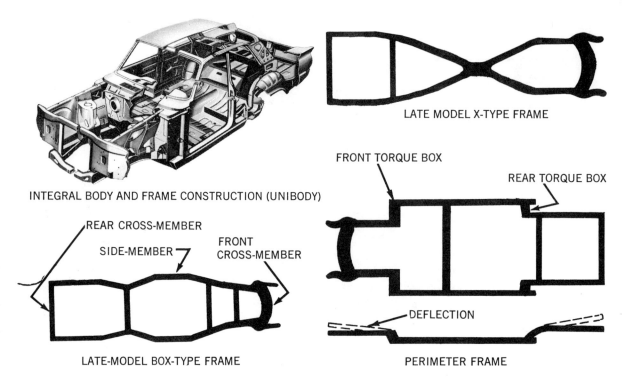

INTEGRAL BODY AND FRAME CONSTRUCTION (UNIBODY)

LATE MODEL X-TYPE FRAME

LATE-MODEL BOX-TYPE FRAME

PERIMETER FRAME

Fig. 3-1   Automobile Frames

Ford Motor Company of Canada Limited

compartment area, reducing the number of humps in the floor. The strength of this type of frame depends entirely upon X-members.

Another popular frame is the *box-girder* type. With this design, resistance to twists and distortion depends upon the box-like construction of the two side-members. In some automobiles the box-girder type side-members are placed at the outer edges of the body compartment and are angled in to permit a narrower frame over the front and rear wheels. This type of construction also reduces the humps in the floor of the passenger compartment.

The perimeter frame uses torque boxes on each side of the frame, located at either, or both, the cowl and rear door areas. These permit the front and rear frame sections to deflect as the wheels move across uneven road surfaces.

Some automobiles do not have a separate frame. Instead, certain of the body members have been greatly reinforced and these, along with the body panels, serve as the automobile frame. The advantages of this type of construction are a reduction in body rattles and squeaks and higher degree of safety. This type of construction is called *integral body and frame construction,* or *unibody.*

SUSPENSION SYSTEM

SPRINGS AND SHACKLES

The wheels and axles are suspended by springs that support the weight (i.e., the

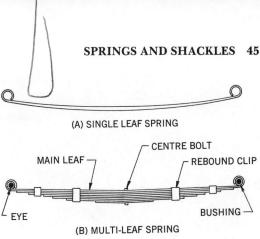

(A) SINGLE LEAF SPRING

(B) MULTI-LEAF SPRING

Fig. 3-3   Leaf Springs

springs partially counteract the force of gravity acting on the mass) of the vehicle. The springs absorb the road shock as the wheels encounter holes or bumps and keep the jarring up-and-down action of the axle from being carried through to the frame and body (Figure 3-2).

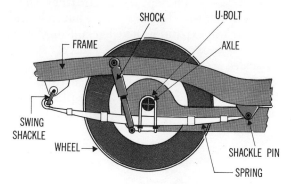

Fig. 3-2   Springs, Shackles, and Shocks

Only the parts of the automobile attached to the frame benefit from the spring action. The weight carried by the springs is called *sprung weight. Unsprung weight* is the name given to the parts of the automobile that are not protected by the spring action. Such parts depend only on the tires for the reduction of road shock. The front and rear axles are examples of unsprung weight.

Springs may be single-leaf, multi-leaf, or coil springs, or a torsion bar may be used.

Leaf Springs. The *multi-leaf spring* is an assembly of flat steel plates, of graduated lengths, called leaves (Figure 3-3). The longest leaf is known as the main leaf and has a *spring eye* at each end, fitted with a bronze or rubber bushing to reduce friction and wear. The other leaves are known as numbers 2, 3, 4 etc. A bolt, called a *spring centre bolt,* passes through the centre of the leaves, holding them together and preventing them from moving lengthwise. *Rebound clips* are placed

near the ends of some leaves to prevent their separating.

The *single-leaf spring* replaces the multi-leaf assembly on some automobiles. The leaf is shaped like the multi-leaf assembly, thin at the ends and thicker in the centre. Its action is the same as the multi-leaf type.

The spring assembly acts as a flexible beam and is usually fastened at both ends to the car frame and at the centre to the axle. To provide flexibility and strength and to reduce flattening, the spring leaves are made of a specially heat-treated steel alloy known as *spring steel.*

When a load is placed on the frame, both types of leaf spring flatten, thus increasing the distance between the spring eyes. If the spring eyes were rigidly fastened to the frame, the distance between the eyes could not change and, therefore, there would be no spring action. To allow the springs to lengthen and shorten, one end of the spring is attached to the frame by means of a pair of swing links known as a *spring shackle* (Figure 3-4). The other end of the spring is attached by a *spring bolt* to a bracket on the frame called a *spring hanger.* The shackle must be free to oscillate; therefore the spring bolt is not clamped tightly. If it were clamped tightly, proper spring action would be prevented and the spring would break.

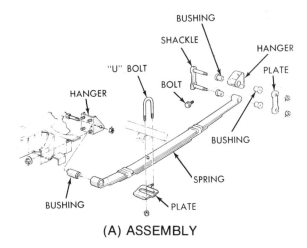

(A) ASSEMBLY

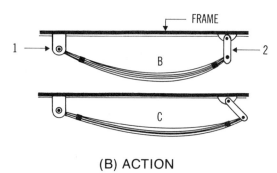

(B) ACTION

Chrysler Canada Ltd.

Fig. 3-4   Spring Shackles

If the spring is attached to the top of the axle, it is said to be *overslung;* if the spring is attached to the underside of the axle, it is said to be *underslung.* Usually, front leaf springs are overslung and rear leaf springs are underslung.

U-bolts fasten the leaf spring to the axle. The nuts holding these U-bolts must be tightened securely in order to prevent spring breakage at or near the centre bolt. Where the spring rests on the axle, the axle is flattened. The flattened part is known as the *spring seat.*

Leaf springs are required to take care of the following forces: the weight of the vehi-

cle, the forward and backward stresses, and the side thrust and rear axle torque.

Coil Springs.   A *coil spring* is a heavy steel coil placed between the frame and the wheels in such a way that it supports the weight of the car. The force of gravity acting on the vehicle's mass puts the spring under an initial compression. The spring will further compress as the wheel passes over a bump in the road or will expand if the wheel encounters a hole. When coil springs are used, spring shackles are not required. The flexing action of the spring is taken up by the surrounding support mechanism. On coil spring suspended rear axles, special support arms,

(A) SPRING

(B) APPLICATION

Fig. 3-5   Coil Spring

track bars, torque arms and stabilizer bars are required to absorb the forces applied to the rear axle. When coil springs are used in the front suspension system, the upper and lower control arms of the front suspension system absorb these forces.

Torsion Bars. In *torsion-bar suspension,* the torsion bar replaces the spring. Spring action is produced by torsion, a twisting effect, along a long bar. The rear end of the bar is attached to the frame through an adjustable anchor; the front end is attached to the lower control arm. The up-and-down movement of the wheel as it goes over a bump twists the bar, causing a spring action (Figure 3-7).

When the torsion bar loses some of its tension, proper front vehicle height may be maintained by adjusting the anchor cams to compensate for this loss.

Special struts, placed between the lower control arm and the frame, absorb the fore-and-aft movement; the upper and lower control arms absorb all the other forces placed on the front wheels.

rubber ball is dropped on the floor.) This additional action is undesirable and results in an uncomfortable ride. To reduce this additional flexing action *shock absorbers* or "shocks" are fastened between the axles and the frame.

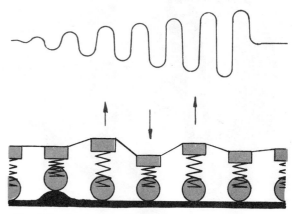

Fig. 3-7   Spring Oscillation

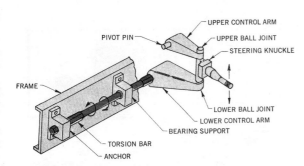

Fig. 3-6   Torsion-bar Suspension

SHOCK ABSORBERS

When a vehicle goes over a bump, the spring compresses, expands, or flexes and will continue to compress, expand, or flex several times before returning to its original position (Figure 3-8). (A similar action is seen when a

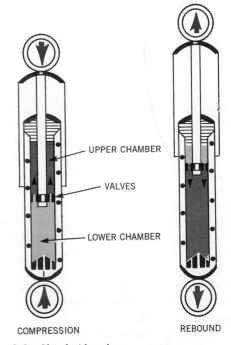

Fig. 3-8   Shock Absorbers

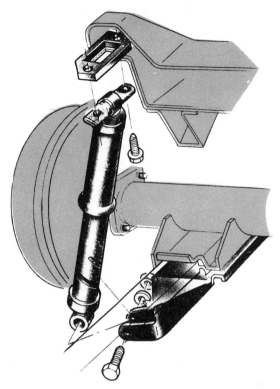

General Motors Products of Canada, Limited

Fig. 3-9   Rear Shock-absorber Mounting

shocks, since better riding qualities are obtained when a longer stroke with less resistance is used.

Insulating rubbers are used to prevent squeaks and rattles between the shock absorber mounting brackets, the frame, and the suspension bracket. Front shocks are usually placed inside the coil spring when coil springs are used. In other types of suspension systems, the shock absorber is mounted in any convenient position.

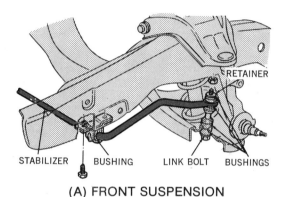

(A) FRONT SUSPENSION

Most late-model shock absorbers consist of a telescoping tube partially filled with a fluid that can pass through a restricted passage from one part of the tube to the other. When the tube is compressed or expanded, the fluid flows through the restricted opening, causing a slowing-down action on the telescoping tube. The rate of flow through the opening varies, depending on the severity of the road shock, and as a result it dampens the additional flexing action of the spring.

Front shock absorbers have resistance in both directions, while rear shocks have more resistance when they are extended than when they are compressed. Rear shocks have less resistance and a longer stroke than the front

(B) REAR SUSPENSION

Fig. 3-10   Stabilizer and Tie-rod Bars

Stabilizer Bars or Sway Bars. Stabilizer bars or sway bars are used to help control the rolling side-to-side motion of a vehicle when the vehicle rounds a curve. They have no influence on the up-and-down motion of the suspension system when the vehicle encounters road bumps.

The stabilizer bar is a spring steel bar bent in the form of an L at each end. Each end is fastened by rubber-mounted links to the lower control arm. The centre portion of the bar is free to twist in rubber-mounted frame brackets.

When the vehicle is level, the bar moves evenly up and down with the lower control arms. When the body tends to roll outwards, as the vehicle rounds a curve, the control arm on one side of the vehicle will be at a different height from the other. This causes a twisting action in the centre portion of the bar. This twist or torque increases the spring pressure on the low side and reduces the pressure on the high side. This helps to resist the rolling action (Figure 3-11).

REAR SUSPENSION

Rear suspension systems may be of either the *leaf spring* or *coil spring* type. When leaf springs are used, they must take care of the following forces: the weight of the vehicle, the forward and backward stresses, side thrust, and rear axle torque.

On coil-spring suspended rear axles, the upper and lower control arms and the sway bar absorb the forces applied to the rear axle. The lower control arm prevents the fore-and-aft movement of the axle and acts as a track bar to maintain proper alignment of the rear wheels; the upper control arm absorbs rear end torque, and acts as a stabilizer when a separate sway bar is not used.

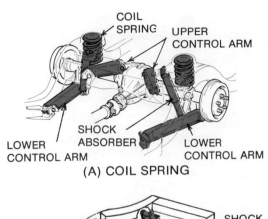

(A) COIL SPRING

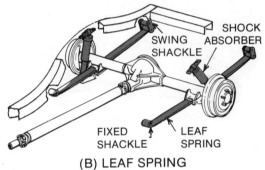

(B) LEAF SPRING

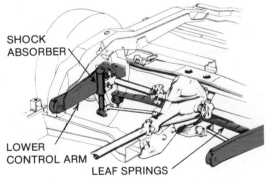

(C) TRANSVERSE LEAF SPRING

Fig. 3-11   Typical Rear Suspensions

FRONT SUSPENSION

Solid Axle.   When a solid front axle is used, both front wheels are tied together by a solid

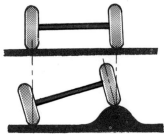

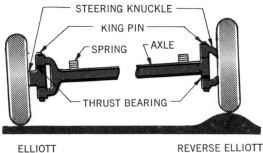

STEERING KNUCKLE

KING PIN

SPRING   AXLE

THRUST BEARING

ELLIOTT   REVERSE ELLIOTT

(A) RIGID

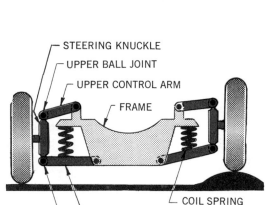

STEERING KNUCKLE

UPPER BALL JOINT

UPPER CONTROL ARM

FRAME

COIL SPRING

LOWER CONTROL ARM

BALL JOINT

(B) INDEPENDENT

Fig. 3-12   Front Axles

I-beam. As one wheel moves up and down to meet the irregularities of the road, the wheel on the opposite end of the axle will be influenced by the movement (Figure 3-12).

With this type of axle, the steering knuckle is attached to the axle and pivoted by a king pin. A thrust bearing between the knuckle and the axle eye end permits easy pivoting while transferring the force of gravity. Bushings between the king pin and the steering knuckle reduce friction and wear. Rigid axle ends may be of the *Elliott* or *Reverse Elliott* type.

Independent Front-Wheel Suspension. In this type of suspension, each front wheel is independently supported by a coil spring, leaf spring, or torsion bar. Since no solid I-beam axle links the two wheels together, either wheel may move up or down without disturbing the other wheel. Independent front-wheel suspension is used on all late-model automobiles.

Independent front-wheel construction consists of an upper and lower control arm and the steering knuckle. The inner ends of the control arms are free to pivot on brackets or shafts, which in turn are attached to the

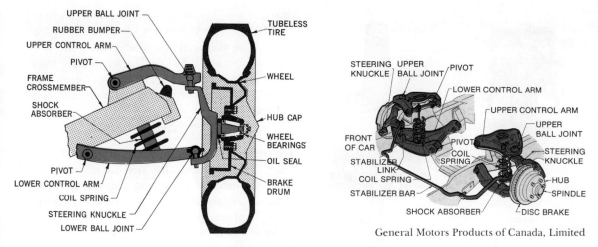

General Motors Products of Canada, Limited

(A) COIL-SPRING SUSPENSION

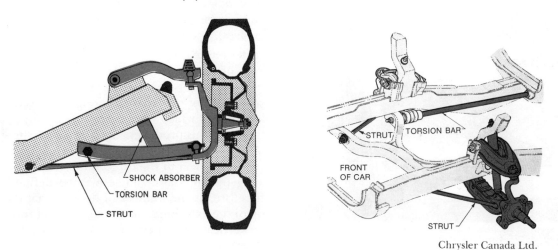

Chrysler Canada Ltd.

(B) TORSION-BAR SUSPENSION

Fig. 3-13 Types of Front Suspension

frame. The outer ends of the control arms are attached to the steering knuckles through ball joints. These ball joints are designed to provide up-and-down movement, pivoting movement, and any combination of both. A coil spring, placed between the lower control arm and the frame, or a torsion bar used in place of the lower control arm mounting

bracket or shaft, transfers the weight of the vehicle from the frame to the suspension system.

The lower control arm is longer than the upper and this, along with the arrangement of the linkage, keeps the point of road contact in a straight up-and-down line as the control arms move up and down over road bumps.

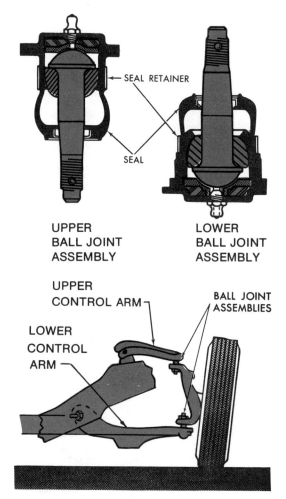

UPPER
BALL JOINT
ASSEMBLY

LOWER
BALL JOINT
ASSEMBLY

UPPER
CONTROL ARM

BALL JOINT
ASSEMBLIES

LOWER
CONTROL
ARM

Fig. 3-14　Control-arm Ball-joint Assemblies

STEERING AND STEERING GEOMETRY

ACKERMAN PRINCIPLE

The automobile uses the Ackerman Principle of steering. Only the wheels and steering knuckles swing, instead of the whole axle, as in a horse-drawn wagon. With this steering principle, the steering knuckle arms are placed at an angle of 100° to 105° instead of 90° to the wheel spindle. As a result of this ar-rangement, the inner wheel turns at a greater angle than the outer wheel when the vehicle makes a turn. When the vehicle is being driven in a straight line, the wheels are paral-lel. The Ackerman Principle of steering is used with both solid and independent front axles.

STEERING GEOMETRY

In order to assure stability and ease of steer-ing, and to minimize tire wear, the front wheels must be in correct alignment. Front-end or steering geometry is the term given to the interrelated angles between the axles, wheels, and other front-end parts and the frame. The names of the angles used in steer-ing geometry are: caster, camber, ball-joint or king-pin inclination, toe-in (measured in mil-limetres), and toe-out-on-turns.

Caster angle is the tilt of the axle towards the front or rear of the vehicle. Because of "cas-ter", the wheels contact the road behind the weight line of the axle. The weight line is the line along which the force of gravity is directed. This produces a trailing effect, simi-lar to that of a furniture caster, which helps to steer the wheel in the direction in which it is being pulled. Caster angle may be defined, therefore, as the number of degrees that the top of the axle, king pin or ball joints tilt from the vertical toward either the front (negative caster) or rear (positive caster) of the vehicle (Figure 3-15a).

Camber angle is the tilt of the front wheels from the vertical that tends to bring the point of contact between the tire and road more di-rectly under the load line. An outward tilt is called positive camber, and an inward tilt is called negative camber (Figure 3-15b).

Ball-joint or **king-pin inclination** is the angle between a line drawn through the centre of the upper and lower ball joints and a vertical line. Its purpose is to return the wheels to the straight-ahead position after a turn has been made (Figure 3-15c).

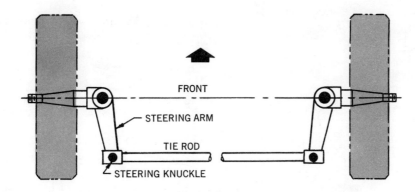

FRONT

STEERING ARM

TIE ROD

STEERING KNUCKLE

(A) WHEN CAR MOVING IN A STRAIGHT LINE

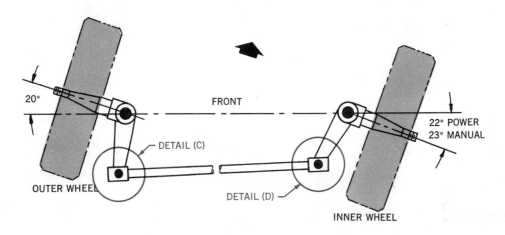

20°

FRONT

22° POWER
23° MANUAL

DETAIL (C)

OUTER WHEEL

DETAIL (D)

INNER WHEEL

(B) WHEN CAR MAKING A TURN

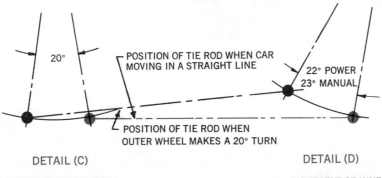

20°

POSITION OF TIE ROD WHEN CAR
MOVING IN A STRAIGHT LINE

22° POWER
23° MANUAL

POSITION OF TIE ROD WHEN
OUTER WHEEL MAKES A 20° TURN

DETAIL (C)

MOVEMENT OF OUTER
WHEEL STEERING KNUCKLE

DETAIL (D)

MOVEMENT OF INNER
WHEEL STEERING KNUCKLE

INNER FRONT WHEEL ON A TURN ALWAYS TURNS A FEW DEGREES MORE THAN OUTER FRONT WHEEL

Fig. 3-15   Ackerman Principle of Steering

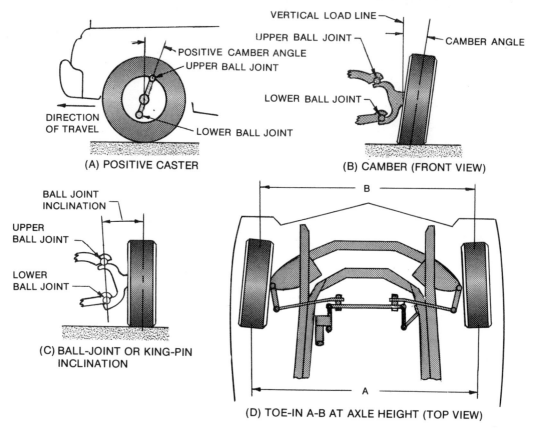

(A) POSITIVE CASTER

(B) CAMBER (FRONT VIEW)

(C) BALL-JOINT OR KING-PIN INCLINATION

(D) TOE-IN A-B AT AXLE HEIGHT (TOP VIEW)

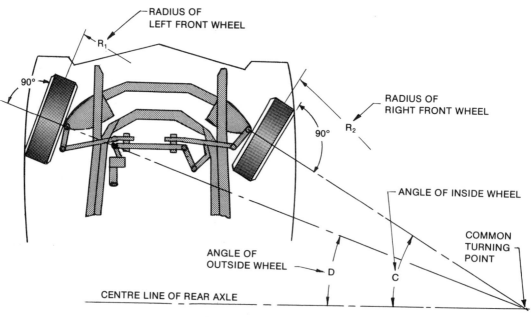

(E) TOE-OUT ON TURNS (TOP VIEW)

Fig. 3-16   Steering Geometry

Toe-in occurs when wheels are angled towards one another so that they are closer together at the front than at the back when viewed from the top. Toe-in is the difference between the centre-to-centre distances. (A − B = toe-in as shown in Figure 3-15d). Its purpose is to offset the undesirable cone rolling effect caused by camber.

Toe-out-on-turns (Figure 3-15e) is the amount of spread, or difference in angles, steered by the inner and outer wheels when the vehicle makes a turn. Since the automobile uses the Ackerman Principle of steering, the inner wheel steers at a sharper angle than the outer wheel; hence the wheels must spread apart at the front during turns.

Before front-wheel alignment can be checked and set, the front suspension parts must be in good condition, and the tracking of the front and rear wheels must be correct.

Tracking means that the front and rear wheels must rotate along parallel lines. Wheels that track properly prevent excessive tire wear and maintain steering stability.

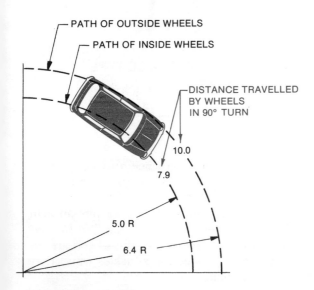

DIMENSIONS IN METRES

Fig. 3-17 Difference in Wheel Travel as Car Makes a 90° Turn

STEERING SYSTEMS

Steering systems vary greatly in design but, regardless of the type used, they achieve practically the same result. They provide me-

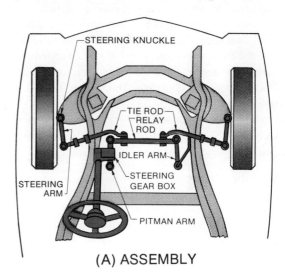

(A) ASSEMBLY

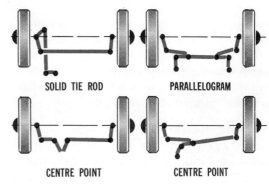

SOLID TIE ROD   PARALLELOGRAM

CENTRE POINT   CENTRE POINT

(B) LINKAGE TYPES

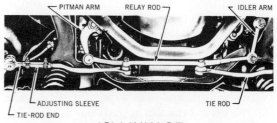

(C) LINKAGE

Ford Motor Company of Canada Limited

Fig. 3-18 Steering System

chanical advantage over the front-wheel *steering knuckles,* offering the driver control of the front wheels with a minimum of effort. They not only assist the driver in turning the steering knuckles in any desired direction, but also aid him in holding the front wheels in position. Without a proper steering system (Figure 3-18), any irregularities in the road would cause the front wheels to be turned or deflected regardless of how the driver held the steering wheel.

The steering gear can be divided into two sections: the steering linkage and the steering gear.

Steering Linkages. Steering linkages of various designs are used, but they all contain similar basic components. The pitman arm, relay rod, tie rods, and steering-knuckle arms are used to transmit the steering effort from the steering box to the steering knuckles. An idler arm, pivoted in a bracket attached to the frame, holds and guides the relay rod at the end opposite to the pitman arm (Figure 3-18). All steering rods are attached to one another through ball joints, which permit movement in any direction. Some of these rods are adjustable in order to maintain proper front wheel alignment (Figure 3-19).

Steering Gears. Two common types of steering gears are the recirculating-ball and the worm-and-roller type. The *recirculating-ball* type consists of a large ball nut or gear rack mounted on a worm shaft. The nut is driven by hardened steel balls, which circulate in grooves in the nut or gear rack and in the worm. As the worm shaft is turned by the steering wheel, the nut or gear rack moves up or down on the worm. This movement rotates a gear on the sector or pitman arm shaft.

In the *worm-and-roller* type, the worm gear on the end of the worm shaft meshes directly with the roller of the sector, or pitman arm

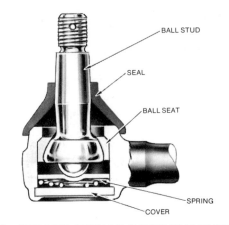

(A) SEALED NONADJUSTABLE TYPE

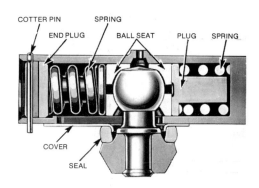

(B) ADJUSTABLE TYPE

General Motors Products of Canada, Limited

Fig. 3-19   Steering Linkage Ball Joints

shaft. As the steering wheel turns the worm shaft, the worm turns the roller and sector shaft (Figure 3-20).

The turning of the sector or pitman arm shaft is transferred to the *steering-knuckle arms* by means of *tie rods.* Since the wheels are attached to the steering-knuckle arms, they turn with them.

The steering box is connected to the steering wheel by the steering shaft which is en-

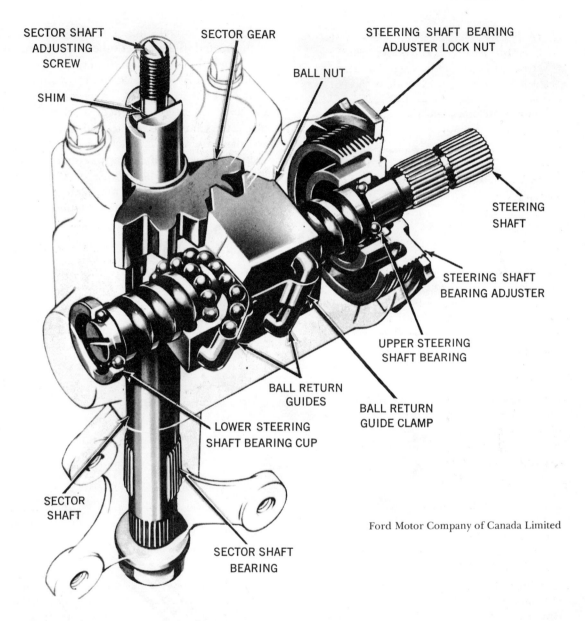

SECTOR SHAFT ADJUSTING SCREW

SECTOR GEAR

STEERING SHAFT BEARING ADJUSTER LOCK NUT

SHIM

BALL NUT

STEERING SHAFT

STEERING SHAFT BEARING ADJUSTER

UPPER STEERING SHAFT BEARING

BALL RETURN GUIDES

BALL RETURN GUIDE CLAMP

LOWER STEERING SHAFT BEARING CUP

SECTOR SHAFT

SECTOR SHAFT BEARING

Ford Motor Company of Canada Limited

Fig. 3-20   Recirculating-ball Type Steering Gear

closed in a mast or jacket tube. The assembly is known as the *steering column*. This column also includes the necessary gear-shift operating mechanism and the electrical connections required for the operation of the horn and turn-signal lights (Figure 3-22).

The steering wheel is attached to the steering shaft by means of *splines* or a *keyway,* and

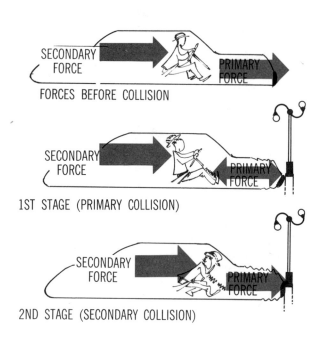

SECONDARY FORCE — PRIMARY FORCE

FORCES BEFORE COLLISION

SECONDARY FORCE — PRIMARY FORCE

1ST STAGE (PRIMARY COLLISION)

SECONDARY FORCE — PRIMARY FORCE

2ND STAGE (SECONDARY COLLISION)

held in position by a nut. The end of the shaft is supported in the jacket tube by a bearing or bushing. The steering shaft may be in one or more sections joined together by universal joints. This arrangement is necessary in order to place the steering wheel at the desired angle and position and to connect it to the steering box which is attached to the frame. A section of the steering column is made in such a manner that it will collapse or telescope if the vehicle is involved in an accident and the driver's body is thrown against the steering wheel.

POWER STEERING

Power steering utilizes hydraulic pressure to reduce the amount of driver effort required to steer the vehicle. A power steering assembly contains four basic units: a pressure pump, a control valve, a cylinder and piston assembly, and the oil lines to transfer the fluid from unit to unit.

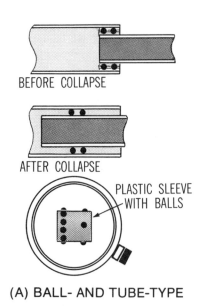

BEFORE COLLAPSE

AFTER COLLAPSE

PLASTIC SLEEVE WITH BALLS

(A) BALL- AND TUBE-TYPE

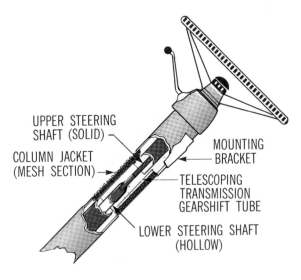

UPPER STEERING SHAFT (SOLID)

COLUMN JACKET (MESH SECTION)

MOUNTING BRACKET

TELESCOPING TRANSMISSION GEARSHIFT TUBE

LOWER STEERING SHAFT (HOLLOW)

(B) JAPANESE-LANTERN TYPE

Fig. 3-22   Collapsible Steering Columns

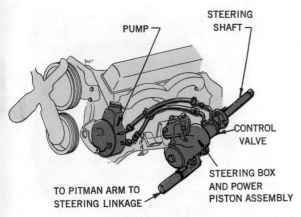

General Motors Products of Canada, Limited

Fig. 3-23   Typical Power Steering for a V8 Engine

Three types of power steering assemblies have been used: the linkage type; the offset integral type; and the in-line integral type. When the steering wheel is turned, the control valve opens passageways to direct oil pressure from the pump to one side of the cylinder and piston assembly and to exhaust oil from the opposite side.

The piston is connected to the linkage (linkage type) or to the pitman arm shaft (in-tegral type). The pressure applied on the piston assists the turning of the wheels. When the desired amount of turning has been attained and the steering wheel is held off centre, the control valve closes, dropping the pressure in the cylinder to retain the desired amount of turning. As the steering wheel is returned to the straight ahead position, the control valve moves to a position to exhaust the pressure from one side of the cylinder and permit pressure into the opposite side. This brings the wheels to the straight-ahead position.

WHEELS AND HUBS

Wheels.   The modern vehicle uses the disc wheel of the *well* or *drop-centre type*. The wheels are provided with a flange at each edge to keep the side walls of the tire from spreading. Around the centre of the rim is a deep groove, or recess, called the *well*. The well is used to facilitate the removal of the tire. When one side of the bead is placed in the well, the opposite side extends beyond the rim. The bead may then be worked over the rim and the tire removed.

The wheel rims must be sealed and provide a sealing surface between the flange and the

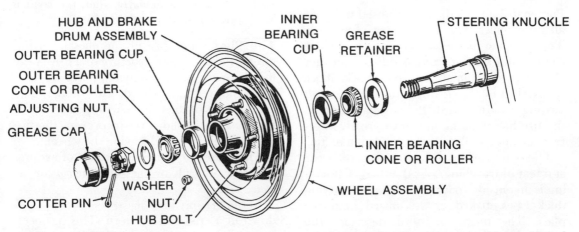

Fig. 3-24   Front Wheel Assembly

Ford Motor Company of Canada Limited

tire bead to prevent loss of tire air pressure. Wheels and rims are available in different diameters and rim widths. The rim width varies according to the tire width.

Hubs. Front wheel hubs are mounted by two cup-and-cone or tapered roller bearings to the front axle or spindle which is part of the steering knuckle. The bearing cups are pressed into the hub and the cone slides easily over the spindle. The bearings must be adjusted to roll freely without the wheel wobbling. A grease retainer or oil seal is pressed into the hub to prevent the lubricating grease from leaking out and causing damage to the brake lining.

Rear axles do not usually use separate hubs; instead, a flange is forged as part of the axle shaft. This flange serves as the wheel hub.

The disc wheel is attached to the hub by four or five wheel studs and nuts, or cap screws. The nuts or cap-screw heads have tapered faces to match the tapered holes in the wheel disc, which assures proper centring of the wheel on the hub.

The brake drum is also attached to the wheel by the wheel studs or cap screws.

TIRES

Pneumatic (air-filled) tires are used today on all automobiles. The tires have two functions. They provide the necessary traction to move the car and keep it from skidding, and they absorb a certain amount of road shock. Shock is absorbed by the flexing action of the tread passing inward against the cushion of air as the tire hits small bumps in the road. In effect, an automobile rides on a cushion of air.

The outer casing of the tire takes the wear and tear of travelling over the road. This casing is an outside coating of rubber of varying thicknesses, baked or vulcanized onto the plies. The term *vulcanized* describes the process of heating rubber under pressure.

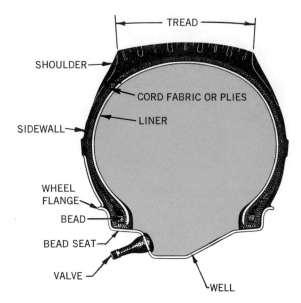

Fig. 3-25   Section View of a Tubeless Tire Rim

This process moulds the rubber into the desired form and tread pattern, and at the same time gives the rubber the characteristics required for flexibility and long wear.

The rubber tread of the tire that makes contact with the road is thicker than the casing and is supplied in a number of different patterns to provide good frictional contact with the road, particularly when the road is wet, snow covered, or muddy.

Tire Plies. The tire ply or plies form the tough, flexible inner structure of a tire. A ply may be made of rayon, nylon, polyester, etc., and is impregnated (filled) with rubber. The carcass plies of the tire are wrapped around a series of steel bead wires to prevent the tire from opening up and leaving the wheel.

There are two general methods of arranging the casing ply or plies—on the *bias* or *radially.*

In the bias-ply tire the carcass plies are laid down in a criss-cross pattern. This has been the conventional method of tire construction

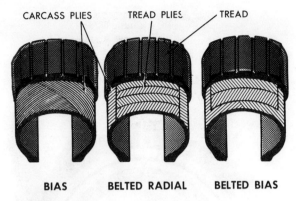

CARCASS PLIES   TREAD PLIES   TREAD

BIAS   BELTED RADIAL   BELTED BIAS

Fig. 3-26   Types of Tire Plies

for many years. In the radial-ply tire the carcass plies are laid down at right angles to the tread centre line. When radial plies are used, extra plies called *tread plies* are required. These plies are placed directly under the tread area. Some radial-ply tires have a layer or two of fine steel mesh embedded in the tread plies to add extra protection against tire damage.

Radial-ply tires flex with a minimal amount of tread distortion which results in longer tread life, better traction, and less rolling resistance; but they are harder to mount, require greater steering effort, and have an appearance of being underinflated.

The belted-bias tire is made up of crisscrossed carcass plies (laid down at a 45° angle to each other) and additional tread plies similar to the radial-ply tire. This type of tire has some of the advantages of the radial-ply tire and lacks some of its disadvantages.

Many new tires use carcass plies of polyester with tread plies of fibreglass.

Ply Ratings. The ply rating is an indication of the tire load-carrying capacity. The load-carrying capacity not only depends upon the number of plies used but to a great extent upon the type of material from which each ply is made. For example: in the modern two-ply/four-ply rated tire, the ply cords are thicker and stronger and as a result produce a tire with the same load-carrying capacity as the older type of four-ply/four-ply rated tire. The two-ply type has the advantage of running cooler, rolling easier and providing better traction and a superior ride.

Because of the increase in ply strength, the use of the standard "ply rating" is being replaced by a "load range" that indicates the maximum mass that can be supported by the tire.

Tubeless Tires. The older type of tires required an inner tube. The inner tube, made of rubber, was the heart of the tire, since it retained the pressurized air. When air was pumped into the tube, it expanded outward against the inner surface of the tire casing, supplying the cushion of air inside the tire.

Late-model vehicles are equipped with tubeless tires, which do not require a separate inner tube. The rim must be sealed and must have a sealed-in tire valve. A thin rubber liner is frequently bonded to the inner surface of the tire casing to prevent air leaks into the ply. The bead, the outside edge of the tire that presses against the wheel, is so constructed that it seals tightly against the rim flange; thus the air is kept within the tire when the tire is inflated.

Tire Sizes. At the present time, tire manufacturers still designate most tire sizes in inches. All types of tires are made in a wide variety of sizes ranging from 6.95 × 14 for passenger cars to 12.00 × 20 for large trucks and buses. The first number in each grouping indicates the width of the tire, and the second number indicates the inside diameter of the tire or the size of the wheel the tire will fit. Some radial tires, especially those from Europe and Asia, designate the width of the tire in millimetres, yet retain the inside diameter in inches; for example, a 165R × 14 size

(A) WHEEL

INSIDE DIAMETER OF TIRE

HEIGHT

TIRE WIDTH

NOTE: Load limits and inflation pressures stamped into tire sidewalls were still being stated in pounds and pounds per square inch, respectively, at the time of publication. Conversion factors are given at the back of the book.

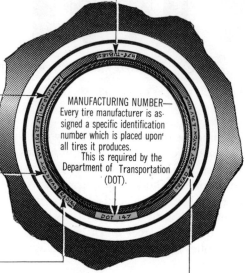

SIZE—In this area may be found the size of the tire. In the example we find it is marked GR70 x 15.

G   Load carrying capacity (1620 lbs. at 32 psi maximum pressure).

R   Radial ply construction.

70   Series (Height to width ratio). The height of the tire   70% of the width.

15   Rim size diameter.

LOAD AND INFLATION—In this area of the tire may be found the maximum load and inflation limits of a tire. In the example, we can see that this tire when inflated to a maximum air pressure of 32 pounds per square inch will support a maximum load of 1620 lbs.

MANUFACTURING NUMBER—Every tire manufacturer is assigned a specific identification number which is placed upon all tires it produces. This is required by the Department of Transportation (DOT).

LOAD RANGE—On the sidewall of every tire may be found the words "load range" followed by a letter. Load range letters are used to identify load and inflation limits and replace the ply rating term. Load range B is for any 4-ply rating tire. Load range C   any 6-ply rating tire. Load range D = any 8-ply rating tire.

CONSTRUCTION TYPE—In this area we may find the type of construction of any tire. In our example, it is readily identified as a radial ply construction.

Sidewall information appearing on today's tires is explained in the above illustration. Note that the manufacturing number is different for each tire maker.

PLY AND MATERIAL IDENTIFICATION—In this area may be found information describing the ply construction and material used. See the example above, on it the following information may be found:

AUTOMOBILE TIRE SIZE CHART					
(Rubber Manufacturers Assn.)					
CONVENTIONAL BIAS PLY Inch	BIAS AND BELTED BIAS PLY		RADIAL PLY		
	"78 Series"	"70 Series"	Metric	Inch "78 Series"	"70 Series"
6.45-14	B78-14	B70-14	165R14	BR78-14	BR70-14
6.95-14	C78-14	C70-14	175R14	CR78-14	CR70-14
	D78-14	D70-14		DR78-14	DR70-14
7.35-14	E78-14	E70-14	185R14	ER78-14	ER70-14
7.75-14	F78-14	F70-14	195R14	FR78-14	FR70-14
8.25-14	G78-14	G70-14	205R14	GR78-14	GR70-14
8.55-14	H78-14	H70-14	215R14	HR78-14	HR70-14
8.85-14	J78-14	J70-14	225R14	JR78-14	JR70-14
		K70-14			KR70-14
		L70-14			LR70-14

NOTE: Since interchangeability is not always possible for equivalent tires due to differences in load ratings, tire dimensions, fender clearances, and rim sizes, automobile manufacturer's recommendations should be checked. Due to differences in handling characteristics, radial ply tires should not be mixed with bias ply tires on the same vehicle.

Fig. 3-27   Tire Sizes

tire is 165 mm wide and 14 inches in diameter. This "dual" type of dimensioning is presently being explored by major North American tire manufacturers, and may become a standard way of expressing tire sizes in the future.

The introduction of the low-profile or wide-oval type of tire has made it necessary to alter the tire size designations so as to indicate the correct load ratings.

The low-profile or wide-oval tire, which is extremely wide in relation to section height, uses a series designation that indicates the relationship between the section height and the width. A "70 series" designation means that the average section height is 70% of the width. The basic width of the tire is indicated by a prefix letter (D, E, F, G, etc.). This letter replaces the number normally used to indicate the width of standard-type tires. The basic width of the tire increases according to the alphabetical listing (E being wider than D, etc.). The tire size D70-14 therefore indicates that the tire is D width or size section, the height is 70% of the section width, and the tire has a 14" diameter across the beads.

Tire Inflation.   Tire inflation pressures vary from 150 to 210 kilopascals (kPa) for passenger cars and up to 840 kPa for large trucks and buses. These readings represent air pressure above atmospheric pressure. It is very important that the tire be inflated to its correct pressure. Too little pressure will cause the side walls of the tire to fail and the outside

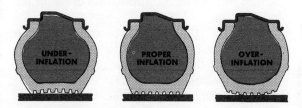

Ford Motor Company of Canada Limited

Fig. 3-28   Tread Contact

edges of the tread to wear rapidly; too much tire pressure will cause rapid tread wear.

Tire Rotation.   Tires wear according to their location on the vehicle. The right-rear tire on most vehicles wears most; the left-rear tire is next, followed by the right front and the left front, which wears the least (assuming that front-end alignment is correctly set). To equalize the amount of wear on each tire, the tires should be rotated. Rotating the tires every 8000 km not only increases the total mileage of a set of tires but also provides an excellent opportunity to inspect the tires for defects.

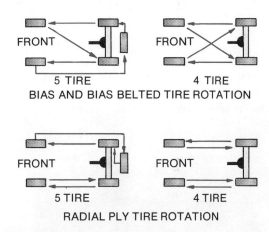

Fig. 3-29   Tire Rotation Patterns

Tire-Tread Wear Indicators.   The potential driving, cornering, and braking traction decreases as tires wear. Furthermore, as the tread depth is decreased the tire has less resistance to road hazards and is more likely to hydroplane on wet pavement. Tread-wear indicators are provided to assist in determining when tires are so worn as to require replacement. These indicators are moulded into the bottom of the tread grooves and will appear as approximately 12 mm wide bands when the tread depth has been reduced to 1.5 mm.

	RAPID WEAR AT SHOULDERS	RAPID WEAR AT CENTRE	CRACKED TREADS	WEAR ON ONE SIDE	FEATHERED EDGE	BALD SPOTS
CONDITION						
CAUSE	UNDER-INFLATION	OVER-INFLATION	UNDER-INFLATION OR EXCESSIVE SPEED	EXCESSIVE CAMBER	INCORRECT TOE	WHEEL UNBALANCED
CORRECTION	ADJUST PRESSURE TO SPECIFICATIONS WHEN TIRES ARE COOL			ADJUST CAMBER TO SPECIFICATIONS	ADJUST FOR TOE-IN 3.0 mm	DYNAMIC OR STATIC BALANCE WHEELS

Fig. 3-30   Tire Wear

Tire replacement because of tread wear is necessary when these indicators appear in two or more adjacent grooves or a localized worn spot eliminates all the tread.

Chrysler Canada Ltd.

Fig. 3-31   Tire-tread Wear Indicator

THE BRAKE SYSTEM

Once the automobile is set in motion, it possesses *momentum*. Brakes are necessary to bring it to an abrupt stop or to slow it down. Automobiles are fitted with two sets of brakes, the *service* or *foot brake* and the *emergency* or *parking brake*. The foot brake is used for stopping the vehicle and is applied by pressure supplied by the driver's foot to the brake pedal. The parking brake, applied by a lever, is used to keep the vehicle from moving when parked.

Brakes consist of brake drums or discs rigidly attached to the wheels and containing semi-stationary brake shoes or brake pads, which can be forced outward against the drums or discs by the application of the brake pedal.

In drum type brakes there are usually two brake shoes, curved to conform to the inner diameter of the brake drum and lined with a tough asbestos material that can withstand wear and high temperatures. With the *hand brakes*, the shoes are forced out against the inner face of the drum by cables and links connected to the hand brake lever.

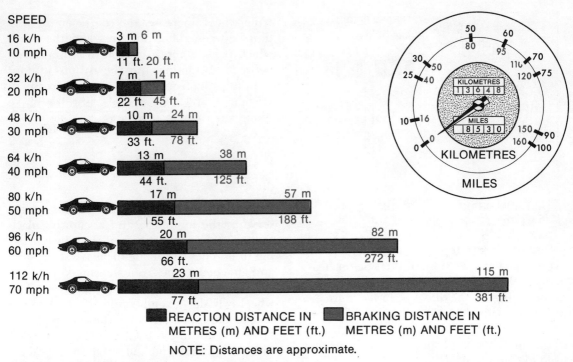

Fig. 3-32   Stopping Distances

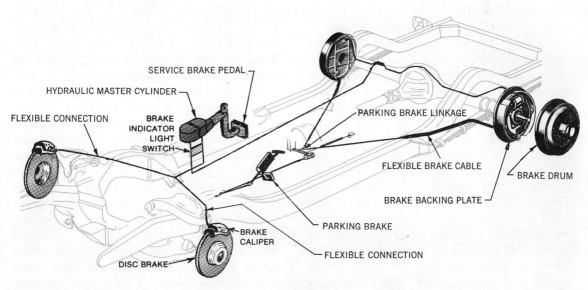

Fig. 3-33   Brake System

General Motors Products of Canada, Limited

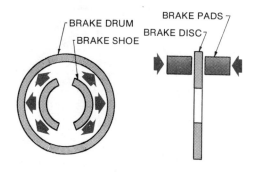

(A) DRUM BRAKE   (B) DISC BRAKE

Fig. 3-34   Brake Principles

Disc brakes are replacing the conventional drum type brake because of their better heat-dissipating properties which result in less brake fading. In the disc type brake there are two brake pads shaped to match the finished surface of the disc. These pads are lined with brake lining made of similar material to that used in drum brakes.

In the hydraulic brake system (Figure 3-39), now universally used for foot brakes, the application of the brake pedal operates pistons in the master brake cylinder. Liquid from this cylinder is forced through tubes to the wheel cylinder in the wheel-braking mechanism. The pressure of the liquid causes pistons in the wheel cylinder to be forced outward, pushing the brake shoes or pads against the drum or disc. The frictional drag of the brake shoes or pads against the brake drums or discs tends to prevent the wheels from rotating, thus stopping the car.

The front wheel brakes usually have larger frictional areas than the rear wheel brake. This is to take advantage of the transfer of inertial force to the front wheels from the rear wheels, when the brakes are applied. Inertial force is force caused by a change in inertia. Inertia is the tendency objects have to remain at rest when at rest, or to remain in motion when in motion. The additional force on the front wheels increases the coefficient of friction between the front tires and the road, which permits more friction to be produced between the lining and the drums without skidding the front wheels. The increase in friction is produced by enlarging the brake lining and drum contact area.

UNITS OF THE DRUM BRAKING SYSTEM

Brake Backing Plates.   Brake backing plates serve as the mounting and anchoring place for the other components of the wheel braking unit. They are made of heavy sheet steel and attached to the front steering knuckle or the rear-axle housing by bolts or rivets. The wheel cylinder assembly and the brake-shoe anchor pins are attached to the backing plate. Holes are cut in the backing plate to provide facilities for adjusting the brake shoes and insertion of the emergency brake cables and the hydraulic brake lines. The backing plate contains flat guides, or pads, against which the brake shoe rests. These guides maintain proper brake-shoe-to-brake-drum alignment.

Brake Drums.   Brake drums are made of cast iron, steel or aluminum alloys, as these materials provide good friction and heat dissipation properties. The brake drum is attached to the wheel by means of the wheel bolts or studs, and revolves with the wheel. The brake shoes are forced against the inner surface of the rim of the drum when the brakes are applied. The energy contained in the momentum of the vehicle is converted into heat energy by the friction developed between the brake lining and the brake drum. This heat must be dissipated by the brake drum. To help dissipate the heat, most brake drums have cooling fins cast around the outside of the drum.

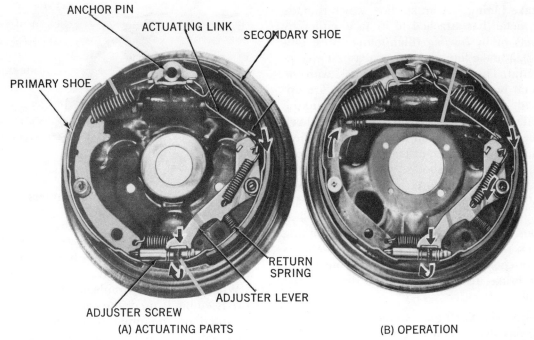

ANCHOR PIN

ACTUATING LINK

SECONDARY SHOE

PRIMARY SHOE

RETURN SPRING

ADJUSTER LEVER

ADJUSTER SCREW

(A) ACTUATING PARTS

(B) OPERATION

Fig. 3-35 Self-adjusting Brake Assembly

General Motors Products of Canada, Limited

Brake Shoes. Brake shoes are made of steel. They are responsible for moving the brake lining toward or away from the brake drum. Brake shoes consist of a web mounted at right angles to a face or table. The web provides the strength that forces the lining against the drum. The face, or table, provides a flat surface to which the lining may be attached. The web is drilled to accommodate the ends of the retraction springs, retaining springs or clips, and sometimes the anchor pin. Surfaces are provided to accommodate the wheel cylinder push rods, emergency brake operating mechanisms, and the anchor pins.

The brake shoe which is ahead of the wheel cylinder, according to the forward rotation of the wheel, is called the primary shoe. The one behind the wheel cylinder is called the secondary shoe. Primary and secondary shoe linings frequently have different coefficients of friction; the design of the braking system determines which shoe has the greater coefficient of friction.

The toe of a brake shoe is at the end farthest from the anchor, and the heel of the shoe is at the end nearest to the anchor.

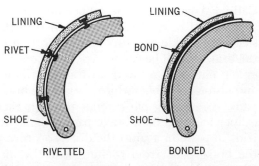

LINING

LINING

RIVET

BOND

SHOE

SHOE

RIVETTED

BONDED

Fig. 3-36 Brake Shoes and Lining

Brake Lining. A brake shoe, which is made of metal, has attached to its face, either by rivets or by *bonding* (high-temperature gluing), a brake lining of a special asbestos compound. This lining comes in contact with the metal brake drum when the brakes are applied. The friction between the lining and the brake drum resists the turning of the wheel. The lining is designed to withstand the heat and dragging effect, or friction, that develops when the brake shoe is forced against the brake drum. This force may reach as high as 4500 N. Temperatures as high as 260°C are not uncommon under extreme brake applications. To prevent damage to the brake lining from these high temperatures, most vehicles have cooling fins attached to the outside of the brake drums, that help to dissipate the heat.

Retraction Springs. Retraction springs of various shapes and lengths are used to pull the brake shoe and lining away from the brake drum when the brakes are released.

UNITS OF THE DISC BRAKE SYSTEM

Brake Disc. The brake disc is made of cast iron and is attached to and rotates with the wheel hub. The disc has a series of vent louvers which increase the cooling area and permit the circulation of air through the disc.

Caliper Assembly. The caliper assembly is a U-shaped casting which is attached to the steering knuckle and surrounds a portion of the brake disc. The caliper assembly contains either one, two or four hydraulic cylinder and piston assemblies which actuate the brake pads. A retaining pin extends through each caliper half and both brake pads to hold the pads in position against the disc. To prevent the brake pads from rotating with the disc when the brakes are applied, the end of the

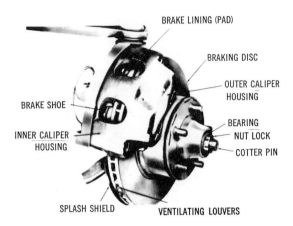

Fig. 3-37 Disc Brake

brake pad butts against machined surfaces within the caliper assembly.

When only one hydraulic cylinder and piston assembly is used, the caliper assembly is mounted on mounting pins and is free to slide sideways along these pins when the brakes are applied, in order to bring both brake pads in contact with the disc.

When two or four hydraulic cylinder and piston assemblies are used, the cylinders are distributed equally in each leg of the U. The caliper assembly is rigidly attached to the steering knuckle. When hydraulic pressure is applied, both pads are forced against the disc by the pistons.

Brake Pads. Each caliper assembly contains two brake pads. A brake pad consists of a steel shoe with brake lining either riveted or bonded to it to provide the necessary friction required for braking.

UNITS OF THE HYDRAULIC SYSTEM

The Master Cylinder. The master cylinder converts mechanical pressure to hydraulic pressure. It is usually mounted on the engine side of the fire wall and is connected to the brake pedal by a mechanical linkage. The master cylinder consists of a reservoir for

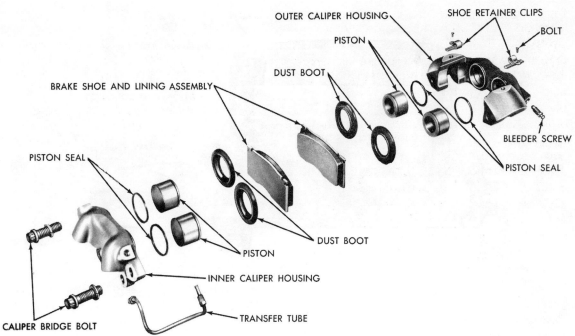

OUTER CALIPER HOUSING

SHOE RETAINER CLIPS

PISTON

BOLT

DUST BOOT

BRAKE SHOE AND LINING ASSEMBLY

BLEEDER SCREW

PISTON SEAL

PISTON SEAL

DUST BOOT

PISTON

INNER CALIPER HOUSING

CALIPER BRIDGE BOLT

TRANSFER TUBE

Fig. 3-38   Exploded Caliper Assembly   Chrysler Canada Ltd.

extra brake fluid, a cylinder, a piston and cup assembly, and seals. Since 1967, all automobiles have been equipped with dual or split

hydraulic brake systems. This system consists basically of two separate brake systems, controlled by a common brake pedal. One system operates the front brakes; the other system operates the rear brakes. If one system should fail, the other is adequate to bring the vehicle to a stop, although the pedal travel and pedal effort substantially increases. Loss of pressure in one system illuminates the brake alarm-indicator light on the instrument panel.

The two separate brake systems are operated by a dual master cylinder, consisting of separate reservoirs, pistons, and outlets in a common body casting. Fluid from the reservoir of each section of the master cylinder flows through the inlet and bypass ports to fill the cylinder. The filler plug of the reservoir, which provides an opening to add fluid, is provided with a vent hole that allows atmospheric pressure on the fluid in the reservoir.

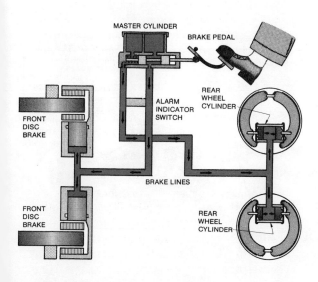

MASTER CYLINDER

BRAKE PEDAL

REAR WHEEL CYLINDER

ALARM INDICATOR SWITCH

FRONT DISC BRAKE

BRAKE LINES

FRONT DISC BRAKE

REAR WHEEL CYLINDER

Fig. 3-39   Brake Hydraulic System

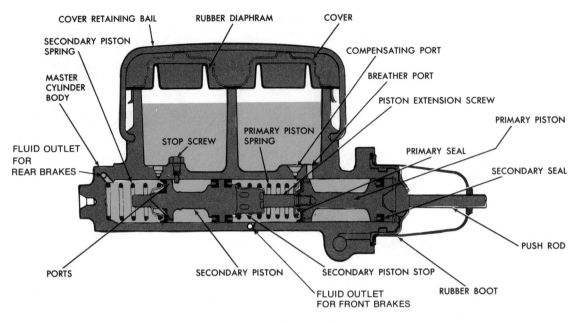

(A) OPERATION

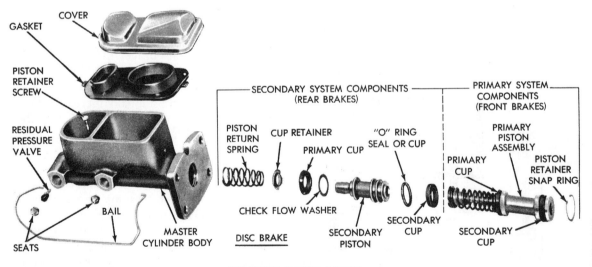

(B) EXPLODED VIEW

Fig. 3-40   Dual-type Master Cylinder   Chrysler Canada Ltd.

A primary cup, mounted at the forward end of each piston, prevents leakage past the piston when mechanical pressure is applied to the piston.

A secondary cup, mounted on the outer end of each master-cylinder piston, acts as a seal between the piston and cylinder and prevents leakage of the fluid. A boot over the open end of the cylinder and around the master-cylinder operating rod acts as a protective covering and keeps out any dirt that might score the cylinder.

The two pistons within the master cylinder receive mechanical pressure from the brake pedal push rod and transmit it through the brake lines as hydraulic pressure to the wheel cylinders. A special brake pipe distribution and switch assembly, mounted near the master cylinder, controls the brake alarm-indicator light.

Drum brakes require a check valve, mounted in the cylinder outlet between the piston and the brake lines. It is so designed that a pressure of 40 kPa to 50 kPa is maintained in the brake line and wheel cylinders. This pressure keeps the wheel cups expanded against the cylinder walls and prevents fluid leaking out and air leaking in. Disc brakes do not require such a valve.

Wheel Cylinders.   Wheel cylinders of drum brakes consist of a cylinder, two wheel cups and pistons, a bleeder screw, and seals. The fluid, under pressure, enters the wheel cylinders between two cups, which act as seals and prevent the fluid from leaking past the pistons. The pressure forces the pistons outward against the brake shoes, and the brake shoes are expanded, thus making contact with the brake drums. Boots are provided at the ends of the wheel cylinders to prevent dirt from entering these cylinders. A compressed spring, placed between the two cups, keeps the cups in contact with the pistons at all times.

The wheel cylinders of disc brakes are machine-bored into the caliper assembly. They are only open at the brake pad end. The piston assembly includes a seal-ring to prevent fluid leakage and a dust boot on the pad end to prevent dust from entering the cylinder. Fluid enters through a tapped hole in the closed end of the cylinder to force the piston toward the disc during brake application. See Figure 3-42.

The bleeder screw in the wheel cylinder provides a means of forcing out any air in the system. Air, unlike liquids, can be compressed and is very dangerous if allowed to enter the brake system. A hydraulic brake with air in it results in a spongy brake pedal. Therefore, it is always necessary to *bleed* the hydraulic brake system after completing a repair job on the system, such as master or wheel cylinder overhaul or brake line repair. Bleeding removes all the air from the hydraulic system.

Brake Lines.   Brake lines are steel tubing and high pressure, flexible, neoprene hoses that transmit hydraulic pressure from the master cylinder to the wheel cylinders. Each section of the line has the proper fittings to connect it to the next unit.

Brake Fluid.   Brake fluid is a specially formulated liquid that:

(a) Must flow easily at all temperatures
(b) Must not evaporate easily
(c) Must be chemically stable over long periods of time
(d) Must lubricate
(e) Must be noncorrosive to metal parts
(f) Must be noninjurious to rubber
(g) Must not expand or contract with temperature changes

Standard brake fluid specifications are set by law and only approved brake fluid must be used in the braking system.

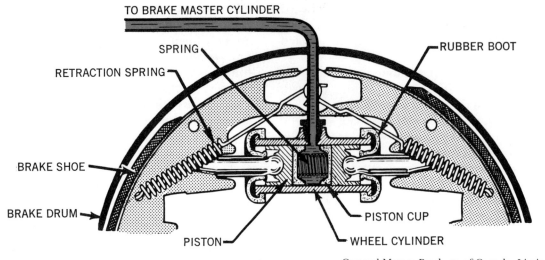

TO BRAKE MASTER CYLINDER

SPRING

RETRACTION SPRING

RUBBER BOOT

BRAKE SHOE

BRAKE DRUM

PISTON

PISTON CUP

WHEEL CYLINDER

General Motors Products of Canada, Limited

(A) OPERATION

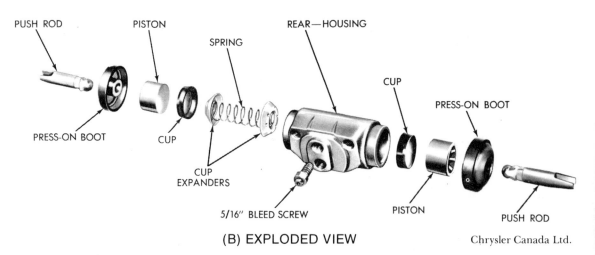

PUSH ROD   PISTON   REAR—HOUSING

SPRING

CUP

PRESS-ON BOOT

PRESS-ON BOOT   CUP

CUP
EXPANDERS

5/16" BLEED SCREW

PISTON

PUSH ROD

(B) EXPLODED VIEW   Chrysler Canada Ltd.

Fig. 3-41   Brake Wheel Cylinder

OPERATION OF HYDRAULIC BRAKES

The operation of the hydraulic brake system is based on Pascal's Law, which states that pressure, when exerted upon a mass of liquid in a closed container, is transmitted without loss in all directions.

When the brake pedal is in the released position, the pistons of the master cylinder are back against the piston stops.

When the pedal is depressed, the pressure is transmitted through the push rod to the pistons. As the pistons and primary cups

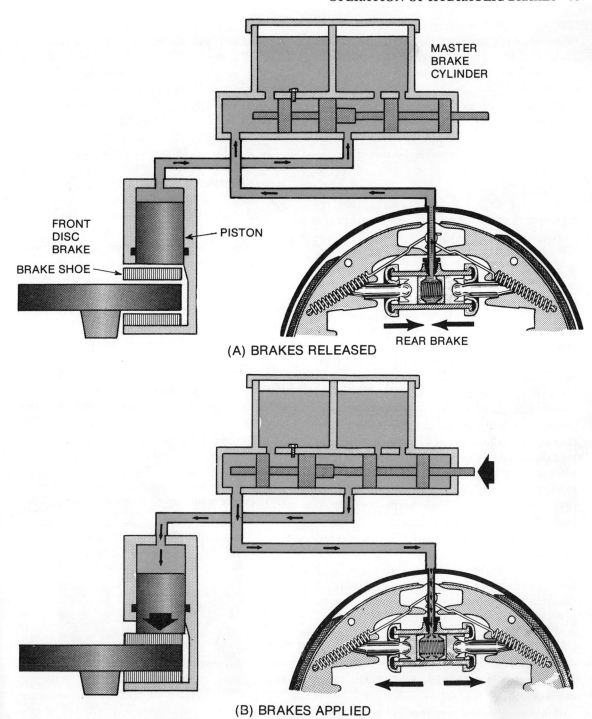

MASTER
BRAKE
CYLINDER

FRONT
DISC
BRAKE

PISTON

BRAKE SHOE

REAR BRAKE

(A) BRAKES RELEASED

(B) BRAKES APPLIED

Fig. 3-42 Hydraulic Brake Operation

move forward, the bypass ports are closed and the fluid is forced out of the outlet fitting, and through the brake pipe lines to the wheel cylinders.

The fluid under pressure enters the wheel cylinder of drum brakes between the two cups, forcing the cups and pistons outward against the brake shoes. The brake shoes are expanded, thus making contact with the brake drums.

When the brake pedal is released, the return spring in the master cylinder pushes the piston and primary cup back against the piston stop. At the wheels, the brake-shoe *retraction springs* pull the shoes back together. This forces the piston inward, and the fluid is forced back to the master cylinder. This returning fluid must have sufficient pressure to force from its seat the check valve, which is held in position by the piston return spring. As this return of fluid is much slower than the return of the master cylinder piston, a vacuum is created in the fluid between the piston and check valve. This vacuum is relieved by fluid which passes in the inlet port, through the drilled holes in the piston, and past the lip of the primary cup. As more fluid returns from the wheel cylinder, it enters the master cylinder, and any excess of fluid returns to the reservoir through the bypass port. This system keeps the cylinder full of fluid at all times and ready for application of the brakes.

When the brakes are applied in the two- or four-piston types, hydraulic pressure from the master cylinder applies pressure to the pistons in the caliper assembly. This pressure moves the pistons inward, deflecting the piston seals and forcing the linings against both sides of the disc. The shoes create a pinching action upon the disc which provides the braking action.

When the brakes are applied in the one-piston type, the hydraulic pressure first moves the piston against the inside face of the disc. The pressure then causes the caliper assembly to slide along its mounting pins to bring the outer pad against the outer face of the disc. Applying additional pressure pinches both pads against the disc to create the braking action.

When the brake pedal is released, the piston seals retract to their normal position and pull the piston and shoe assembly away from the disc to release the brakes.

When disc brakes are used on the front wheels and drum brakes on the rear, a proportioning valve, located in the hydraulic system between the master cylinder and the rear brake wheel cylinders, meters the hydraulic pressure to provide a balance between the front and rear braking system. This valve prevents premature lockup of the front wheels when the brakes are applied.

POWER BRAKES

Power brakes permit the use of a *low brake pedal* and reduce the amount of driver effort required to stop the vehicle. The unit is mounted on the *engine side* of the fire wall, and is connected directly to the brake pedal linkage.

The assembly is a self-contained *hydraulic* and *vacuum* unit, using engine-manifold vac-

Chrysler Canada Ltd.

Fig. 3-43   Power Brake Unit

uum and atmospheric pressure to produce power. The unit contains a *vacuum diaphragm* in a chamber, a *control valve*, a *master cylinder and plunger assembly,* and a *fluid reservoir.* A vacuum line and check valve is connected between the control valve and the manifold. The master cylinder outlet is connected to the brake lines.

When the brake pedal is depressed, the control valve is opened to permit engine vacuum to be applied to one side of the vacuum diaphragm. The pressure produced is applied to the *master cylinder plunger,* which in turn applies the brakes. When the required amount of braking effort has been attained and the brake pedal is held partially depressed, the control valve closes, trapping engine vacuum in the diaphragm chamber and maintaining the braking effort.

When the brake pedal is released, the control valve is in a position to dissipate the vacuum in the chamber and therefore releases the braking effort.

BRAKE ADJUSTMENTS

Each time the brake is applied, a small amount of wear takes place on each brake lining. This wear increases the clearance between the brake lining and the brake drum. As this clearance increases, the brake pedal must travel further to operate the brakes. In this condition, since the travel of the brake pedal is limited by the floor boards, the brake shoes cannot be forced against the brake drum with sufficient pressure to create the necessary friction to stop the wheel from turning. Therefore, a means of adjusting the shoes is necessary to compensate for the wear. When the lining has worn considerably, and further adjustment is not possible, the brake shoe must be removed to have a new lining installed.

Two popular types of mechanism have been designed for adjusting the brakes on modern automobiles. the *cam* type used in *Lockheed* brakes and the *expanding-bolt* type used in *Bendix* brakes.

SELF-ADJUSTING BRAKES

The automatic adjusting mechanism of self-adjusting brakes only operates when the vehicle is moving rearward, and then only when the secondary brake shoe can move toward the drum beyond a predetermined point. The movement of the secondary shoe causes a cable to pull the adjusting lever upward against the end of a tooth on the adjusting screw *starwheel.* As the brake lining wears, the upward travel of the lever increases. When the lever can travel upward far enough, it passes over the end of the tooth and engages the tooth. When the brakes are released, the adjusting lever is pulled downward by a spring, causing the adjusting screw starwheel to turn and expand the brake shoes. The starwheel is turned one tooth at a time, as the brake linings wear.

PRACTICAL ASSIGNMENTS

a. *On an Assigned Automobile Chassis:*
   1. Locate all the units listed on the chassis diagrams in this chapter.
   2. Measure: (a) the wheel base, (b) the wheel tread, and (c) the road clearance.
   3. Determine the type of frame construction.

b. *Disassemble and Assemble a Leaf Spring.*
Procedure:
   1. Place the spring sideways in the vise, so that all leaves are grasped by the vise jaws.
   2. If rebound clips are present, remove them.
   3. Take the nut off the centre bolt and push the bolt through with a punch.
   4. Slowly release the vise jaws.

5. Be prepared to identify all parts.
6. Reassemble the spring, using a punch to line up the centre bolt holes.
7. Make sure that the long end of each leaf is facing toward the rear of the spring.
8. Place the spring in a vise and tighten the vise.
9. Remove the punch; insert the centre bolt and tighten it.
10. Have the instructor inspect your work.

c. Remove and Replace Wheel and Tire Assembly.
Procedure:
1. Remove the hub cap, using a suitable pry bar.
2. Loosen the wheel nuts about one full turn.
3. Jack up the vehicle in accordance with the manufacturer's instructions.
4. Remove the wheel nuts and wheel. (Note the location of the tapered portion of the nuts.)
5. Replace the wheel and wheel nuts.
6. Tighten the wheel nuts as tight as you can by hand.
7. Tighten the wheel nuts, using the pattern shown in Figure 3-45 to ensure proper alignment between the wheel and axle.

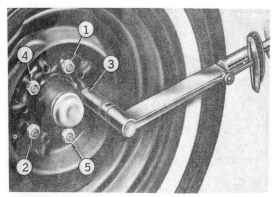

Chrysler Canada Ltd.

Fig. 3-44   Wheel Stud Nut Tightening Sequence

8. Lower the vehicle and give the nuts the final tightening.
9. Have the instructor inspect your work.
10. Replace the hub cap.

d. Remove and Replace a Tire.
Removal:
Dismounting tubeless tires presents no problems if the correct procedures are used and the following precautions observed.
1. Remove the valve cap and valve core. Let out all the air.
2. Press the inner side of the tire into the rim well. Use bead loosening tool or if regular tire irons are used, take particular care not to injure or tear the sealing ribs on the bead.
   CAUTION: Never use tire irons with sharp edges or corners.
3. Using tire irons on the opposite side, remove bead, taking small "bites" around the rim.
4. Turn the tire over, and use two tire irons, one between the rim flange and the bead to pry the rim upward, the other iron to pry outward between the bead seat and the bead.

Installation:
Extreme care must be exercised to prevent injury to the sealing bead and circumferential bead when forcing tire over rim.
1. Apply a light film of suitable rubber lubricant to sealing bead of tire.
   NOTE: The use of excessive lubrication may lead to rim slippage and subsequent breaking of air seal.
2. Carefully mount the outer bead in usual manner by using tire irons, taking small "bites" around rim, being careful not to injure the tire bead.
   CAUTION: DO NOT use a hammer, as damage to the bead will result.

Fig. 3-45 Tire Servicing Equipment

3. Install the inner bead in the same manner.

NOTE: If a seal cannot be effected in the foregoing manner with the rush of air, it can be accomplished by applying to the circumference of the tire a tire mounting band or heavy sash cord and tightening with the use of a tire iron. On tire mounting machines, bouncing the tire assembly is not required. The tire should be lifted on the rim to force the top tire bead against the top rim flange. Force of gravity will seat the bottom bead.

e. Repair a Tire. When a tire loses all or most of its air pressure, particularly when driving at high legal speeds on today's super highways, recommended procedure is to remove it from the wheel for complete inspection, to be sure no tire damage has occurred.

There are several types of rubber plugs—some are inserted from the inside of the tire; others are inserted from the outside of the tire without demounting the tire from the rim.

When using the plug method be sure to clean and lubricate the hole with repair cement before inserting the plug. Your tire supplier has available complete kits containing materials, tools, and detailed instructions for making repairs with plugs. Follow instructions in the kit that you use.

f. Remove and Replace the Complete Front Wheel. There are many reasons for removing the front wheel assembly, such as brake-lining inspection and brake repairs, repacking of front-wheel bearings, and repairs of steering linkage.

Procedure:

1. Jack up the front of the car so that the wheels are clear of the floor.
2. Place the proper rigid supports under the vehicle.
3. Remove the hub cap, grease cap, cotter pin, and nut-and-tongue washer.
4. Pull the wheel off the spindle and catch the outer wheel bearing, as it passes over the end of the spindle.
5. Notice whether the inner wheel bearing and grease retainer remain on the spindle or in the wheel hub. If these parts remain on the spindle, slide the bearing and grease retainer along the spindle to remove them. If the bearing is held in place by a pressed-in grease retainer, drive out the retainer by means of a punch. This operation will usually damage the grease retainer, which therefore, should be replaced.
6. Clean, inspect, and lubricate all parts.
7. Have the instructor inspect your work.
8. Reassemble the parts.

9. To adjust the wheel bearing, tighten the spindle nut until you feel a slight drag during the rotation of the wheel, then back off the nut one-eighth of a turn, plus whatever is necessary to line up the cotter pin hole with the slot in the nut. Some manufacturers specify that the spindle nut must be tightened to a given number of newton metres of torque, then backed off sufficiently to insert the cotter pin.

10. Install a new cotter pin and lock it properly.

11. Replace the grease cap and hub cap.

12. Remove the axle stands and jack.

g. *Disassemble and Assemble a Steering Box—Recirculating Ball Type.*

Procedure:

1. Loosen the lock nut on the end of the sector shaft.

2. Turn the lash adjuster counterclockwise two turns to release the load on the worm bearings.

3. Loosen the lock nut on the worm-bearing adjuster, and turn the adjusting nut counterclockwise two turns.

4. Remove the side cover attaching bolts, cover, and sector shaft from the housing. (It may be necessary to turn the worm shaft in order to allow the sector shaft to clear the housing.)

5. Remove the lock nut and worm-bearing adjuster.

6. Withdraw the ball nut or gear rack and worm assembly from the housing.

7. Remove the upper and lower worm-shaft bearings.

8. Be prepared to identify all parts.

9. Place the upper bearing over the worm shaft, and insert the shaft and nut assembly into the housing.

10. Place the worm bearing in the worm-bearing adjuster and install the adjuster

and lock nut in the lower end of the housing.

11. Rotate the worm shaft until the ball nut or gear rack is in the centre of its travel.

12. Place the sector shaft in position, meshing it in the centre of the nut or gear rack.

13. Tighten the cover nuts.

14. Have the instructor inspect your work.

h. *Adjust Steering Box—Recirculating-Ball Type.* NOTE: Before any steering box adjustment can be made, the steering gear linkage must be disconnected from the box.

Procedure:

1. To adjust worm-shaft end play.
   Tighten the worm-bearing adjuster until you feel a slight tension as the worm shaft is turned; then tighten the lock nut (Figure 3-47).

2. Centralize the steering box by turning the worm shaft from one stop to the next, while counting the number of turns. Now turn the shaft back exactly half the number of turns.

3. Turn the sector shaft adjusting screw, or lash adjuster, until all the lash between

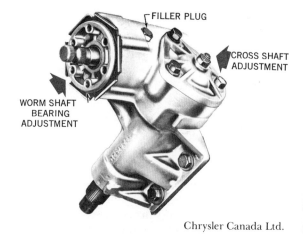

Chrysler Canada Ltd.

Fig. 3-46   Steering Gear Adjustment Locations

the sector shaft roller and the ball nut, or
gear rack, or worm assembly is just removed; then tighten the lock nut.
4. Have the instructor inspect your work.

i. Overhaul Master Cylinder.

Procedure:
1. If the master cylinder is installed on an
   automobile, follow the manufacturer's
   instructions for removal.
2. Remove the rubber boot from the cylinder.
3. Clean off all outside dirt with a wire
   brush.
4. Remove the filler-plug and/or top cover
   from the master cylinder and drain off
   the fluid.
5. Remove the lock ring, piston stop, piston,
   return spring, check valve, and the two
   cups.
6. Wash all parts in alcohol. Absolute cleanliness is essential.
7. Check the cylinder for scores, and hone
   them if necessary.
8. Install the new valve and rubber parts.
   Assemble all parts in reverse order to disassembly.
9. Have the instructor inspect your work.
10. Replace the master cylinder in the vehi-
    cle according to the manufacturer's in-
    structions.
11. Adjust the brake-pedal lash to the manu-
    facturer's specifications.
12. Fill the master cylinder with new brake
    fluid and bleed the brakes.
13. Have the instructor inspect your work.

j. Overhaul Wheel Cylinder.

Procedure:
1. If the wheel cylinder is installed on an
   automobile, jack up the car and remove
   the wheel.

2. Remove the brake-shoe retracting
   springs.
3. Disconnect the brake line.
4. Remove the studs, holding the cylinder
   to the backing plate.
5. Remove the rubber dust caps.
6. Remove the pistons, rubber caps, and
   spring.
7. Wash all parts in alcohol. Absolute cleanliness is essential.
8. Inspect the cylinder bore. If it is scored
   or rough, clean it with a brake-cylinder
   hone.
9. Check the fit of the piston according to
   the manufacturer's specifications.
10. Dip new pistons and rubber cups in
    brake fluid.
11. Place the spring in the centre of the
    housing and the rubber cups at each end
    of the spring. Then place the pistons
    against the cups and place the dust caps
    over the end of the cylinder.
12. Assemble the cylinder to the backing
    plate, and reassemble the brake shoes in
    reverse order to disassembly.
13. Replace the wheel and bleed the brakes.
14. Have the instructor inspect your work.

k. Bleed Brakes.

Procedure:
1. Jack up the automobile and place it on
   safety stands.
2. Clean away dirt from the master-cylinder
   filler plug.
3. Check and fill the master cylinder with
   brake fluid.
4. Select the wheel furthest from the master
   cylinder and remove the bleeder set
   screw, if used.
5. Attach the bleeder hose to the bleeder
   valve and place the other end of the hose
   in a jar, with sufficient brake fluid to
   cover the end of the bleeder hose.

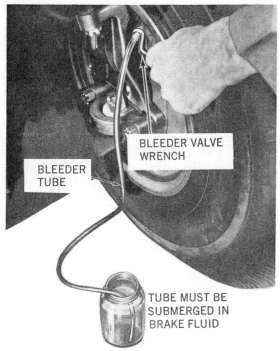

BLEEDER VALVE WRENCH

BLEEDER TUBE

TUBE MUST BE SUBMERGED IN BRAKE FLUID

General Motors Products of Canada, Limited

Fig. 3-47   Bleeding Brakes

6. Open the bleeder valve about three-quarters of a turn.
7. Work the brake pedal up and down slowly several times, until bubbles cease to appear in the jar.
8. Release the brake pedal slowly and close the bleeder valve while the tube is still in the fluid.
9. Remove the bleeder hose and replace the bleeder set screw.
10. Check and refill the master cylinder with brake fluid.
11. Repeat the operation for all wheels.
12. Have the instructor inspect your work.

l. Adjust Lockheed Single-Cylinder Brakes.

Procedure:
1. Jack up all four wheels, and place the automobile on safety stands.

2. Locate the adjusting nuts.
3. Rotate the adjusting cam on the forward shoe until a slight drag is felt when the wheel is rotated in the forward direction of the car.
4. Back off the adjusting cam until the wheel rotates freely.
5. Repeat this operation for the other brake shoe.
6. Repeat operations 3, 4, and 5, for all wheels.
7. Work the brake pedal up and down two or three times.
8. Check and refill the master cylinder.
9. Remove the safety stands and jack.
10. Have the instructor test the brakes.

m. Adjust Lockheed Two-Cylinder Brakes.

Procedure:
1. Jack up all four wheels, and place the automobile on safety stands.
2. Locate the adjusting nuts.
3. Rotate the adjusting cam on the forward shoe, until a slight drag is felt when the wheel is rotated in the forward direction of the car.
4. Back off the adjusting cam until the wheel rotates freely.
5. Repeat this operation for the other brake shoe.
6. Repeat operations 3, 4, and 5, for all wheels.
7. Work the brake pedal up and down two or three times.
8. Check and refill the master cylinder.
9. Remove the safety stands and jack.
10. Have the instructor check the brakes. (See Figure 3-41).

n. Adjust Bendix Duo-Servo Brakes.

Procedure:
1. Jack up all four wheels and place the automobile on safety stands.

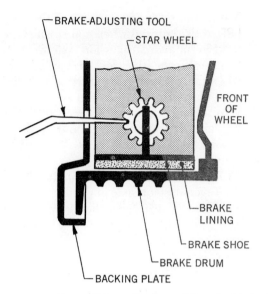

General Motors Products of Canada, Limited

Fig. 3-48   Brake Adjustment on Standard
             Bendix Brakes

2. Remove the dust clip from the adjustment slot.
3. Insert a brake-adjusting tool in the slot of the backing plate until it engages the starwheel on the adjusting screw, and move the end of the tool upward to expand the brake shoe.
4. Expand the brake shoes until the car wheel can just be turned by hand.
5. Back off the adjusting screw ten notches.
6. Check to see that the wheel turns freely without drag. It may be necessary to tap the backing plate to permit the shoes to centralize, before the wheel will spin freely.
7. Repeat steps 2, 3, 4, 5, and 6 at all four wheels.
8. Work the brake pedal up and down two or three times.
9. Check and refill the master cylinder.
10. Remove the safety stands and jack.
11. Have the instructor test the brakes.

o. Backing-off Self-adjusting Brakes to Remove Brake Drum

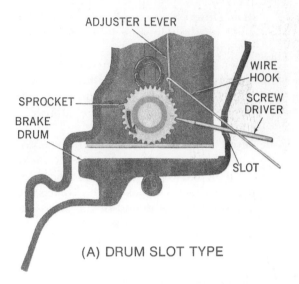

(A) DRUM SLOT TYPE

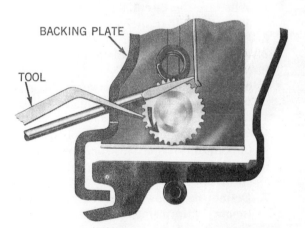

(B) BACKING PLATE SLOT TYPE

General Motors Products of Canada, Limited

Fig. 3-49   Backing-off Brake Adjustment on
             Self-adjusting Brakes

Procedure:
1. Jack up all four wheels and place the automobile on safety stands.
2. Remove the dust clip from the adjusting slot.
3a. When the adjusting slot is in the brake drum, insert a wire hook through the slot and pull the adjusting lever away from the adjusting starwheel.
3b. When the adjusting slot is in the brake backing plate, insert a small screwdriver or awl through the slot to push the adjusting lever away from the adjusting starwheel.
4. Insert a brake adjusting tool into the slot while holding the adjusting lever away from the starwheel, until the tool engages the starwheel. To back off the brake shoe adjustor, move the end of the adjusting tool upward (backing plate slot type) or downward (drum slot type).
5. Replace dust clips.

REVIEW QUESTIONS

1. What are the essential characteristics of an automobile frame?
2. What is the purpose of the X- or K-members of an automobile frame?
3. What is a frame gusset?
4. State the difference between integral frame and body construction, and separate frame and body construction.
5. What are the advantages of unibody type of body and frame construction?
6. Name the two functions of chassis springs.
7. Define the following terms: (a) sprung weight (b) unsprung weight.
8. Name three types of springs used in modern cars and briefly explain their operation.
9. State why a spring shackle is necessary and describe its operation.
10. Name and state the purpose of the support rods required when coil springs are used in the rear suspension system.
11. What absorbs the fore-and-aft forces when (a) coil springs, (b) torsion bars are used in the front suspension system?
12. Why are shock absorbers necessary?
13. Explain briefly the operation of a shock absorber.
14. Why are stabilizer bars used?
15. By means of a sketch, illustrate (a) Elliott (b) Reverse Elliott axle ends.
16. Explain the difference between a solid axle and independent front-wheel suspension.
17. Why is it necessary to turn the front wheels at different angles when the vehicle turns the corner?
18. Describe briefly the Ackerman Principle of steering.
19. Give three reasons why front-end alignment must be correct.
20. By means of sketches, illustrate the angles used in steering geometry.
21. What is the one factor of front-end alignment which is used to offset the undesirable effect of another factor?
22. What is the purpose of the steering gear?
23. Describe mechanical advantage.
24. Name the major divisions of the steering system.
25. Make a sketch of a typical steering-gear linkage and identify the main components.
26. Make a sketch of the recirculating ball type of steering gear and identify the major components.
27. Describe the actions that take place in the steering system when the steering wheel is turned.
28. Why is the modern steering column colapsible?
29. What is the purpose of the wheel well?

30. What is the purpose of (a) the front wheel hub, (b) the rear axle flange?
31. Why do wheel nuts have tapered faces?
32. What two functions do tires perform?
33. What does the term "plies" mean?
34. What determines the number of plies a tire will have?
35. Describe three methods of arranging tire plies.
36. What effects do overinflation and underinflation have on a tire?
37. What do the figures in the tire size E70 × 15 signify? What about these figures: 165R 13?
38. How is the air retained in a tubeless tire?
39. Why is tire rotation recommended?
40. Name and state the purpose of the two types of braking systems on a vehicle.
41. State the purpose of the following brake parts: (a) backing plate, (b) brake shoes and lining, (c) retraction springs, (d) master cylinder, (e) wheel cylinder, (f) brake lines.
42. How is (a) the primary brake shoe, (b) the toe of the shoe determined?
43. What material is used for brake linings? Why?
44. Why do front brake shoes have a larger lining area than rear brake shoes?
45. What is the purpose of (a) the primary cup, (b) the secondary cup of the master cylinder?
46. What effect does air in the braking system have on the feel of the brake pedal? Why?
47. What is the purpose of the master-cylinder check valve?
48. Name and describe the scientific law upon which hydraulic brakes work.

49. Describe the operation of a hydraulic brake system (a) when the brakes are applied, (b) when the brakes are released.
50. Why must brakes be adjusted?
51. Describe two methods of adjusting brakes.
52. Explain how self-adjusting brakes adjust themselves.
53. Make a sketch of the (a) master cylinder, (b) wheel cylinder, and identify all parts.
54. Why is it necessary to close the bleeder valve each time the pedal is depressed when a bleeder tube and bottle are not used?
55. List three service brake repair operations that must be followed by the bleeding of brakes.
56. List the four major units of the power-steering system.
57. Name three types of power-steering systems.
58. Describe briefly the actions that take place in a power-steering system when the steering wheel is turned.
59. What is the advantage of a dual or split braking system?
60. Why is a brake alarm-indicator light necessary?
61. State two advantages of power brakes.
62. What is used to produce the power necessary to operate power brakes?
63. Explain how the braking effort required by the driver is reduced when power brakes are used.
64. What are the advantages of disc brakes?
65. Describe the action of the brake shoes in a disc brake when the brakes are applied.

THE ENGINE 4

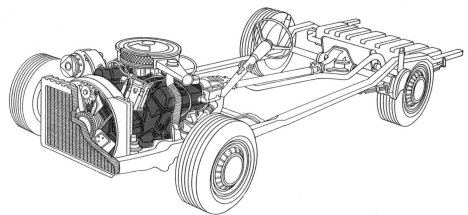

Power is required to propel a vehicle. There are two popular methods of producing power for land transportation: the *internal-combustion* engine, which uses gasoline or diesel fuel, and the *external-combustion* engine, which burns fuel such as coal or wood to produce steam. The latter is not used in automobiles today.

INTERNAL-COMBUSTION ENGINES

The internal-combustion engine (Figure 4-1) has affected the rapid progress of modern transportation methods more than any other kind of motor. The development of this engine has been responsible for the widespread use of the bus, automobile, truck, tractor, and airplane. Its popularity is due primarily to the fact that it is a self-contained unit, capable of operating for a prolonged period on a relatively small amount of fuel.

In a steam engine, steam is produced by heating a boiler. It is then forced under great

pressure into a *cylinder*. The pressure of the steam forces a *piston* to move in the cylinder, causing the engine to operate. The fuel that produces the steam is burned *outside* the engine; hence the name, external-combustion engine.

The operation of the internal-combustion engine depends upon the fact that a gas expands when heated. If the expansion of a heated gas is confined, pressure will develop. The energy required is provided by the fuel, the most popular fuel being gasoline. The potential energy contained in gasoline must be released and converted into another form of energy before it can be applied mechanically.

When a proper mixture of fuel enters a cylinder and is ignited, instant combustion occurs. The great heat of combustion causes the gases in the cylinder to expand, forcing the piston to move downward in the cylinder. The downward motion of the piston can be

Fig. 4-1   An Automobile Engine

General Motors Products of Canada, Limited

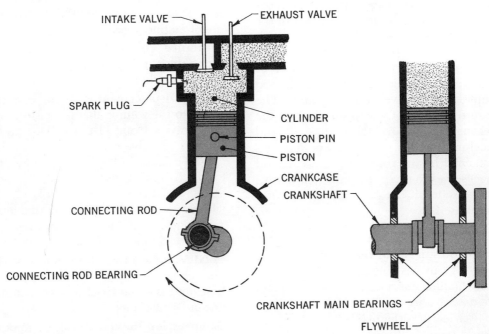

Fig. 4-2   Basic Internal-combustion Engine

classified as *mechanical energy,* which can easily be put to useful work.

Internal-combustion engines have many parts, but only the more important ones will be considered here, using a simple one-cylinder gasoline engine (Figure 4-2) as an example. The cylinder is open only at the lower end and is fitted with a piston having a solid top or head. The piston is free to travel up and down in the cylinder but must fit well enough to provide a gas-tight seal. The seal is provided by *piston rings.* Below the cylinder is the *crankcase,* which houses a pair of bearings, called main bearings, that support the *crank-shaft.* A *connecting rod,* connecting the piston to the crankshaft, is attached to the piston by a *piston pin,* and to the *crankshaft crank* by a *crankpin.* The connecting rod is free to oscillate, or move back and forth, on the piston pin, and the crankpin is free to turn in the *connecting-rod split bearing.* At one end of the crankshaft, the *flywheel* is mounted.

If a charge of gasoline is placed in the chamber at the top of the cylinder and ignited, the expanding gases formed force the piston down in the cylinder. The action of the piston is referred to as *reciprocating* (up-and-down) action, and must be converted into rotary motion to supply a practical form of power. The crankshaft and connecting rod accomplish this conversion of power. The downward motion of the piston causes the connecting rod to turn the crankshaft and flywheel in the main bearings. The momentum attained by the rotating crankshaft and flywheel serves to carry the piston back to its original position if the pressure in the cylinder is released.

BASIC ENGINE TERMS

In order to understand the operation of an internal-combustion engine it is necessary to become familiar with a number of terms which describe its mechanical, operational, and power features (Figure 4-3).

Top Dead Centre (TDC) is the farthest point of upward travel of the piston in its cylinder.

Bottom Dead Centre (BDC) is the lowest point of downward travel of the piston in the cylinder.

Stroke is the distance in millimetres travelled by the piston in its movement from top to bot-

tom dead centres. The piston makes a stroke while travelling downwards and another stroke while travelling upwards. One downward plus one upward stroke of the piston equals one *revolution* of the crankshaft.

Bore is the inside diameter of the cylinder, measured in millimetres.

Throw is the distance in millimetres from the centre of the crankshaft main bearing to the centre of the crankpin, or connecting-rod bearing. The length of the throw is equal to one half of the stroke.

Revolutions Per Minute (r/min) is the unit of measurement used to determine the speed of rotating parts. For example, if an engine is operating at 2000 r/min it means that the crankshaft is rotating 2000 times in each minute of engine operation.

Clearance Volume (CV) for one cylinder is the volume of the combustion chamber above the piston when the piston is at TDC.

Piston Displacement (PD) for one cylinder refers to the volume that the piston displaces as it travels from TDC to BDC, and is expressed in cubic centimetres (cm^3) or litres (ℓ). To calculate PD for one cylinder, the following formula is used:

$$PD = \pi \times r^2 \times stroke$$

where r = one half of the bore diameter. Total Piston Displacement for engine = PD for one cylinder × number of cylinders.

Total Volume (TV) of a cylinder is the volume above the piston when the piston is at BDC and is equal to Clearance Volume plus Piston Displacement.

Compression Ratio (CR) for a cylinder is the ratio of the Total Volume of a cylinder to the Clearance Volume. It is calculated by dividing the Total Volume by the Clearance Volume, and is expressed as a ratio (e.g., 10:1).

Volumetric Efficiency is the ratio between the amount of fuel-air mixture that enters the cylinder on the intake stroke and the amount

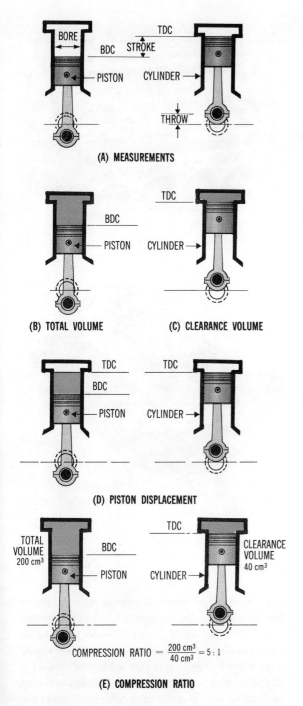

(A) MEASUREMENTS

(B) TOTAL VOLUME

(C) CLEARANCE VOLUME

(D) PISTON DISPLACEMENT

(E) COMPRESSION RATIO

$$\text{COMPRESSION RATIO} = \frac{200 \text{ cm}^3}{40 \text{ cm}^3} = 5:1$$

Fig. 4-3   Engine Nomenclature

required to completely fill the cylinder to atmospheric pressure. It is expressed as a percentage (e.g., 80%).

Engine Power. In the metric system the power output of an engine is measured in kilowatts (kW). The watt (W) is the unit of power and is used to measure both mechanical power and electrical power. Since power is the rate at which work is done (the work done per second), one watt of power is equal to one joule of work done in one second. If an engine is rated at 108 kW, this is the amount of power the engine can produce at a particular r/min at full throttle. Engine power can be determined by connecting the flywheel of the engine to either a *prony brake* or a *dynamometer*. The prony brake is an adjustable friction braking device mounted to the flywheel with a lever that rests on the platform scale. As the braking device is tightened, the lever produces a greater pressure on the scale. The engine power may be determined by using the following formula:

$$N \cdot m \cdot rad/s \ (0.104 \ 72 \ N \cdot m \cdot r/min) = W$$

when N = newtons of force applied on the scale

m = length of the lever in metres

r/min = engine speed

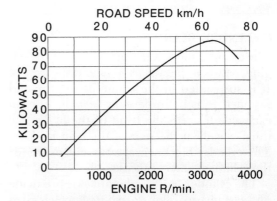

Fig. 4-4   Engine Power Curve

When a dynamometer is used to determine engine power, it also is connected to the engine flywheel. A dynamometer is also a braking device, which uses either a water pump or an electric generator to place a load upon the engine. In both types, instruments are used to measure the engine r/min and load. The instrument readings are given in kW, thereby indicating the engine power being produced.

Prior to the introduction of the metric system of measurement, engine power was given in horsepower. One horsepower is the amount of power required to lift 33 000 pounds a distance of one foot in one minute. The horsepower which an engine developed was referred to as brake horsepower, which was measured by either a prony brake or a dynamometer. When a prony brake was used, the Brake Horsepower was determined by using the following formula:

$$\frac{2\pi \times r \times w \times r/min}{33\ 000} = \text{brake hp}$$

where r = length of arm in feet
w = load on the scale in pounds
r/min = engine speed

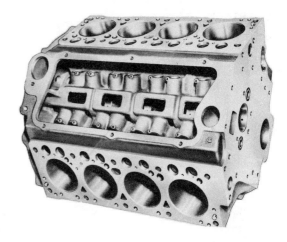

(A) TOP VIEW

(B) BOTTOM VIEW

Chrysler Canada Ltd.

Fig. 4-5   Cylinder Block

ENGINE STATIONARY PARTS

CYLINDER BLOCK

The cylinder block is the main body of the engine, between the *cylinder head* and the *oil pan*. It is suspended in the frame of the car and fastened to it by three *motor mounts*, one on each side towards the front of the block, the third usually at the rear of the transmission. The cylinder block serves as an enclosure for the cylinders and crankcase.

The cylinder block and crankcase are made of a cast ferrous alloy or *semi-steel*, which gives greater wear resistance than the older type of grey cast iron. Some engines use cylinder blocks of cast aluminum with steel cylinder liners. The upper part of the block contains the cylinders and water jackets. The lower part forms the crankcase, which serves as a support and cover for the crankshaft and camshaft which are supported by suitable bearings.

CYLINDER HEAD

The cylinder head is made of aluminum or cast semi-steel. Cylinder head design varies with the type of engine. All heads contain the *combustion chambers* and *threaded spark-plug holes,* and have hollow water compartments that connect to the water jackets of the cylinder block. In some engines the head contains the *valves* and *valve operating mechanisms,* including passageways, or ports, to allow the fuel and air mixture to enter, or allow exhaust gases to leave the cylinder. In some engines these ports are in the cylinder block.

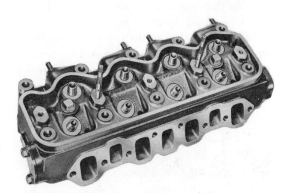

(A) TOP VIEW

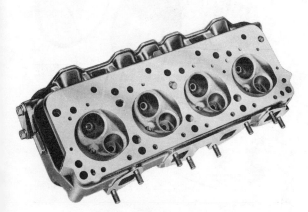

(B) BOTTOM VIEW

Chrysler Canada Ltd.

Fig. 4-6   Cylinder Head

A cylinder-head gasket is placed between the cylinder head and the block to prevent compression and liquid leakage. When bolting the cylinder head to the block, it is necessary to use a torque wrench. Tighten the bolts in a circular pattern, starting from the centre and working out. The tightening of cylinder heads in this manner prevents cylinder head and block distortion.

Oil Pan.   The oil pan (Figure 4-7) serves as a reservoir for the engine oil and as a bottom cover for the crankcase. It is usually a sheet steel pan, pressed into the required shape. Bolts attach it to the bottom of the crankcase and a cork or Velumoid gasket is used to make the union leakproof. The oil pan must be removed before the mechanic can examine or work on any of the parts located in the crankcase.

Chrysler Canada Ltd.

Fig. 4-7   Oil Pan

Manifolds.   Vaporized fuel from the carburetor is carried to the intake ports through a pipe known as the *intake manifold.* In the cylinder, the vacuum caused by the downward movement of the piston on the intake stroke draws the fuel through the manifold and into the engine.

On V8 engines, the intake manifold is located between the cylinder banks. On in-line engines, it may be attached to either the right or left side of the cylinder head and directly above the exhaust manifold. The carburetor is bolted to an opening in the centre of the manifold.

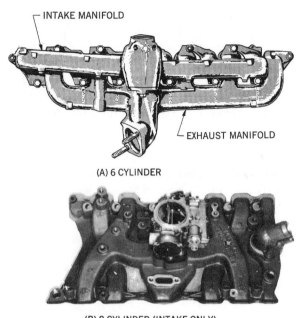

(A) 6 CYLINDER

(B) 8 CYLINDER (INTAKE ONLY)

Fig. 4-8   Manifolds

The *exhaust manifold* is a pipe, bolted to the exhaust ports, that carries hot exhaust gases to the exhaust pipe. It is usually made of cast iron to withstand the excessive heat of the exhaust gases. The intake and exhaust manifolds are bolted together so that the heat from the exhaust manifold may pass to the intake manifold and thereby aid in vaporizing the fuel (Figure 4-8).

ENGINE MOVING PARTS

CRANKSHAFT

The crankshaft, made of forged steel, is located in the crankcase directly below the cylinders. Forged steel is steel that has been heated until red-hot and then hammered or pressed into the proper shape. The bearing surfaces of the shaft are accurately ground to size, and the entire shaft is delicately and accurately balanced. The shaft is supported in the crankcase by bearings known as *main bear-*

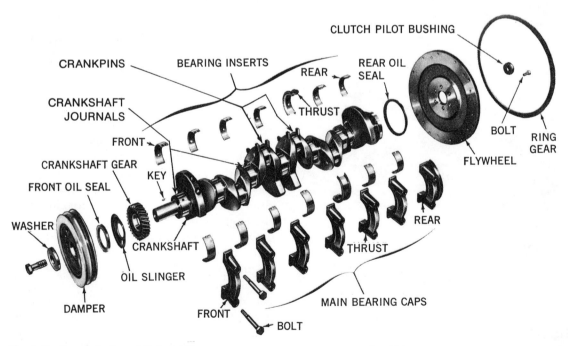

Fig. 4-9   Crankshaft and Related Parts

Ford Motor Company of Canada Limited

ings. Each main bearing fits on a main-bearing journal.

On a bicycle, your feet push only in a downward direction on the bicycle pedals, causing the crank to revolve. This up-and-down motion (reciprocating motion) is changed into rotary motion. Similarly, the purpose of the crankshaft is to change the reciprocating motion of the piston in the cylinder to the rotary motion of the flywheel. This conversion of motion is accomplished by the use of offset cranks called *throws.* There is a throw for each cylinder of an in-line engine, while on V8 engines one throw serves a cylinder in each bank. The throw has a bearing

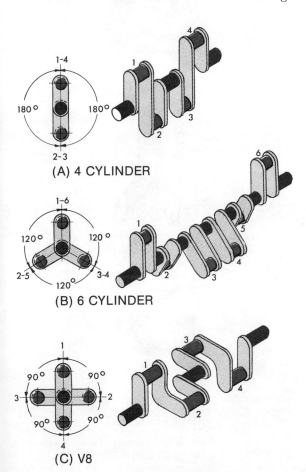

(A) 4 CYLINDER

(B) 6 CYLINDER

(C) V8

Fig. 4-10 Crankshaft Throws

surface known as a *crankpin,* to which the connecting rod is attached (Figure 4-10).

Crankshaft Bearings. Both the main bearings and connecting-rod bearings are liners made of a long-wearing tin and lead alloy known as *babbitt.* The liner is of the split-shell design and is fused to a steel or bronze backing to provide the necessary strength. Many bearings used in late model engines have an overlay of copper alloy or cadmium-silver placed on the face of the babbitt to increase the wearing properties of the bearing.

The bearing shells are held in place and prevented from turning by small tangs or locking lugs. The tangs fit into recesses in the crankcase and cap. One main bearing will be made with side flanges to take care of the end thrust of the crankshaft. The rear main bearing is designed to include an oil seal which prevents leakage of oil along the shaft and out the rear of the engine.

Flywheel. The flywheel is a heavy, carefully machined, perfectly balanced wheel, usually bolted to a flange on the rear end of the crankshaft. When a heavy wheel is turned, there is a force known as momentum which tends to keep it turning. Because of its momentum, the flywheel tends to keep the crankshaft, and other moving parts of the engine, moving or turning when there is no downward push on the cranks. An engine with many cylinders does not need as heavy a flywheel as an engine with fewer cylinders because of *power lap.*

CONNECTING RODS AND PISTONS

Connecting rods join the pistons to the crankshaft. They are fastened to the pistons by hollow steel pins called piston pins or wrist pins. The piston pin may be held in position in one of four ways: it may be locked to the connecting rod or to the piston-pin boss by a lock bolt; it may be pressed into the connecting rod and rely on the tightness of the fit to keep it in its proper position; or it may be allowed to float in both the piston bosses and the connecting rod and held in position by snap rings located in grooves in the piston. Bronze bushings are sometimes placed on the oscillating piston or connecting rod to help reduce wear.

Each connecting rod is fastened to a crankpin on the crankshaft by a plain split bearing, which permits easy removal of the bearing cap and the connecting rod from the crankshaft. These bearings are lined with babbitt for long wear (Figure 4-11).

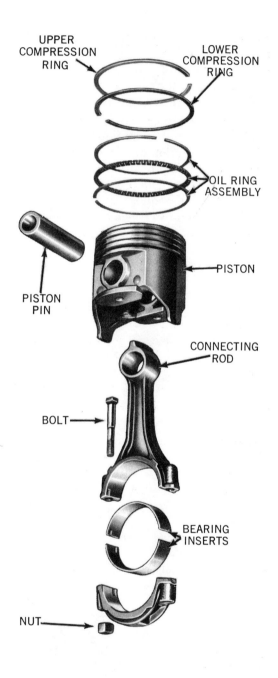

(A) ASSEMBLED

Chrysler Canada Ltd.

(B) EXPLODED

Ford Motor Company of Canada Limited

Fig. 4-11   Piston and Connecting Rod Assembly

Pistons. The pistons move up and down in the cylinders. They are the first moving part to receive the push of the burning and expanding fuel in the cylinders.

Some engines have pistons made of cast iron, but cast-iron pistons have the disadvantage of being too heavy for high-speed operation. Other engines use pistons made of lightweight aluminum alloy. Light pistons can be moved up and down in the cylinder faster without wasting as much power.

The top of the piston is called the *piston head,* and the lower part is called the *skirt.* Grooves are cut around the head, and the piston rings fit into these grooves. As aluminum expands more rapidly than cast iron when heated, aluminum pistons usually have slots in the skirt to prevent the piston from overexpanding and seizing in the cylinder. The hole in the piston skirt through which the piston pin passes is reinforced for strength and to provide a greater bearing surface. These reinforced areas around the piston-pin holes are called *piston-pin bosses.*

Piston Rings. Piston rings are located in the ring grooves around the head of the piston, and on some pistons one ring is located around the skirt. Three purposes are served by the piston rings: they seal the space between the cylinder wall and the piston, preventing the escape of burning gases from the combustion chamber; they control the flow of oil over the cylinder walls; and they dissipate heat to the cylinder walls. Piston rings are made slightly larger in diameter than the cylinder they are to fit. The ring is then cut at one place so that it can be expanded over the piston for installation. The ring must then be compressed to close the gap where it was cut, in order to install the piston and ring assembly in the cylinder. This compressing of the ring puts the ring under tension, so that it is always pressing outwards against the cylin-

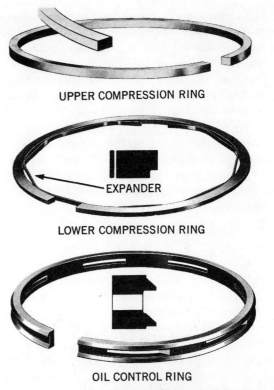

UPPER COMPRESSION RING

LOWER COMPRESSION RING

EXPANDER

OIL CONTROL RING

The Hastings Manufacturing Company

Fig. 4-12   Piston Rings

der wall, providing the necessary sealing action.

There are many types of piston rings: the compression ring, the oil ring, and the compression scraper ring, to name but a few.

Compression rings are usually located in the top grooves of the piston. They are smooth and their principal purpose is to prevent the loss of compression from the combustion chamber above the piston.

Compression scraper rings are placed in the second ring groove. They are dual purpose rings, because they assist the compression ring in forming a seal, and the oil ring in removing excess oil from the cylinder walls.

Oil rings are located in the lower ring grooves. These rings are used to regulate the amount of oil on the cylinder walls, thereby preventing loss of oil into the combustion chamber. Slots are cut through the oil rings and as surplus oil is scraped from the cylinder walls by the rings, it flows through the slots to the back of the rings, then on through oil holes to the inside of the piston, where it drops back into the oil pan. Sometimes thin steel rings, called *inner rings,* are used under the compression and oil rings to make them exert more pressure on the cylinder walls.

Timing Gears. The crankshaft gear is on the end of the crankshaft and the camshaft gear is on the end of the camshaft. The camshaft must rotate at half the speed of the crankshaft. This is accomplished by using a crankshaft gear having exactly one-half the number of teeth of the camshaft gear. The camshaft must rotate at half the speed of the crankshaft because each valve opens only once in every two revolutions of the crankshaft. For example, the exhaust must be removed on every other stroke (Figure 4-13).

Some engines use a silent *timing chain* and *sprockets* to drive the camshaft, instead of timing gears. Timing gears are not always made of the same material. Combinations of fibre, steel, or aluminum gears are used to achieve quiet operation and longest wear.

Overhead camshaft type engines frequently use a cogged type of belt to drive the camshaft.

Both timing gears and sprockets are marked to show the point of mesh. These timing marks must be aligned according to the manufacturer's specifications to assure proper relationship between the opening and closing of the valves, according to the position of the piston in the cylinder.

Camshaft. The camshaft (Figure 4-14) on four and six cylinder in-line engines is located

(A) TIMING SPROCKET MARKS

TIMING MARKS

(B) TIMING GEAR MARKS

General Motors Products of Canada, Limited

Fig. 4-13   Timing Gears and Timing Chains

in the crankcase to one side and slightly above the crankshaft. In V8 type engines it is directly above the crankshaft and between the two cylinder banks. In overhead camshaft engines the camshaft is attached to the cylinder head above the valves. The shaft is usually supported by three or four sleeve bearings. It

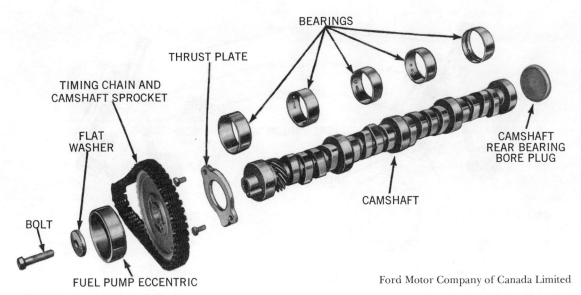

Ford Motor Company of Canada Limited

Fig. 4-14   Camshaft and Related Parts

is equipped with two cams for each cylinder. When the camshaft revolves, the cams cause the valve lifters to rise, opening the valves in the proper order at the correct time. A gear near the centre of the camshaft is used to drive the *oil-pump shaft* and the *distributor shaft* at the same speed as the camshaft. The camshaft also operates the fuel pump, which is located on the side of the crankcase.

Valve Lifters.   Valve lifters may be solid or hydraulic and are located directly above the camshaft, with their lower ends resting on the cams of the camshaft. The valve stem, or push rod, contacts the upper surface of the lifter. As the high point of the cam passes under the lifter, the lifter rises and causes the valve to open. The valve lifters slide up and down in *lifter guides,* which are cylindrical holes in the cylinder block above the camshaft. In some engines the lifter guides are removable sleeves. The action between the cam and the lifter is a rolling motion. Therefore, the bottom of the lifter has to be hard enough to withstand wear.

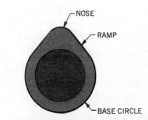

(A)   CAM NOMENCLATURE

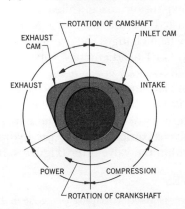

(B)   CAM ARRANGEMENT

Fig. 4-15   Cam Nomenclature

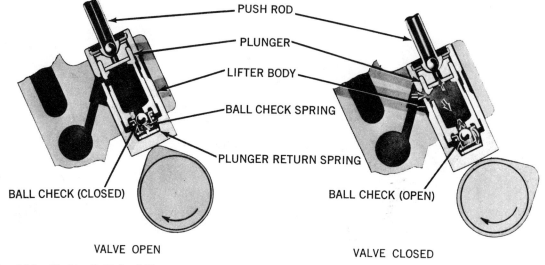

PUSH ROD

PLUNGER

LIFTER BODY

BALL CHECK SPRING

PLUNGER RETURN SPRING

BALL CHECK (CLOSED)

BALL CHECK (OPEN)

VALVE OPEN

VALVE CLOSED

Fig. 4-16   Hydraulic Valve Lifters   General Motors Products of Canada, Limited

In order to maintain proper running clearance and to assure complete closing of the valves, it is necessary to allow space for the expansion of the valve stem as it becomes heated. The valve lifter or tappet provides a convenient place to allow for this expansion.

On L-head engines using solid lifters, the valve expansion space, called *valve clearance*, is adjusted by the use of a *tappet-adjusting screw*, which changes the overall length of the tappet. On I-head engines, valve clearance is adjusted by *rocker arm adjusting screws*.

Most late-model engines have *hydraulic valve lifters*, which are very quiet, as they assure zero valve clearance. The expansion of the valve is compensated by the hydraulic action within the valve lifter (Figure 4-16).

VALVES

A valve is used to open or close a hole, or port. The engine valves are located in the exhaust and intake ports with the stem extending to the valve lifter or rocker arm. Each cylinder has two valves: an intake valve, which

opens and closes the intake port, and an exhaust valve, which opens and closes the exhaust port (Figure 4-17). As the exhaust valve must withstand the excessive heat of the exhaust gases, a special heat-resisting alloy of

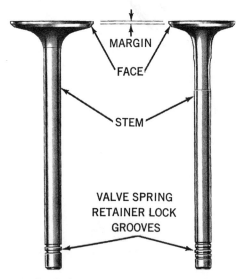

MARGIN

FACE

STEM

VALVE SPRING
RETAINER LOCK
GROOVES

Fig. 4-17   Valves   Chrysler Canada Ltd.

nickel, tungsten, and silicon-chrome steel is commonly used in its construction. Some exhaust valves are hollow and filled with sodium, which helps to dissipate the excessive

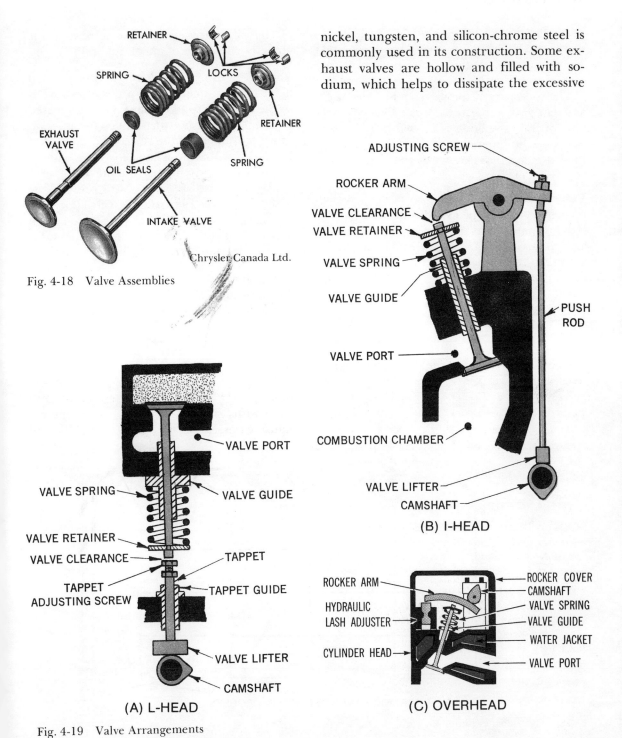

Fig. 4-18 Valve Assemblies

Chrysler Canada Ltd.

RETAINER

SPRING

LOCKS

RETAINER

EXHAUST VALVE

OIL SEALS

SPRING

INTAKE VALVE

ADJUSTING SCREW

ROCKER ARM

VALVE CLEARANCE

VALVE RETAINER

VALVE SPRING

VALVE GUIDE

PUSH ROD

VALVE PORT

COMBUSTION CHAMBER

VALVE LIFTER

CAMSHAFT

(B) I-HEAD

VALVE PORT

VALVE SPRING

VALVE GUIDE

VALVE RETAINER

VALVE CLEARANCE

TAPPET

TAPPET ADJUSTING SCREW

TAPPET GUIDE

VALVE LIFTER

CAMSHAFT

(A) L-HEAD

Fig. 4-19   Valve Arrangements

ROCKER ARM

HYDRAULIC LASH ADJUSTER

CYLINDER HEAD

ROCKER COVER

CAMSHAFT

VALVE SPRING

VALVE GUIDE

WATER JACKET

VALVE PORT

(C) OVERHEAD

heat. The intake valve is made of chrome-nickel steel; chromium gives hardness and wear resistance to the steel, and nickel increases its strength.

The wide part of the valve is the *valve head* and below it is the *valve stem*. The tapered part of the valve head is known as the *valve face*, and the tapered part of the port where the valve face fits is known as the *valve seat*.

Valve Seats. Intake valve seats are usually formed as part of the cylinder head or block. Exhaust valve seats are usually special steel alloy inserts designed to withstand the high temperatures of the exhaust gases. They can be replaced should they become cracked, burnt or damaged.

The valve face and seat are accurately machined to an angle of either 30° or 45°.

Valve Guides. Valve guides may be reamed holes or semi-steel inserts pressed into holes in the cylinder head or block. They are used as a slipper bearing that guides the up-and-down movement of the valve. The valve must be guided within close limits to assure that the valve face fits accurately on the valve seat. The guides also act as a seal to prevent the gases from escaping from the valve port into the valve chamber, and to prevent oil from leaking from the valve chamber into the valve port on overhead valve engines.

Valve Springs. Valve springs are located on the valve stem and are fastened at the end of

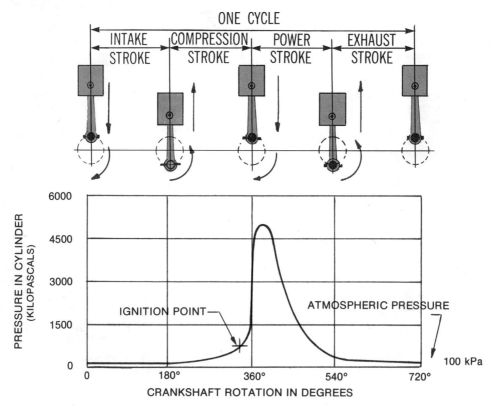

Fig. 4-20   Cylinder Pressure in One Cycle

the stem by a pin or key, held in place by the spring pressure. The purpose of the spring is to keep the valve closed when it is not being forced open by the action of the camshaft. Before a valve can be removed, the valve spring must be compressed and the key or pin removed. The tool used for this purpose is called a *valve-spring compressor*.

Valve Push Rods and Rocker Arms.   Valve push rods and rocker arms are required on overhead valve engines. The push rod is used to transfer the up-and-down motion of the valve lifter to the rocker arm. The rocker arm reverses the upward motion of the valve lifter to push the valve downward to open. A push rod and rocker arm is required for each valve of the engine. The rocker arms may be pivoted on a common rocker-arm shaft or individually on rocker-arm studs. The rocker-arm shaft is attached to the cylinder head by mounting brackets. The individual rocker-arm studs are pressed into the cylinder head.

AIR PRESSURE IN ENGINE

In order to produce power from the burning of fuel, it is necessary to (a) secure fuel for combustion, (b) prepare the fuel for combustion, (c) ignite and burn the fuel to develop the power, and (d) remove the burnt and waste products of combustion. In the internal-combustion engine, these four operations are accomplished by the changing of the air pressure inside the cylinder.

From elementary science we learn that the air around us has a given pressure called *atmospheric pressure*, which is normally equal to approximately 100 kPa. In engineering, atmospheric pressure is sometimes talked of as zero pressure. This refers to air pressure which, at sea level, is zero. Pressures below this level are stated in numbers smaller than 100 kPa, while pressures above it are measured in numbers larger than 100 kPa. By

various means it is possible to raise or lower air pressure and atmospheric pressure.

To understand the operation of the internal-combustion engine it is necessary to make a comparison of the pressures inside the cylinder on each stroke.

During Securing of Fuel or Intake Stroke. When the piston on the intake stroke moves from TDC to BDC, the volume of the cylinder chamber is enlarged. This enlargement of the cylinder chamber causes a decrease in air pressure which creates a partial vacuum inside the cylinder. Since the movement of air is always from a high-pressure area (atmospheric pressure in this case) to a lower-pressure area (partial vacuum in this case), it is possible for atmospheric pressure to force the necessary charge of fuel for combustion into the cylinder.

During Preparation or Compression Stroke.   As the piston moves from BDC to TDC during the compression stroke, it can readily be seen that the volume of the cylinder decreases. Since the fuel mixture has no means of escape, it is squeezed into a smaller space. This increases the pressure above atmospheric pressure. The name given to this pressure in the automotive service trade is *compression pressure* and, depending on the type of engine, it usually ranges between 850 kPa and 1000 kPa.

During Combustion or Power Stroke. When the compressed fuel and air mixture is ignited and combustion follows, the burning gases expand rapidly, and a much greater pressure is created inside the cylinder. This pressure increase is approximately five times greater than the compression pressure, being between 4200 kPa and 4900 kPa. It is this pressure that pushes the piston down from TDC to BDC in the cylinder and creates the mechanical effort necessary to operate the engine.

During Cleaning or Exhaust Stroke. To rid the cylinder of the burnt or waste gases, it is necessary to create a pressure higher than atmospheric pressure in order to force the waste gases out into the atmosphere. During the exhaust stroke the piston moves from BDC to TDC and the volume of the cylinder is again decreased, thus increasing the pressure. This increase in pressure forces the burnt gases out of the cylinder through an exhaust opening.

THE FOUR-STROKE-CYCLE PRINCIPLE

It has been shown that four operations are required to complete one cycle, namely, the collection of the fuel, the preparation of the fuel, the burning of the fuel, and the disposing of the burnt fuel. Since each of these operations requires one stroke, the internal-combustion engine is said to operate on the *Four-Stroke-Cycle Principle*. In the trade the four strokes are known as the intake, compression, power, and exhaust strokes (Figure 4-21).

In order to accomplish these strokes, it is necessary to open and close, by means of valves, small openings called *ports* in the upper cylinder chamber. When these ports are open, they allow either fuel to enter the cylinder or burnt gases to escape. A valve-operating mechanism opens the intake valve only during the *intake stroke* and opens the exhaust valve only during the *exhaust stroke*.

The four-stroke-cycle principle can be described as follows:

1. During the intake stroke, the piston travels downward in the cylinder from TDC to BDC, creating a partial vacuum in the cylinder. Atmospheric pressure forces air through the *carburetor*, where it mixes with gasoline and enters the cylinder through the open intake valve. The exhaust valve

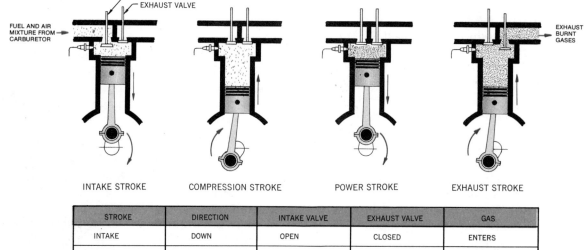

STROKE	DIRECTION	INTAKE VALVE	EXHAUST VALVE	GAS
INTAKE	DOWN	OPEN	CLOSED	ENTERS
COMPRESSION	UP	CLOSED	CLOSED	COMPRESSED
POWER	DOWN	CLOSED	CLOSED	BURNT
EXHAUST	UP	CLOSED	OPEN	EXPELLED

Fig. 4-21   The Four-stroke-cycle Principle

remains closed during this stroke and the crankshaft turns through half a revolution.

2. The intake valve closes, the piston moves up from BDC to TDC, and the gas in the cylinder is compressed in the combustion chamber. This stroke is called the *compression stroke*. Both valves remain closed throughout this stroke. The crankshaft has now completed one revolution.

3. The fuel is now ready to be ignited. This is accomplished by an electric spark at the spark plug. Combustion immediately takes place, and the gas, as it burns, heats and expands instantly. The rapid expansion of the gas greatly increases the pressure in the cylinder and forces the piston down from TDC to BDC, causing the crankshaft to turn. This is known as the *power stroke*. Both valves remain closed during this stroke.

4. The crankshaft has now rotated 1.5 revolutions, and the cylinder has become filled with burnt gases that must be removed. The exhaust valve opens, and the piston moves from BDC to TDC, forcing the burnt gases out of the cylinder. This is known as the *exhaust stroke*. During this stroke the intake valve remains closed. Now the crankshaft has completed two revolutions. The piston is at top dead centre and the engine is ready to repeat the cycle of operations.

Since one stroke is equal to 0.5 revolutions of the crankshaft, 2 revolutions of the crankshaft are required to complete one four-stroke cycle. In order to keep the engine in continuous operation, the momentum of the *flywheel* is used to carry the engine through the exhaust, intake, and compression strokes.

VALVE TIMING

During the discussions of the four-stroke-cycle principle, it was assumed that the valves opened and closed at TDC or BDC, and that a cycle was 720° in length (2 revolutions of crankshaft). In practice the valves do not open and close on the dead centres but open before or close after dead centre is reached.

The changing of stroke length by valve timing is done to increase engine power. This may seem odd at first, as the power stroke is shortened by 45°. However, by the time the power stroke reaches 45° before BDC, the pressure in the cylinder has dropped considerably and the crankshaft throw is not in a position to effectively produce turning effort. It is more advantageous, therefore, to open the exhaust valve earlier and allow the remaining pressure to force the exhaust gases through the exhaust system. Leaving the exhaust valve open for 5° after TDC takes advantage of the inertia of the moving gases to further *scavenge* (remove burnt gases from) the cylinder.

As the exhaust gases rush past the area of the intake valve, they create a low pressure in that area. Opening the intake valve 5° before TDC of the intake stroke utilizes this low pressure to start the fuel-air mixture flowing into the cylinder. Leaving the intake valve open for 45° after BDC also makes use of the inertia of the moving gases to fill the cylinder more completely. The more fuel-air mixture that enters the cylinder on the intake stroke, the higher the Volumetric Efficiency and the more power produced. (See Figure 4-22.)

The opening of a valve before either TDC or BDC is called *valve lead*. The closing of a valve after TDC or BDC is called *valve lag*. When the valves are open at the same time between the exhaust and intake strokes it is called *valve lap*.

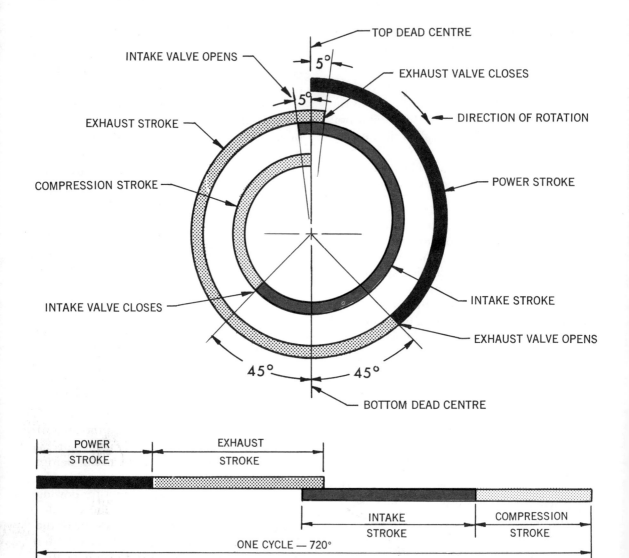

Fig. 4-22   Relationships Between Theoretical and Actual Strokes

STROKE	THEORETICAL LENGTH	START OF STROKE	END OF STROKE	ACTUAL LENGTH
Power	180°	TDC	45° before BDC	135°
Exhaust	180°	45° before BDC	5° after TDC	230°
Intake	180°	5° before TDC	45° after BDC	230°
Compression	180°	45° before BDC	TDC	135°
One Cycle	720°			730°

MULTI-CYLINDER ENGINES

The simple one-cylinder engine that has been described would not be satisfactory for the operation of the modern motor car. Nowadays most motor vehicles use either a *four-cylinder, six-cylinder* or *eight-cylinder* engine. The power strokes of multi-cylindered engines are so timed that they occur at intervals of 180° of crankshaft rotation in a four-cylinder, 120° in a six-cylinder, and 90° in an eight-cylinder engine.

The greater the number of cylinders an engine has, the shorter the interval between the power strokes. In the six-cylinder and eight-cylinder engines, the second power stroke starts before the first power stroke finishes. This overlap of power strokes is known as *power lap*.

Regardless of the number of cylinders in an engine, each cylinder operates as a single self-contained unit, following the basic four-stroke-cycle principle. Each unit is connected

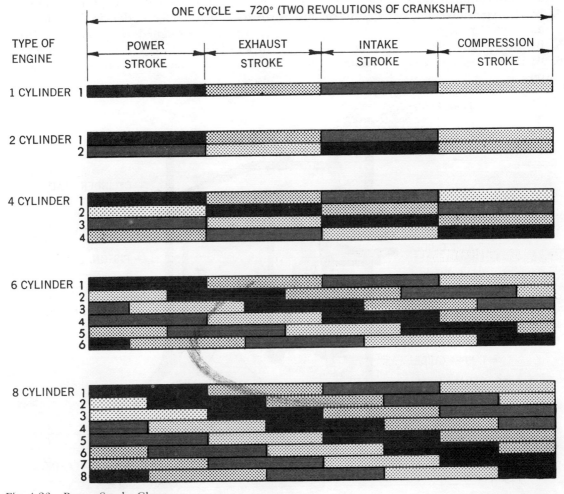

Fig. 4-23   Power Stroke Chart

to a common crankshaft and uses a common fuel supply, exhaust, and ignition system. (See Figure 4-23).

TYPES OF ENGINES

Engines may be classified in many different ways:

1. By the number of cylinders—4, 6, or 8
2. By the arrangement of the cylinders—in line or V
3. By the types of valve arrangement—I, L, T, or F (the I and L arrangements being the most common today)
4. By the type of cooling system—air or liquid
5. By the type of cycle—two or four strokes
6. By the type of fuel used—gasoline or diesel

Because most automobiles use liquid-cooled, gasoline, internal-combustion, four-cycle engines, we shall be concerned only with the valve and cylinder arrangements.

CYLINDER ARRANGEMENTS

Four-cylinder in-line engines have the cylinders cast vertically in a single row in the engine block. The crankshaft is supported by either three or four main bearings, and the throws are set 180° apart, with the throws for 1 and 4 cylinders in one position and the throws for 2 and 3 cylinders in the other. The camshaft is designed to produce a firing order of either 1, 3, 4, 2, or 1, 2, 4, 3. Either I-head or L-head valve arrangements may be used.

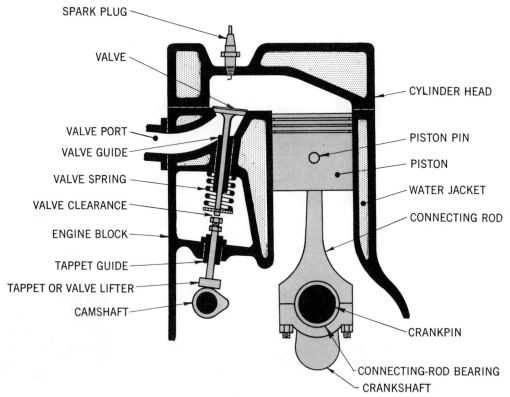

Fig. 4-24 L-Head Engine

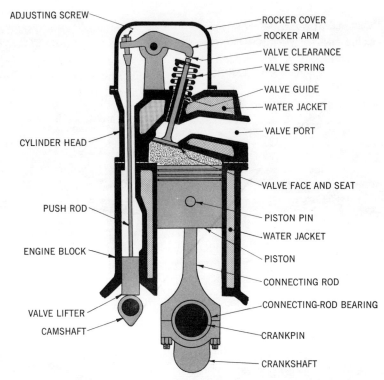

ADJUSTING SCREW

ROCKER COVER

ROCKER ARM

VALVE CLEARANCE

VALVE SPRING

VALVE GUIDE

WATER JACKET

CYLINDER HEAD

VALVE PORT

VALVE FACE AND SEAT

PUSH ROD

PISTON PIN

WATER JACKET

ENGINE BLOCK

PISTON

CONNECTING ROD

CONNECTING-ROD BEARING

VALVE LIFTER

CAMSHAFT

CRANKPIN

CRANKSHAFT

Fig. 4-25 I-Head Engine

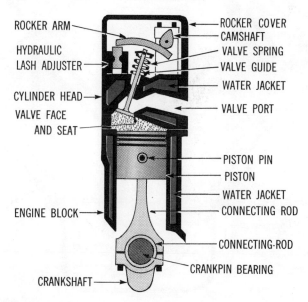

ROCKER ARM

ROCKER COVER

CAMSHAFT

HYDRAULIC
LASH ADJUSTER

VALVE SPRING

VALVE GUIDE

WATER JACKET

CYLINDER HEAD

VALVE PORT

VALVE FACE
AND SEAT

PISTON PIN

PISTON

WATER JACKET

CONNECTING ROD

ENGINE BLOCK

CONNECTING-ROD

CRANKPIN BEARING

CRANKSHAFT

Fig. 4-26 Overhead Camshaft Engine

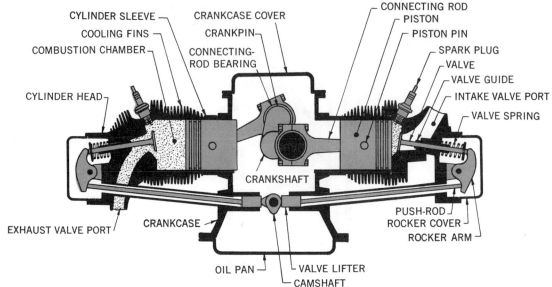

Fig. 4-27   Horizontal Opposed Engine

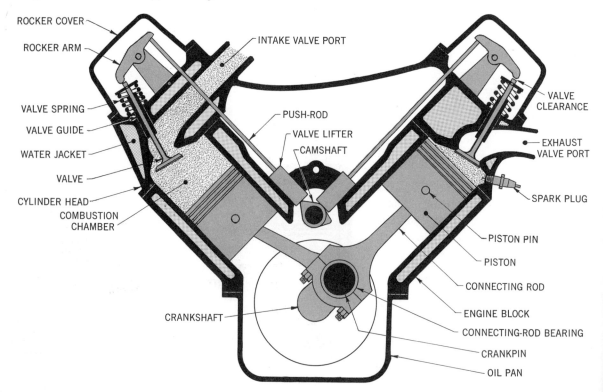

Fig. 4-28   I-Head V8 Engine

Six-cylinder in-line engines have the cylinders cast in the engine block in a single row. The cylinders are placed either vertically or at an angle of 30° from the vertical. The crankshaft, supported by three or four main bearings, has the throws placed 120° apart, with the throws for 1 and 6 cylinders in one position, 2 and 5 in the second position, and 3 and 4 in the third position. The camshaft is designed to produce a firing order, the most common being 1, 5, 3, 6, 2, 4. Either L-head or I-head valve arrangements may be used.

Six-cylinder horizontal opposed engines (pancake) have the cylinders in two rows, 180° apart. See Figure 4-27. The cylinders are individual cast-iron sleeves and are attached in groups of three to an aluminum cylinder head. The heads contain integral intake valve ports, combustion chambers, and valves for each cylinder. The cylinders are attached to each side of the aluminum crankcase, which can be split into halves. The crankcase supports the camshaft and the crankshaft, the latter being mounted on four main bearings. The crankshaft throws and the camshaft are arranged to give a firing order of 1, 4, 5, 2, 3, 6.

V6 cylinder engines have two banks of three cylinders set at an angle of 60° to each other. The crankshaft has four main bearings. The crankshaft throws and the camshaft are arranged to give a firing order of 1, 6, 5, 4, 3, 2. The valve arrangement is of the overhead valve type. These engines are sometimes coupled together to form a V12 engine for heavy trucks.

V8 cylinder engines have two banks of four cylinders each, usually set at an angle of 90° to each other. (See Figure 4-28.) The crankshaft is supported by four main bearings. The connecting rods are attached in pairs, one from each bank, to the crankpins. Late-model V8 engines are of the I-head type, although the L-head type has been used. Due to the wide variety of cylinder-numbering systems used, the firing orders vary greatly.

Cylinder Numbering. The numbering of the cylinders in multi-cylinder engines varies, depending upon the manufacturer (Figure 4-29).

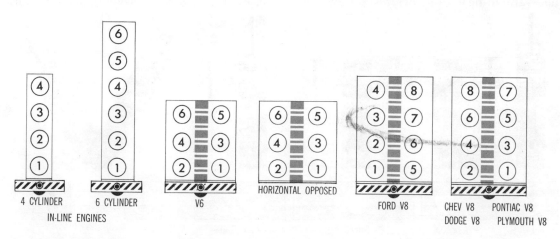

Fig. 4-29   Cylinder Numbering

VALVE ARRANGEMENTS

L-Head Valve Arrangement. In an L-head valve arrangement, sometimes referred to as "valve-in-block" or "flat head," the cylinders and combustion chamber form an inverted L (Figure 4-30). The intake and exhaust valves of each cylinder are located side by side in the engine block beside the cylinder. In L-head V8 engines the valves are located between the two banks. Only one camshaft is required in both cases. The valve operation is as follows: as the high point of the cam passes under the valve lifter, or tappet, the lifter is raised, which in turn raises the valve. As the valve is raised, the valve spring is compressed between the engine block and the retaining washer, the latter being locked to the valve stem by the valve lock or keeper. As the high point of the cam moves away from the lifter, the valve spring expands, closing the valve.

The L-head engine has lost its popularity because its larger combustion chamber makes it very difficult to produce the high compression ratios which are required for today's powerful engines.

I-Head Valve Arrangement. In the I-head type valve arrangement, sometimes known as the "valve-in-head" or "overhead valve arrangement," the valves are located side by side in the cylinder head. A series of rocker arms are mounted on top of the cylinder head and are operated by push rods. These rods are located beside the cylinders in an in-line engine or between the banks of a V6 or V8 engine. In both cases only one camshaft is used.

The valve operation is as follows: as the high point of the cam passes under the valve lifter, the lifter is raised, which in turn raises the push rod, which lifts one end of the rocker arm, causing the rocker arm to pivot around its axis. Since the rocker arm is a first class lever, when one end moves up, the other end moves down. This downward motion is applied to the valve stem, which opens the valve and compresses the valve spring between the cylinder head and the retaining washer. The retaining washer is locked to the valve stem by the valve keeper. As the high point of the cam moves away from the lifter, the valve spring expands, closing the valve.

ENGINE AUXILIARY SYSTEMS

In order to maintain continuous engine operation, certain other auxiliary systems are necessary, such as the cooling system, lubri-

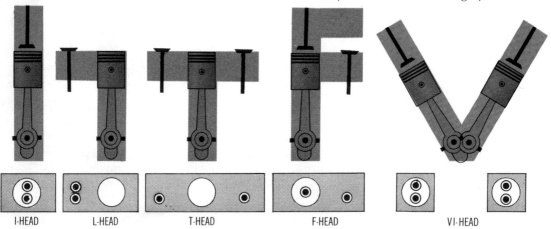

I-HEAD   L-HEAD   T-HEAD   F-HEAD   VI-HEAD

Fig. 4-30   Valve Arrangements

cating system, fuel system, exhaust system, starting system, ignition system, and generating system. These systems and the basic engine parts combine to form a complete self-contained power plant.

Cooling System.   The heat generated by the burning of the fuel inside the cylinder is sufficient to heat the cylinder walls red-hot. This great heat is capable of burning off the lubricating oil and thus causing the pistons to expand and seize in the cylinder. It is necessary, therefore, to cool the cylinder walls in order to keep them at an efficient operating temperature of approximately 87°C. Water and air are most commonly used for cooling purposes.

Lubricating System.   Oil for the lubricating system is carried in the oil pan. The oil is pumped by the oil pump to many moving parts of the engine so that they will operate smoothly and with very little friction. The oil, as it travels through the engine, picks up a considerable amount of heat. It transfers this heat to the oil pan, where the oil is cooled by the air passing under the bottom of the oil pan. If the lubricating system fails, the engine will seize and stop, and many parts will be damaged beyond repair.

Fuel System.   Fuel for the engine must be vaporized, that is, converted to a gas, and combined with the proper proportion of air to make a very explosive mixture. The fuel system consists of the parts which hold and carry the gasoline and prepare the proper mixture for the engine.

Exhaust System. Poisonous burnt gases leave the cylinder through the exhaust port with considerable noise. Therefore, they must be silenced and, in addition, must be conveyed to the rear of the automobile, away from the passenger compartment. This is done by the exhaust system, made up of the exhaust manifold, exhaust pipe, muffler and tailpipe.

Starting System. The starting system consists of the battery and the starting motor and its controls. When the engine is starting, the starting motor receives electrical energy from the battery and converts this energy into the mechanical energy necessary to crank the engine.

Ignition System.   The ignition system consists of the battery, ignition switch, ignition coil, distributor, and spark plugs. When the switch is turned on and the engine started, the coil receives electrical energy from the battery and produces high-voltage surges of current. These high-voltage surges flow to the distributor, which distributes them to the spark plugs. The spark at the spark plug ignites, or sets fire to, the fuel in the cylinders.

Charging System.   The charging system consists of the alternator and its controls. In most cases, the alternator is driven by the fan belt. Electricity is produced by the alternator to recharge the battery and supply the other units of the electrical system.

TWO-STROKE-CYCLE ENGINES

Small two-stroke-cycle engines are used as the power plant for lawn mowers, snow blowers, and small garden tractors, and as marine outboard engines. These engines may be *air cooled* (lawn mowers, etc.) or *liquid cooled* (outboards). They are lubricated by mixing the lubricating oil with the gasoline, and have *magneto-type* ignition systems.

The most common type of large two-stroke-cycle engine is the diesel engine, although some large two-stroke-cycle gasoline engines are manufactured for special applications.

In a two-stroke-cycle engine, only two strokes of the piston (one revolution of the crankshaft) are required to complete one

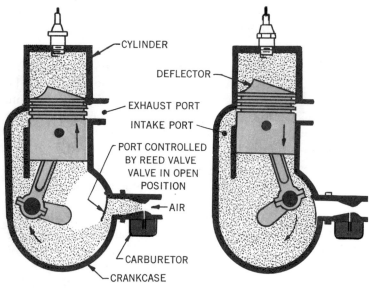
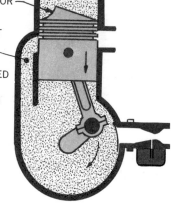
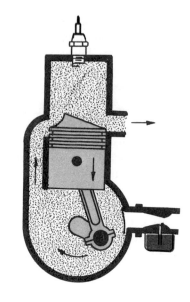

CYLINDER

DEFLECTOR

EXHAUST PORT

INTAKE PORT

PORT CONTROLLED
BY REED VALVE
VALVE IN OPEN
POSITION

← AIR

CARBURETOR

CRANKCASE

(A) COMPRESSION STROKE   (B) POWER STROKE   (C) INTAKE AND EXHAUST STROKE

2-PORT TYPE

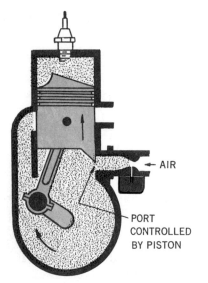
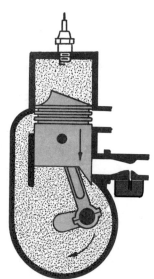
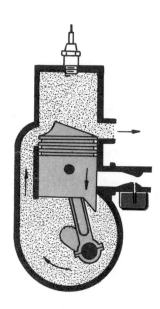

← AIR

PORT
CONTROLLED
BY PISTON

(A) COMPRESSION STROKE   (B) POWER STROKE   (C) INTAKE AND EXHAUST STROKE

3-PORT TYPE

Fig. 4-31   Two-stroke-cycle Engine

cycle. To accomplish the four operations (intake, compression, power, and exhaust) with only two strokes of the piston, both the top and bottom sides of the piston are utilized. The underside of the piston is used to create the low pressure in the crankcase which is required to bring the fuel and air mixture in through the carburetor, and to partially compress this fuel and air mixture in the crankcase just before the piston uncovers the intake port.

Several types of two-stroke-cycle engines have been produced: the two-port type, the three-port type, and the exhaust-valve type, all of which require sealed crankcases; and a type which uses a blower or supercharger to produce the initial pressure to force the fuel and air, or air only (diesels) into the cylinder. The latter type does not require a sealed crankcase.

CONSTRUCTION

Crankcase. In order to utilize the underside of the piston, the two-stroke-cycle engine must have an enclosed and air-tight crankcase which has a separate sealed compartment for each cylinder.

The two-port-type engine requires a *reed* or *flapper* type valve mounted between the carburetor and the crankcase. This valve opens to permit the entrance of fuel and air into the crankcase when the pressure in the crankcase is less than atmospheric pressure, and closes when the crankcase pressure is above atmospheric pressure.

In the three-port-type engine, the carburetor-to-crankcase passageway is located at the bottom of the cylinder. The piston skirt acts as a valve which uncovers and covers the port that admits the fuel-air mixture into the crankcase. This occurs when the crankcase pressure is lower than atmospheric pressure.

Provision for the main bearing supports in the crankcase is similar to that of the four-stroke-cycle engine.

Cylinder Block, Cylinder Head, Piston and Rod Assembly. The cylinder block may be cast separately or may be an integral part of the cylinder head. It may consist of a steel cylinder assembly and a separate cast head. The assembly may be made of cast iron, aluminum, or die cast alloys, and is designed to include the cooling fins or water jackets and the inlet transfer passageway.

Instead of using valves to control the entry of the fuel-air mixtures into the cylinder, or the exhaust gases from leaving the cylinder, most two-stroke-cycle engines use *ports* (holes in the cylinder walls). The ports are covered and uncovered as the piston travels up and down in the cylinder and are located on opposite sides of the cylinder just above BDC of the piston travel. The exhaust port is located higher up in the cylinder than the intake port so that it will be uncovered first on the exhaust stroke.

When exhaust ports are used, a *deflector*, formed on the inlet side of the piston head, diverts the fresh fuel-air mixture up into the cylinder while the exhaust gases are leaving the cylinder on the opposite side.

Some two-stroke-cycle engines use one or two exhaust valves located in the cylinder head, instead of the cylinder wall port. This valve is operated and timed by a camshaft and timing gears.

The piston, piston rings, piston pins, and connecting rods are similar to those used in four-stroke-cycle engines.

Crankshaft. The crankshaft is similar in design to the four-stroke-cycle type except that it must include machined surfaces for the crankcase seals. These seals are placed around the crankshaft between each cylinder and at each end and form an air tight seal for each crankcase compartment.

The magneto cam is mounted on one end of the shaft, and the drive pulley or coupling on the other.

OPERATING CYCLE (TWO-PORT TYPE)

Crankcase Action.   As the piston is moved from BDC to TDC, it creates a partial vacuum in the crankcase, causing the crankcase-to-carburetor valve to open and admit a charge of fuel-air mixture. When the piston travels from TDC to BDC, the fuel-air mixture in the crankcase is slightly compressed. Near the end of the stroke, the upper edge of the piston uncovers the intake port, and the compressed fuel-air mixture in the cylinder passes through the passageway into the cylinder.

Cylinder Action.   As the piston is moved from BDC to TDC, first the inlet port, then the exhaust port, is covered by the piston, and the fuel-air mixture is compressed. Near the end of the compression stroke, the mixture is ignited, causing combustion. The resulting pressure forces the piston from TDC to BDC to turn the crankshaft and develop power. Near the end of the power stroke, the piston uncovers the exhaust port and the burnt gases escape. As the piston moves further down in the cylinder, it uncovers the inlet port to admit the next charge of fuel-air mixture.

Since the actions above and below the piston are simultaneous, the four operations of intake, compression, power, and exhaust are completed in one revolution of the crankshaft.

PRACTICAL ASSIGNMENTS

a. Engine Parts Identification.   Use the cutaway diagram or model engine in the shop and locate all the stationary and moving parts discussed in this chapter.

b. Remove and Replace Cylinder Head—Block Assembly Only.

Procedure:

For an I-head engine do all steps.
For an L-head engine eliminate steps 2, 3, 4, 12, and 13.

1. Remove the spark plugs and place them in order in the spark-plug rack.
2. Remove the intake and exhaust manifolds.
3. Remove the rocker covers, rocker arm, and shaft assembly or rocker arms from the pivot studs.
4. Remove the push-rod covers and push rods, placing the rods in the proper order in a push-rod rack.
5. Remove cylinder-head bolts or nuts.
6. Lift off the cylinder head. Do not pry between the cylinder head and block, as parts could be damaged. Remove and discard the used gasket.
7. Clean the cylinder-head and cylinder-block gasket surfaces.
8. Have the instructor inspect your work.
9. Place a little oil around the pistons in each cylinder.
10. Make sure that the new gasket is in proper alignment and place it over the cylinder-head studs or guide pins which have been temporarily installed in the cylinder-head bolt holes.
11. Install the cylinder-head bolts or nuts finger tight. Using a torque wrench, tighten the nuts or bolts in several steps to proper torque specifications, following the proper tightening sequence.
12. Install the push rods, making sure that they are properly seated in the valve lifters; install rocker arms and shaft assembly or rocker arms on pivot studs.
13. Tighten the rocker-arm shaft, attaching bolts to torque specifications.
14. Adjust valve clearance as outlined in practical assignment d., page 113.

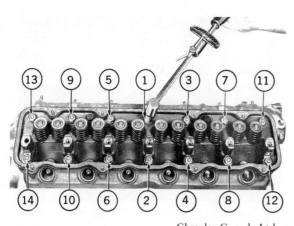

Chrysler Canada Ltd.

Fig. 4-32   Cylinder Head Tightening Sequence

c. Remove and Replace Valves.

Procedure:

1. Remove the cylinder head as outlined in the preceding assignment.
   CAUTION: On L-head engines, cover any holes in the block through which the valve retainers could drop.
2. Using the correct valve-spring compressor, compress the valve spring and remove the valve-spring lock or keeper.
3. Release the valve-spring compressor, and

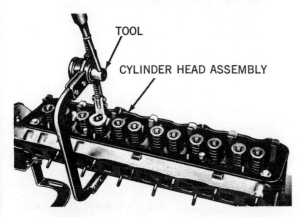

TOOL

CYLINDER HEAD ASSEMBLY

Chrysler Canada Ltd.

Fig. 4-33   Removing Valves

remove the valve spring and retaining washer.
4. On L-head engines remove the valve from the block.
   On I-head engines remove the valve from the underside of the head.
5. Place the valve you have removed in the valve rack.
6. Repeat steps 2 to 5 for the remaining valves.
   CAUTION: Place the valves in their proper order on the valve rack.
7. Identify all the parts.
8. Reassemble all the valves, springs, retaining washers, and retaining locks or keepers.
9. Have the instructor inspect your work.

d. Adjust Valves on Engines with Solid Lifters.

Procedure:

Start the engine and allow it to run at a fast idle until it reaches its normal operating temperature. After the engine reaches normal operating temperature, run it at a slow idle and then proceed with the checking and adjusting of the valves. You may set valves with the engine stopped by turning the crankshaft until the valve lifter is on the low point of the cam. Check and adjust the exhaust valves first.

For L-Head Engines

1. If the tappet screw has a lock nut, loosen it slightly.
2. Insert a feeler gauge of the proper thickness between the end of the valve stem and the top of the adjusting screw. If the feeler gauge cannot be inserted, turn the adjusting screw in with one wrench while holding the valve lifter with another (Figure 4-34).
3. Turn the adjusting screw until the feeler gauge can be moved in and out with a slight drag.

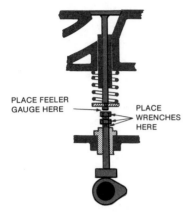

PLACE FEELER
GAUGE HERE

PLACE
WRENCHES
HERE

Fig. 4-34   Valve Adjustment of L-Head Engine

4. Tighten the lock nut (where used) and recheck the adjustment with the feeler gauge.
5. Repeat for all other valves.
6. Have the instructor inspect your work.

For I-Head Engines

1. Insert a feeler gauge of the proper thickness between the valve stem and the end of the rocker arm (Figure 4-35). If the

WRENCH

STEP-TYPE FEELER GAUGE

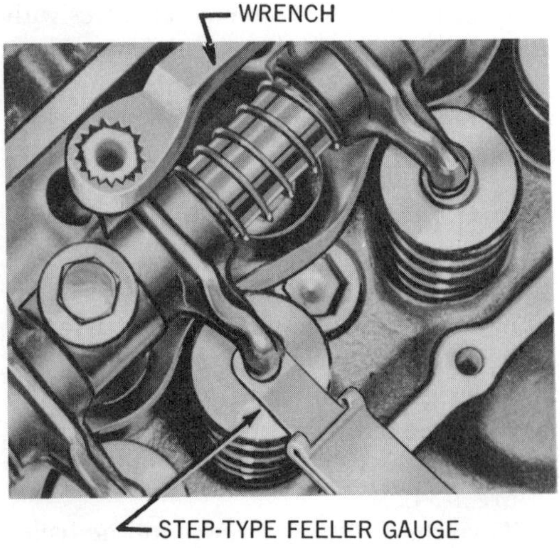

Ford Motor Company of Canada Limited

Fig. 4-35   Valve Adjustment of I-Head Engine

gauge will not slide in, use a screwdriver to prevent the adjusting screw from turning and, with a wrench, loosen the lock nut. Back out the screw sufficiently to allow the gauge to slip in between the valve stem and the end of the rocker arm.

2. To adjust the valve clearance, tighten the screw (the lock nut must be loosened) until the feeler gauge is gripped firmly between the valve stem and the rocker arm. Then loosen the screw until the feeler gauge can be moved in and out with a slight drag. Hold the screw in this position and tighten the lock nut. Then, recheck the clearance to make sure that tightening the lock nut has not changed the adjustment.

3. Adjust the remaining valves in the same manner.

4. Have the instructor inspect your work.

e. Adjust Hydraulic Valve Lifters.   Hydraulic valve lifters must not be adjusted while in service. After the lifters have been cleaned, it is necessary to make a basic initial adjustment. Procedure:

1. Crank the engine until the valve lifter is on the low point of the cam.

2. Back off the adjusting nut (rocker-arm stud nut) until there is play in the valve push rod.

3. Tighten the adjusting nut to just barely remove the clearance between the push rod and rocker arm. This is accomplished by rocking the push rod as the nut is tightened. When the rod does not move readily in relation to the rocker arm, the clearance has been eliminated (Figure 4-36).

4. Tighten the adjusting nut an additional three-quarters of a turn to place the *hydraulic lifter plunger* in the centre of its travel.

5. Have the instructor inspect your work.

General Motors Products of Canada, Limited

Fig. 4-36   Hydraulic Valve-lifter Adjustment

f. Remove and Replace Oil Pan—Block Assembly Only.

Procedure:

1. Remove the drain plug and allow the engine oil to drain from the engine.
2. Remove the screws holding the pan to the block. To prevent the pan from dropping, steady it before taking out the last two screws.
3. If the pan sticks, pry it loose. Proceed carefully to avoid distorting the pan.
4. If the pan does not clear the crankshaft, turn the crankshaft a few degrees, so that the "counterweights" move out of the way.
5. Clean the pan by washing it with cleaning solvent, and remove all traces of gasket materials from the pan and block.
6. Have the instructor inspect your work.
7. Coat the new gasket (or gaskets) with grease and place it in position, aligning the gasket with the pan bolt holes.

8. Lift the pan into position and attach it with two screws, one on each side. Examine the gaskets to make sure that they are still in alignment. Install the remainder of the screws, tightening them uniformly so that the gaskets are compressed evenly.
9. Replace the oil plug and add the proper grade and amount of engine oil.
10. Have the instructor inspect your work.

g. Remove and Replace Piston and Connecting-Rod Assembly.

Procedure:

1. Remove cylinder head as outlined in practical assignment b., page 112.
2. Remove the oil pan as outlined in practical assignment f., page 115.
3. Examine the rod and rod cap for cylinder number identifying marks. These marks assure replacement of the rod and piston assembly in the cylinder from which it was removed. The marks are usually on the camshaft side of the rod and the cap.
4. If the rod and cap are not marked, stamp numbers on them. This should be done before the assembly is removed, to avoid distorting the cap and the rod. Likewise, the piston should have an identifying mark.
5. Remove the connecting-rod nuts and caps from one connecting rod.
6. Slide the rod and piston assembly up in the cylinder and away from the crankshaft.
   NOTE: To protect the crankpin, some manufacturers specify the use of guide sleeves, which are placed over the rod bolts before the rods are pushed away from the crankshaft. These sleeves prevent the bolt threads from scratching the crankpins.

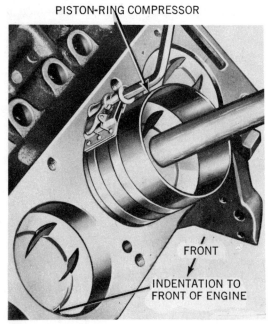
PISTON-RING COMPRESSOR

FRONT

INDENTATION TO FRONT OF ENGINE

Ford Motor Company of Canada Limited

Fig. 4-37   Typical Piston Installation

7. Push the assembly out through the top of the cylinder and remove it. Replace the cap on the connecting rod. Tighten the nuts (finger tight only).

8. Repeat for the other pistons. It will be necessary to turn the crankshaft in order to remove the remaining pistons.

9. Have the instructor inspect your work.

10. To replace a rod and piston assembly, first check the markings to make sure that they match and that the assembly is going back into the same cylinder from which it was removed. Take off the cap nuts and the cap.

11. Position the piston rings so that their gaps are uniformly spaced around the piston.

12. Put the piston-ring compressor in place so that the rings are compressed into their grooves.

13. After installing the rod bolt guide sleeves, if specified, place the assembly on the cylinder block, with the rod in the cylinder. Make sure that the rod markings are on the correct side.

14. Push the piston down into the cylinder. It should slip down without a great deal of pressure. A hammer handle is normally used to tap the piston into place (Figure 4-37). If the piston does not go down easily, remove the assembly to see what is holding the piston up. Do not use heavy pressure or hard blows.

15. Lubricate the crankpin and pull the rod assembly down until it rests in a normal position on the crankpin. Remove the rod bolt guide sleeves (where used) and replace the cap and nuts, tightening them to torque specifications.

16. Repeat for the remaining connecting-rod assemblies.

17. Install new cotter pins or palnuts on the connecting-rod bolts.

18. Have the instructor inspect your work.

REVIEW QUESTIONS

1. Describe the difference between internal- and external-combustion engines.

2. State the scientific law upon which the operation of the internal-combustion engine depends.

3. Define the following terms: (a) stroke (b) bore (c) TDC (d) r/min (e) piston displacement (f) compression ratio (g) power.

4. Define reciprocating motion.

5. A four-cylinder engine has a bore of 100 mm and a stroke of 150 mm with a clearance volume of 150 cm³. Its volumetric efficiency is 85%. Calculate (a) piston displacement, (b) compression ratio, (c) compression pressure.

6. Name the types of metals that are used in the manufacture of cylinder blocks and explain why these metals are used.
7. What is the lower part of the engine block called? What is its purpose?
8. What is the purpose of the ports in the cylinder heads or cylinder blocks?
9. Describe the procedure to be followed when tightening cylinder heads. Why is this procedure necessary?
10. What is the purpose of the oil pan?
11. Name the two types of manifolds and state why each is necessary.
12. Describe the manufacture of crankshafts.
13. What is (a) a crankpin, (b) a crank journal?
14. How is a crankshaft supported in the crankcase?
15. What is a crank throw? What is its purpose?
16. Describe the construction of crankshaft bearings.
17. How are bearing shells held in place?
18. Define momentum.
19. Which requires a heavier flywheel, a four-cylinder engine or an eight-cylinder engine? Why?
20. How are connecting rods attached to (a) the crankshaft, (b) the piston pin?
21. Sketch a piston and label all parts.
22. What are the advantages of an aluminum piston?
23. Why must aluminum pistons have a split skirt?
24. Name and state the purpose of two types of piston rings.
25. What are piston-ring expanders? Why are they used?
26. Describe two methods of driving the camshaft.
27. Explain why the camshaft must rotate at one-half crankshaft speed.
28. What is the purpose of the timing marks?
29. Name the parts of a camshaft and state the purpose of each.
30. What is the purpose of the valve lifter?
31. What are the advantages of hydraulic valve lifters?
32. Sketch a valve and identify the important parts.
33. Define (a) valve face, (b) valve seat, (c) valve margin.
34. Name the types of metals used in the manufacture of valves and state why these metals are used.
35. What are the common valve face and seat angles?
36. What are the valve guides? Where are they located?
37. What is the purpose of a rocker arm?
38. Describe two methods of mounting rocker arms.
39. What is valve clearance? Why is it necessary?
40. How can the intake and exhaust valves be identified in an assembled engine?
41. Define the word "cycle."
42. (a) Name, in their correct order, the four strokes of the four-stroke-cycle principle.
    (b) Compare the pressure inside the cylinder to atmospheric pressure for each stroke of the cycle.
    (c) Explain the purpose of each stroke of the cycle.
    (d) State the position of each valve during each stroke of the cycle.
43. How many degrees and revolutions does the crankshaft make during (a) one cycle, (b) one stroke?
44. When should the spark occur at the spark plug?
45. Give two reasons for changing the stroke length by valve timing.

46. Define the terms (a) valve lead, (b) valve lag, (c) valve lap.

47. Define the term "power lap."

48. State the number of degrees of crankshaft rotation between the power strokes of (a) four-cylinder, (b) six-cylinder, (c) eight-cylinder engines.

49. State five ways in which engines may be classified.

50. Describe three types of cylinder arrangements.

51. By means of sketches, illustrate the cylinder numbering arrangements as used by (a) Chevrolet six-cylinder, (b) Ford eight-cylinder, (c) Plymouth eight-cylinder engines.

52. Sketch four different types of valve arrangements.

53. Compare the valve-operating mechanism of an L-head engine to that of an I-head engine.

54. Why have most manufacturers changed to I-head engines?

55. Explain why each of the following engine auxiliary systems is necessary for continuous engine operation: (a) cooling system, (b) lubricating system, (c) ignition system.

56. How many degrees of crankshaft rotation are required for one cycle of a two-stroke-cycle engine?

57. Describe the actions that take place (a) above, (b) below the piston as the piston moves downward in a two-port two-stroke-cycle engine.

58. Why must a two-port two-stroke-cycle engine have a sealed crankcase?

59. What are "reed" valves? Why are they necessary?

THE COOLING SYSTEM 5

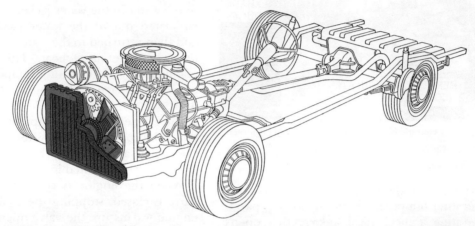

An engine's cooling system is designed to conduct heat away from the metal surrounding the combustion chamber. The heat developed by combustion may be as high as 2000°C, and approximately one-third of this heat is removed by the cooling system. If this heat were not dissipated, the metal parts would expand and the lubricating oil would be burnt off. Either condition could cause scoring of the pistons and cylinders or seizure of the engine.

Although the dissipation of heat is the primary job of the cooling system, the system must perform two other important functions:
1. Maintain a minimum operating temperature of between 82°C and 93°C, because the engine does not operate efficiently when cold.
2. Provide a convenient means of heating the passenger compartment in cold weather.

Two general types of cooling systems are used, *liquid-cooling* and *air-cooling*. The liquid-cooling system is the more popular.

AIR-COOLED ENGINES

In an air-cooled engine many thin, heat-radiating fins are attached to the outside of the cylinder head and walls. Heat from the burning fuel is transferred to the fins. A constant stream of cooled air passes over the fins, absorbing the excess heat and carrying it away.

This air is directed around each cylinder and cylinder head by sheet-metal forms, called *shrouds,* which encase the engine (Figure 5-2). The amount of air circulated is controlled by a blower and a thermostatically controlled valve. The blower is a centrifugal type fan, belt-driven from a pulley attached to the crankshaft. The thermostat that operates the air-regulator valve is of the bel-

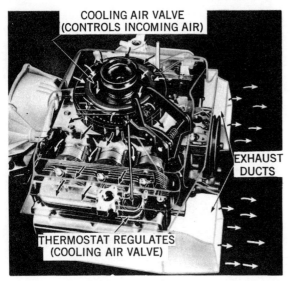

COOLING AIR VALVE
(CONTROLS INCOMING AIR)

EXHAUST
DUCTS

THERMOSTAT REGULATES
(COOLING AIR VALVE)

General Motors Products of Canada, Limited

Fig. 5-1   Engine Air-cooling System

lows type. As the engine reaches its normal operating temperature, the bellows expand, operating a mechanical linkage that opens the valve. The valve is located near the top of the engine; as the valve opens, it allows the fan to circulate more air past the fins of the cylinders and cylinder heads. The air picks

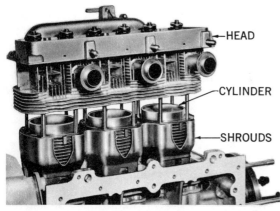

HEAD

CYLINDER

SHROUDS

General Motors Products of Canada, Limited

Fig. 5-2   Air-cooled Engine Heads

up the excess heat and carries it away through an opening in the lower rear portion of the shrouds.

LIQUID-COOLED ENGINES

In the liquid-cooled engine a passageway called a *water jacket* surrounds each cylinder. The heat of combustion is conducted through the cylinder walls and is transferred to the water in the water jackets. The water is circulated out of the water jackets, cooled, and then returned to the water jackets, ready to accumulate more heat. This circulation maintains a safe operating temperature and prevents damage to the engine parts (Figure 5-3).

An efficient engine temperature is maintained by controlling the water circulation by the use of a *thermostat,* which is a heat-controlled valve, mounted in the upper hose.

When the engine is cold, the thermostat valve is closed, stopping the coolant. As the engine warms up, the valve opens to permit sufficient coolant circulation to maintain proper operating temperatures. (See Figure 5-3).

UNITS OF THE COOLING SYSTEM

Water Pump. To circulate water through the cooling system, a water pump is used. Usually mounted at the front end of the cylinder block, between the block and the radiator, the pump is driven by a belt connected to the *drive pulley,* attached to the front end of the engine crankshaft.

Most water pumps are of the *impeller* type, consisting of a housing, with water inlet and outlet, and an impeller, a series of curved blades or vanes attached to one end of a sealed pump shaft. As the impeller rotates, the water between the blades is thrown outward by centrifugal force, and forced through the pump outlet into the cylinder block. Cooled water from the bottom of the

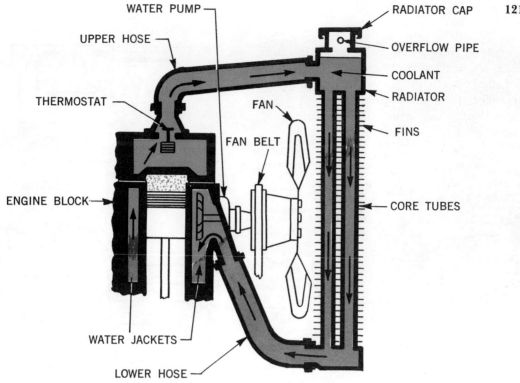

Fig. 5-3 Basic Liquid Cooling System

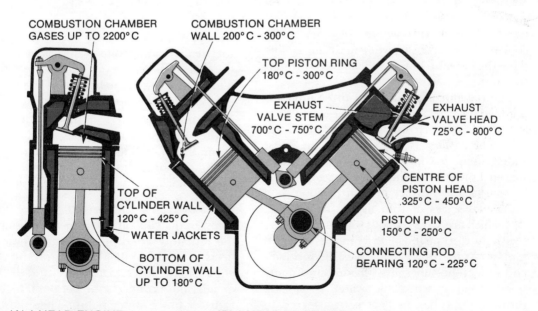

(A) I-HEAD ENGINE   (B) I-HEAD V8 ENGINE

Fig. 5-4 Typical Water Jackets

radiator is drawn into the pump through a hose connected to the water-pump inlet. The impeller shaft is supported by one or more bearings, and a seal is used to prevent water from leaking out around the bearing. (See Figure 5-5.)

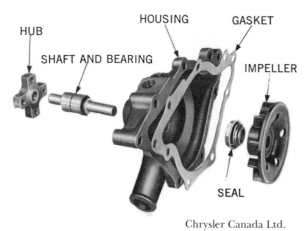

Fig. 5-5   Water Pump

Chrysler Canada Ltd.

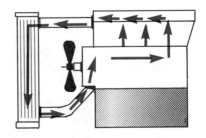

(A) DOWN-FLOW RADIATOR

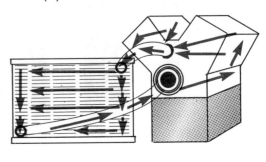

(B) CROSS-FLOW RADIATOR

Fig. 5-6   Radiators

Radiator.   Two general types of radiator designs are used, the *down flow* and the *cross flow* types. In the down flow type of radiator the coolant flows vertically, while in the cross flow type the coolant flows horizontally through the core.

The radiator is made up of three units assembled together: the *top tank,* the *bottom tank,* and the centre or cooling section, called the *core.* The *tubular* type of core is the most widely used. It consists of many small tubes placed in rows, running from the top to the bottom tank. They are held in position by a horizontal series of thin metal strips called *fins,* which are spaced about 3 mm apart. The fins help to transfer heat from the water to the air. As the hot water leaves the top tank and enters the tubes, it is divided into many small streams; while the water is passing through the tubes, its heat is transferred to the tubes. This heat is rapidly conducted to

the fins and carried away by air passing through the radiator core.

An overflow pipe, which serves as an outlet for steam and surplus water, is attached to the filler neck on the top tank of the radiator. This pipe leads to the bottom of the radiator. The lower end is open to the atmosphere.

A drain cock, fitted in the bottom of the lower tank, permits draining of the coolant from most cooling systems. Some systems have additional drain cocks mounted in the engine block.

Radiator Hoses.   Radiator hoses are used to transfer the coolant between the engine and the radiator. The upper or outlet hose connects the water outlet housing on top of the engine to the top radiator tank, and the lower or inlet hose connects the bottom tank of the radiator to the water pump. These hoses are made of rubber which is able to withstand the

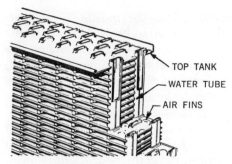

(A) RADIATOR CORE CONSTRUCTION

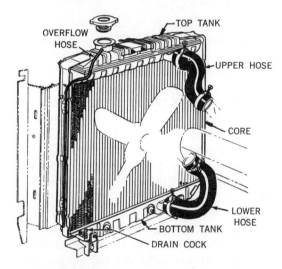

(B) RADIATOR AND CONNECTIONS

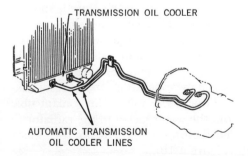

(C) COOLING THE AUTOMATIC TRANSMISSION

Ford Motor Company of Canada Limited

Fig. 5-7   Radiators and Connections

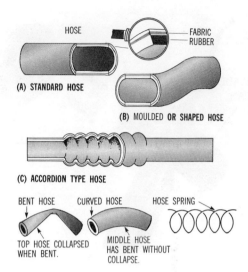

Fig. 5-8   Radiator Hoses

vibration between the engine and the radiator.

Some lower hoses have a coil of spring
wire, which is the same diameter as the inside
of the hose, fitted inside them. This coil prevents the hose from collapsing because of the
low pressure produced by the water pump.

Hose clamps of the spring tension, screw,
or worm-tightened band type are used to secure the hose to the connection and to prevent leakage.

Hose connections between the radiator and
engine may deteriorate, resulting in leakage
or inadequate passage of water. The appearance of the hose and connections will usually
indicate their condition. If the hose is rotted
or soft, and collapses easily when squeezed, it
should be replaced. To calculate the size of
radiator hose used, measure either the inside
diameter of the hose or the outside diameter
of the connection.

Fan.   When the engine is running, the fan
draws air through the radiator core, cooling
the water in the radiator. The fan is usually
mounted on the end of the water-pump shaft

4 BLADE
FAN

SPACER

PULLEY

Chrysler Canada Ltd.

Fig. 5-9   Standard Fan Drive

and is driven by the fan belt. The cooling action of the air caused by the fan is most important while the engine is idling or being operated at city driving speeds. At highway driving speeds, the fan is not as important, because the forward motion of the vehicle is sufficient to force the required amount of air through the radiator for cooling purposes (See Figure 5-9.)

Fan Belt.   A fan belt is necessary to drive the water pump, fan assembly, alternator, and other accessories. Most fan belts are made in a V or wedge shape. The wedge of the belt fits firmly into the pulley grooves, so that belt slippage is eliminated by the extra friction.

Fan-belt tension is adjusted by moving the alternator away from the engine block. This adjustment varies according to the type of alternator mounting. A general rule to be followed when adjusting the fan-belt tension is to tighten the belt so that when a light thumb pressure is applied at a point midway between the drive and one of the driven pulleys, the belt will sag approximately its own width.

Thermostat.   The thermostat is a heat-operated valve that controls the flow of the coolant to the radiator. It maintains the proper engine operating temperature, which is usually between 82°C and 93°C. The thermostat is usually located inside the *water-outlet housing* near the top front section of the engine block or cylinder head. Two types of thermostats are used, the *pellet* and the *bimetal spring*. Both work on the basic scientific principle that materials and gases expand when heated (Figure 5-10).

Pellet-type thermostats are used in most modern automobiles. This type of thermostat contains a copper-impregnated wax pellet that expands when heated and contracts when cooled. The pellet is connected to the thermostat control valve through a piston. As the pellet is heated, it expands and moves the piston which opens the valve. Cooling the pellet reverses the action to close the valve. The pellet-type thermostat is not pressure-sensitive and works well in pressurized cooling systems.

The cooling system is designed to provide the necessary cooling for high-speed operation in hot weather. This amount of cooling is not required for light driving or for cool weather. Under the latter conditions, the thermostat valve controlling the flow of water to the radiator remains nearly closed, and the water pump either recirculates the coolant through the engine water jackets by means of a bypass pipe, or the water stops circulating completely. As the engine warms up, the thermostat valve-operating mechanism expands and opens the valve. Hot coolant now flows from the water jacket to the radiator to be cooled before it returns to the water jackets (Figure 5-10).

Thermostats are designed to open at specific temperatures. A thermostat marked 87°C should start to open between 85°C and 90°C and be fully opened at 100°C.

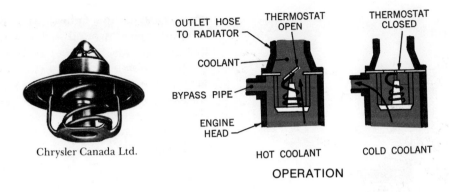

OUTLET HOSE TO RADIATOR
THERMOSTAT OPEN
THERMOSTAT CLOSED
COOLANT
BYPASS PIPE
ENGINE HEAD
HOT COOLANT
COLD COOLANT
OPERATION

Chrysler Canada Ltd.

(A) BIMETAL SPRING TYPE

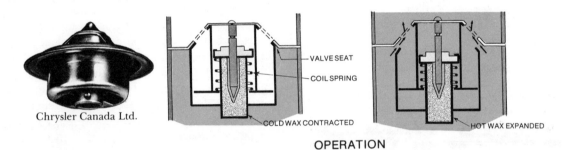

Chrysler Canada Ltd.

VALVE SEAT
COIL SPRING
COLD WAX CONTRACTED
HOT WAX EXPANDED
OPERATION

(B) PELLET TYPE

Fig. 5-10   Thermostat Operation

Radiator Pressure Cap. The radiator pressure cap is a device which permits higher operating temperatures, increased cooling efficiency, and reduced evaporation and surge losses.

At sea level, water boils at 100°C. When the air pressure is increased, the boiling point of the water is increased. Each additional 10 kPa increases the boiling point of the water approximately 2°C. Present-day automotive cooling systems are designed to operate under pressures ranging from 50 kPa to 120 kPa. In a cooling system operating at 50 kPa the boiling point of water is raised to 112°C. In a 120 kPa system the boiling point of water

would be raised to about 130°C. In this way water can be circulated through the cooling system without boiling at temperatures above 100°C. As the temperature of the coolant rises above 100°C, the difference between air and coolant temperatures becomes greater. This causes the heat to be transferred more quickly to the air, resulting in improved cooling efficiency.

Two valves are included in the pressure cap. One valve prevents excess pressures in the cooling system by allowing the excess pressure to escape through the overflow pipe. The other valve prevents a vacuum from forming in the cooling system after the engine has been shut off and the coolant begins to cool.

Chrysler Canada Ltd.

(A) RADIATOR CAP

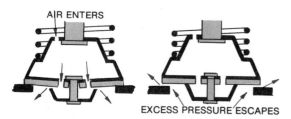

VACUUM VALVE OPEN   PRESSURE VALVE OPEN

(B) OPERATION

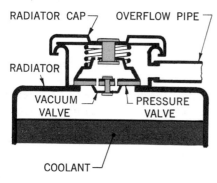

(C) ASSEMBLY

Fig. 5-11   Radiator Pressure Cap

Water-Distribution Tubes. In order to prevent "hot spots" around such parts as the exhaust-valve seats, a portion of the water from the water pump is directed through a water-distribution tube. This is a long tube which fits in the water jackets and has holes or nozzles in it to direct the water to the hot spots. Without the tubes, damage would occur at the hot spots.

SEALED AND CLOSED TYPE COOLING SYSTEMS

The sealed and closed types of cooling systems are similar to the conventional cooling system except that they include a separate expansion tank or reservoir either in place of or in conjunction with the radiator overflow pipe. This tank is usually made of translucent plastic which is marked to indicate when the system is at operating level or requires additional coolant. The tank is used in place of the expansion space usually provided in the top radiator tank. In a sealed or closed system the radiator is filled to capacity. In both types the tank accommodates the increased volume of the coolant as the coolant temperature is increased. The tank prevents the loss of coolant as the temperature increases.

The expansion tank or reservoir usually includes a removable cap to permit the addition of coolant if required or the testing of the freezing point of the solution.

Sealed Type of Cooling System. In this type of system the expansion tank is connected directly to the top tank of the radiator. The radiator does not use a pressure-type radiator cap. However, the expansion tank is equipped with a combination pressure-vacuum valve which is similar in operation to the valves in a pressure-type radiator cap.

During normal engine operation the level of the liquid in the tank is constantly changing as the temperature of the coolant in-

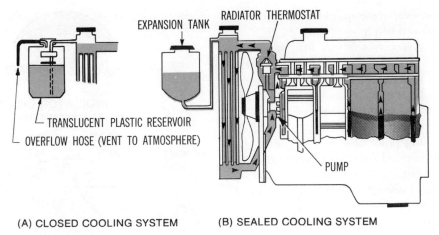

(A) CLOSED COOLING SYSTEM   (B) SEALED COOLING SYSTEM

Fig. 5-12   Cooling Systems

creases or decreases. The normal expansion of the coolant is absorbed by the cushion of air in the tank. As the cushion of air is compressed, it provides the pressure increase required to raise the boiling point of the coolant during high temperature operation. The pressure valve opens when the cooling system pressure, caused by the expanding coolant, reaches a predetermined value. The vacuum valve opens when the coolant cools and contracts, thereby lowering the system pressure below that of atmospheric pressure.

The Closed-Type Cooling System. This system has the reservoir attached to the overflow outlet of the radiator filler neck. The system uses a type of pressure radiator cap which is referred to as a "drop valve vented cap." The valve in the cap is temperature operated and is in the open position until the coolant approaches the boiling point, at which time it closes, sealing off the reservoir from the cooling system. The reservoir is vented to the atmosphere so that the system can operate at atmospheric pressure when the engine is comparatively cool.

As the engine warms up, the coolant expands and the excess coolant is forced into the reservoir. Should the coolant reach near the boiling point the temperature-controlled drop valve closes, preventing the coolant from reaching the reservoir and the engine cooling system operates as a normal pressurized cooling system. When the engine cools, the drop valve opens to permit the coolant to flow back from the reservoir into the top tank of the radiator.

ANTIFREEZE SOLUTIONS

In winter weather, plain water in the radiator and water jackets would freeze. This would result in serious damage to the cooling system parts as the expansion, due to freezing, would burst these parts. Various mixtures known as antifreeze solutions are used to prevent freezing. Some of the substances used in antifreeze solutions are ethylene glycol, glycerine, and alcohol. The most popular is ethylene glycol.

Antifreeze solutions of alcohol and water will give satisfactory results in some cooling systems. However, since alcohol starts to boil at 78°C, it is not recommended for automobiles whose cooling systems operate at 87°C or higher. Another disadvantage is that alcohol tends to evaporate quickly; therefore it must be replaced often.

Ethylene glycol is sold as an antifreeze under various trade names. A solution of ethylene glycol and water is suitable for protection against temperatures to −30°C and will not boil until a temperature of 105°C is reached. Since this is considerably higher than the boiling point of water, ethylene glycol is recommended for use in late-model automobiles whose cooling systems operate above 87°C. However, ethylene glycol must not be used undiluted, as it will *slush up* at relatively high temperatures. The maximum possible protection of −60°C is obtained with a mixture of 68% ethylene glycol and 32% water.

Figure 5-13 indicates the proportions of ethylene glycol and water which are necessary to withstand various temperatures without freezing.

| FOR 5 ℓ OF COOLANT | | RATIO OF | |
QUANTITY OF WATER	QUANTITY OF ETHYLENE GLYCOL	WATER TO ETHYLENE GLYCOL	FREEZING POINT
3.75 ℓ	1.25 ℓ	3:1	−10°C
3.3 ℓ	1.9 ℓ	2:1	−20°C
3.0 ℓ	2.0 ℓ	3:2	−30°C
2.5 ℓ	2.5 ℓ	1:1	−35°C

Fig. 5-13

TEMPERATURE GAUGES

Motor vehicles are equipped with a gauge which indicates the temperature of the coolant in the water jackets, or with temperature warning lights that indicate when the coolant is cold or hot. Both types are electrically operated.

Gauges. The gauge type is comprised of a *sending unit* and a *dash unit*. The sending unit contains a flat disc that changes its electrical resistance as the temperature rises. The higher the temperature rises, the lower the resistance falls.

TEMPERATURE IN FAHRENHEIT

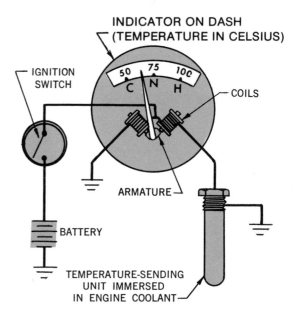

BALANCING COIL TYPE

Fig. 5-14   Temperature Dash-gauge Units

In the *balancing coil type* of dash unit, the resistance changes in the sending unit alter the magnetic strength of one of the two coils in the dash unit. The needle is attracted to the stronger field, thus indicating an increase in temperature. (See Figure 5-14.)

INDICATOR LIGHTS

When indicator lights are used, the sending unit contains a *bimetal spring* which, when cold, closes a set of contacts to complete the circuit through to the cold indicator light. As the engine warms up to the normal operating temperature, the circuit to the cold indicator light is broken by the change in position of

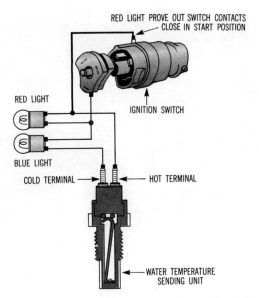

Ford Motor Company of Canada Limited

Fig. 5-15   Cold and Hot Temperature Indicator
Light Circuit

the bimetal spring, and the light is turned off.
Should the engine overheat, the bimetal
spring moves farther and closes a second set
of contacts which completes the circuit to the
hot indicator light (Figure 5-15).

PRACTICAL ASSIGNMENTS

a. On a cutaway or model engine locate all the
parts of the cooling system.

b. Remove and Replace the Fan Belt.
Procedure:
1. Loosen the alternator-clamp bolt "B."
2. Loosen alternator-clamp bolts "A" at the
front and rear of the alternator.
3. Move the alternator towards the block to
free the belt from the alternator pulley.
4. Work the fan belt off the drive pulley.
5. Work the fan belt up between the fan
blades and the radiator.

6. Reinstall the fan belt on the fan, alternator, and drive pulleys.
7. Tighten the alternator-clamp bolts sufficiently to hold the alternator in position.
8. Adjust the fan belt to the proper tension
(Figure 5-16).

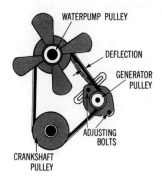

Fig. 5-16   Fan Belt Adjustment

9. Securely tighten all clamp bolts.

c. Remove and Replace the Radiator Hose.
Procedure:
1. Drain the water from the radiator by
opening the drain valve under the radiator.
2. On some engines a second drain valve,
located on the engine block, is used to
drain the water jackets, since the engine
block does not entirely drain through the
radiator drain valve.
3. Unscrew the bolts in the radiator hose
clamps.
4. Slide the hose clamps to the centre of the
hose.
5. Twist the hose on each connector to
loosen.
6. Bend the hose slightly in the centre and
remove from one connector.
7. Remove the hose from the other connector.
8. Measure the outside diameter of each
connector to determine the hose size.

9. Measure the distance between the ends of the connectors and add 75 mm to allow for overlapping. This would be the length of a new hose should one be needed.
10. Examine the hose clamps and if they are distorted or broken, replace them.
11. Install the hose and the clamps on the connectors with the same amount of overlap at each end.
12. Place the clamps 5 mm from each end of the hose and tighten.
13. Refill the radiator to within 50 mm of the top. This space allows for the expansion of the water when heated.
14. Check all connections for water leaks.

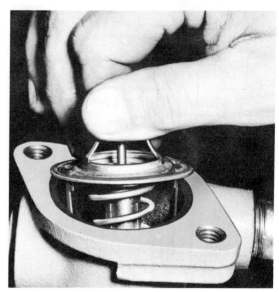

General Motors Products of Canada, Limited

Fig. 5-17   Replacing Thermostat

d. Remove, Test, and Replace a Thermostat.

Procedure:

1. Drain the water from the cooling system.
2. Remove the top radiator hose.
3. Unscrew the bolts or nuts which fasten the thermostat housing to the engine block or cylinder head.
4. Remove the thermostat housing by lifting if off. (See Figure 5-17.) Remove the gasket.
5. Remove the thermostat from its seat.
6. Using a putty knife, scrape the gasket surfaces clean.
7. Scrape the thermostat seat clean.
8. Test the thermostat by placing it in hot water to see at what temperature it opens. The water temperature may be taken with a thermometer.
9. Compare the temperature at which the thermostat opens with the temperature stamped on the thermostat, to see if the thermostat is working properly.
10. Install the thermostat, a new gasket, the thermostat housing, and the radiator hose in the reverse order of their removal.
11. Tighten the thermostat-housing bolts evenly to avoid cracking the housing.
12. Fill the cooling system with water.
13. Check the system for leaks.

e. Remove and Replace the Water Pump.

Procedure:

1. Drain the cooling system.
2. Disconnect the lower radiator hose from the water pump.
3. Loosen the alternator and remove the fan belt.
4. Remove the water-pump bolts, being careful not to drop the water pump when the last bolt is removed.
5. Clean the gasket surfaces on the block and pump.
6. Apply a light coat of grease or gasket paste to the gasket surface of the block. This will hold the gasket in position during the installation of the pump.

7. Place the pump in position and insert the bolts. Tighten them evenly to avoid cracking the pump housing.
8. Reinstall the fan belt and radiator hose. Fill the cooling system with water.
9. Check the cooling system for leaks.

f. Test Antifreeze Solutions. Obtain several samples of antifreeze solutions and an antifreeze tester.

Procedure:
1. Heat the mixture sufficiently for testing purposes.
2. Test the mixtures with the antifreeze tester and determine the amount of protection offered by each sample.

REVIEW QUESTIONS

1. Name three important functions of the cooling system.
2. Name and describe two methods of cooling an engine.
3. What is the purpose of (a) cooling fins (b) shrouds?
4. Explain how the air circulation is controlled in an air-cooled engine.
5. State the purpose of the following units of the liquid-cooling system: (a) radiator, (b) water pump, (c) thermostat, (d) water distribution tubes.
6. Trace the path followed by the coolant through the cooling system.
7. Name the three main sections of a radiator.
8. Why are some lower radiator hoses fitted with an internal coil spring?
9. How is the size of radiator hose determined?
10. How is fan-belt tension tested?
11. Explain the operation of a thermostat.
12. What are the advantages of a pressurized cooling system?
13. Calculate the boiling point of water in a cooling system operating under 98 kPa.
14. Under what type of driving conditions is the operation of the fan most important?
15. State the advantage of the closed or sealed type of cooling system.
16. What type of antifreeze solution is best for the modern automobile? Why?
17. What is the amount of antifreeze required for a 15 ℓ capacity cooling system to give protection against freezing at (a) $-20°C$, (b) $-30°C$?
18. Name and describe the operation of two types of temperature gauges.

THE LUBRICATING SYSTEM

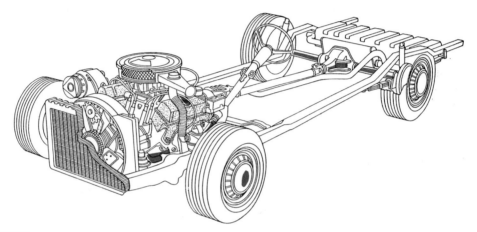

LUBRICATION

In the automobile there are a great many parts that rotate or slide against another part. This motion creates what is known as *friction*. Friction can be described as resistance to motion, caused by the contact of the surfaces of bodies, and it exists in various degrees between all moving parts. The speed, load, type of material, and finish are the main factors affecting friction. Even highly polished surfaces have small projections and irregularities which set up a resisting force (friction) which is converted into heat. The heat can cause abnormal expansion of the parts and ultimately could cause them to bind or seize.

Lubrication helps to reduce friction by placing a film of oil or grease between the moving surfaces. The molecules of a lubricant are very small, flexible and slippery, yet will stick to most surfaces. The lubricating film acts like a layer of small balls which prevents the actual contact of the two metal surfaces.

A good lubricant must have *adhesive* and *cohesive* properties. Adhesion is the property of the lubricant which enables it to stay between the surfaces it is to lubricate. Cohesion refers to the force of attraction of the like particles of the lubricant and is expressed as *viscosity* or *body*.

Lubricating oils must also have *fluidity:* the property which allows the oil to flow through oil lines and then to spread evenly over all the bearing surface.

Lubricants are used in the automobile for five main reasons. First, they form a film between moving parts, thereby reducing friction which causes loss of power. Second, lubricants help to carry away heat from such parts as pistons and valves, in the same way that water does when it is splashed on a hot surface. Third, lubricating oil helps to seal the space around the pistons and piston rings, thereby preventing loss of compression. Fourth, it acts as a cushion to protect the parts and fifth, it acts as a cleaning agent.

REFINING CRUDE OIL

Crude oil, as it comes from the ground, contains many petroleum products. *Refining* is the name given to the process necessary to separate crude oil into gasoline, motor oil, greases, etc. The first step in the process is called *fractionation.*

Fractionation, like distillation, depends upon the vaporization and subsequent condensing of a liquid, and is used to separate liquids having different boiling points. The crude oil is heated in the bottom of a tall vertical tower containing a series of trays. Since the temperature in the tower is lower at the top than at the bottom, the portion of the crude oil having the highest boiling point condenses on the lowest trays, while the portion with the lowest boiling point keeps rising in the form of vapour and condenses on the trays nearest the top of the tower.

Fractionation does not release enough gasoline from crude oil to satisfy today's demands. To obtain sufficient gasoline a process called *cracking* is used.

Cracking is the process of breaking down the original structure of the oil, or breaking the molecules apart so that they can be re-

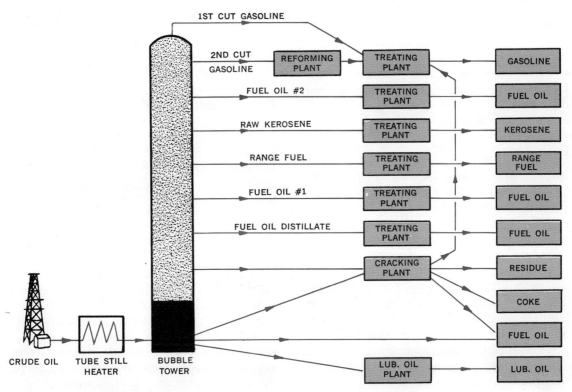

Fig. 6-1   Composite Flow Diagram of a Modern Refinery

formed in a different structure. This process makes it possible to produce large amounts of gasoline from low-grade materials.

After cracking, the manufacturing is divided into three sections: gasoline, lubricating oil, and gear lubricants and greases. During the manufacture of premium or regular grades of gasoline, a product known as *tetraethyl lead* is added to give the gasoline a high *antiknock* rating. This reduces the pinging noise that is technically referred to as *detonation*. A special blending process is used to produce non-leaded gasolines.

Engine lubricating oils are manufactured by blending stocks called neutrals (light oils) and bright stocks (heavy oils) in the correct proportion to produce oils of a given viscosity, such as SAE 10, SAE 20, and SAE 30. Other chemicals called *additives* are used to produce detergent *(heavy duty)* motor oils.

Gear lubricants and greases are manufactured by adding certain chemicals and soaps, which increase the clinging properties of oil. In this category we find transmission and differential oils, and chassis, cup, wheel-bearing, and special greases.

ENGINE OILS

An engine oil must be able to withstand crankcase temperatures as high as 130°C without breaking down and permitting metal-to-metal contact. It must not thicken at low temperatures or it would not circulate through the oil passages of a cold engine to provide the necessary lubrication; it must not contain the lighter, more volatile molecules which evaporate at normal crankcase temperatures; and finally, its tendency to form carbon at normal operating temperatures must be held to a minimum.

During the refining process, dissolved solids and substances such as acids, tar, and paraffin, which create corrosion and gum deposits, must be carefully removed.

Many tests to determine and rate the properties of lubricants have been developed. Some will be discussed here.

Viscosity. The term *viscosity* refers to the tendency of a liquid such as oil to resist flowing. It may be measured by determining the speed at which a given amount of the oil will flow through a given hole at a given temperature. When oil is hot, it has a lower viscosity and will flow faster than when cold. An oil of high viscosity may be termed a heavy oil; an oil of low viscosity, a light oil.

Cold Test. The cold test is used to determine the temperature at which oil congeals and ceases to flow. The *cloud point* of an oil is the temperature at which the solids in the oil begin to crystallize or separate out from the solution.

Flash Point Test. The flash point test is used to determine the temperature at which the lubricant has vaporized sufficiently that when an open flame is passed over its surface a small flash of short duration will occur.

Carbon Residue Test. The carbon residue test is used to determine the amount of carbon that is left after a given quantity of oil has been evaporated.

Volatility Test. The volatility test is used to determine the temperature at which the lubricant will evaporate.

SAE SYSTEM OF OIL CLASSIFICATION

In order to have a convenient and widely understood method of labelling oils according to their viscosity, the Society of Automotive Engineers adopted the system described as the SAE Recommended Practice for Lubricant Viscosity Numbers. With this rating system, the lower the rating number, the lower the viscosity of the oil. The numbers do not indicate proportionate increases in the viscosity according to the increase in the number; an SAE 20 oil, for example, is not necessarily twice as heavy at a given temperature as an SAE 10 oil. The SAE rating does not indicate in any way the quality of the motor oil.

The petroleum industry has developed oils having a low viscosity for winter starting temperatures. These oils are modifications of the SAE 10 and 20 grades that meet winter conditions. They are known as *10W* and *20W*, because they will meet both winter viscosity specifications and the standard SAE specification.

Refiners have added a further oil classification, namely *SAE 10W-30* oil, which has a viscosity rating when cold equal to SAE 10 oil and when hot a viscosity rating equal to SAE 30 oil. In other words, as the temperature rises the oil does not become as thin as a number 10 oil would normally be, but retains a viscosity comparable to SAE 30 oil.

Oil thickens in cold weather. Thick oil makes the engine difficult to start because the oil does not flow readily through the small spaces between the moving parts. If the oil is too thick, the engine loses much of its power in turning over and many of the parts will not be properly lubricated. If the oil is too thin, it will be squeezed from between the surfaces of the moving parts too quickly, causing increased friction and wear. Oil with the correct viscosity should be used in accordance with the temperature and the season of the year.

SAE OILS AND THEIR USES
SAE 40—Used in heavy engines in very hot weather.
SAE 30—Used in almost all automobile engines during summer months.
SAE 20—Used during spring and fall months down to freezing temperatures, or to break in new engines during summer months.
SAE 10—Used during winter months below freezing temperature.

During normal engine operation, carbon and other harmful impurities tend to form deposits on working parts. Engine efficiency is thus decreased. To help overcome this problem, *heavy duty* oils, which contain detergent additives, have been developed. Detergent oil holds the impurities in suspension, preventing the buildup of deposits.

ASTM SERVICE RATINGS OF OIL
In addition to the SAE system of oil classification, which determines the grade of oil, another method of oil classification is used. It is called the *service rating system*. The service ratings are divided into eight groups: *SA, SB, SC,* for gasoline-powered engines, and *CA, CB, CC,* and *CD,* for diesel-powered engines.

SA—typical of engines operated in such a manner that straight mineral oils are satisfactory.

SB—typical of engines operated in such a manner that oils designed for this service provide only antiscuff capability and resistance to oil oxidation and bearing corrosion.

SC—typical of gasoline engines in 1964-through-1967 model vehicles. Oil design for this service provides detergent-dispersive characteristics as well as protection against wear, rust, and corrosion.

SD—typical of gasoline engines beginning with 1968 model vehicles and operating under engine manufacturing warranties. Oils for this service provide more protection from high- and low-temperature deposits, wear, rust, and corrosion.

CA—typical of diesel engines operating in mild to moderate duty with high quality fuels. These oils provide protection from bearing corrosion and high-temperature deposits.

CB—typical of engines operated as at CA but using lower quality level (high sulphur) fuels.

CC—typical of lightly super-charged diesel engines in moderate to severe duty. The oils provide protection from high-temperature deposits.

CD—typical of super-charged diesel engines in high-speed, high-output duty, requiring highly effective control of wear and deposits.

CHANGING ENGINE OIL

Until recently, most manufacturers recommended that engine lubricating oils be changed every 1600 km in summer and every 800 km in winter. Now, most manufacturers suggest longer periods between oil changes, ranging from a low of 1600 km for vehicles used mainly for stop-and-start driving, to a high of 10 000 km for vehicles used mainly for highway driving.

When engine oil is put into the oil pan, it is clear and clean. When it is removed, it is usually black and dirty. The oil becomes dirty during the operation of the engine, when harmful impurities such as carbon, gasoline, water, and metal particles mix with the oil.

As fuel is burned in the cylinders, *carbon* is formed. Most of this is blown out through the exhaust system, but some settles on the cylinder walls. The movement of the pistons and piston rings scrapes this carbon from the cylinder walls, mixing it with the oil and making the oil black and gritty.

When an engine is started, especially in cold weather, it is necessary to use the choke. This prevents most of the air from entering the carburetor and allows the engine to draw a very rich gasoline mixture into the cylinders. If the choke is used too much, not all of the gasoline burns; some seeps down past the pistons and rings, mixing with and diluting the oil. This thinning of the oil causes scored and scratched pistons.

A difference in temperature between the inside and outside of the oil pan, especially in winter, causes water vapour to condense on the inside walls of the oil pan. A similar condensation is noticed on house windows during the winter. This water runs to the bottom of the oil pan and freezes, thereby preventing the flow of oil into the oil pump. Condensation of water in the oil pan is greater in engines that run for a short time and then are allowed to cool off again.

Because the moving parts are constantly wearing, small particles of metal that are worn away mix with the oil and help make it gritty.

The preceding reasons explain why oil becomes contaminated, necessitating a periodic oil change.

ENGINE LUBRICATION

Two types of engine lubrication systems are used in internal-combustion engines: the *splash system* and the *pressure-feed system*. The pressure-feed system, with small modifications, is the more popular for modern automobile engines. The splash system is used on most lawn mower and outboard engines.

Pressure-Feed System. In the pressure-feed system, oil is forced by the oil pump through oil lines and drilled passageways. The oil, passing through the drilled passageways under pressure, supplies the necessary lubrication for the crankshaft main bearings, the connecting-rod bearings, piston-pin bushings, camshaft bearings, valve lifters, valve push rods, and rocker studs. Oil passing through the oil lines is directed to the timing gears and the valve rocker shafts in order to lubricate these parts. The cylinder walls are lubricated by oil thrown off the connecting-rod and piston-pin bearings. Some engines have *oil spit holes* in the connecting rods that line up with drilled holes in the crankshaft journal during each revolution, and throw or spit a stream of oil onto the cylinder walls.

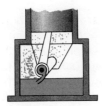

(A) SPLASH LUBRICATING SYSTEM

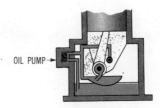

(B) COMBINATION SPLASH AND PRESSURE LUBRICATING SYSTEM

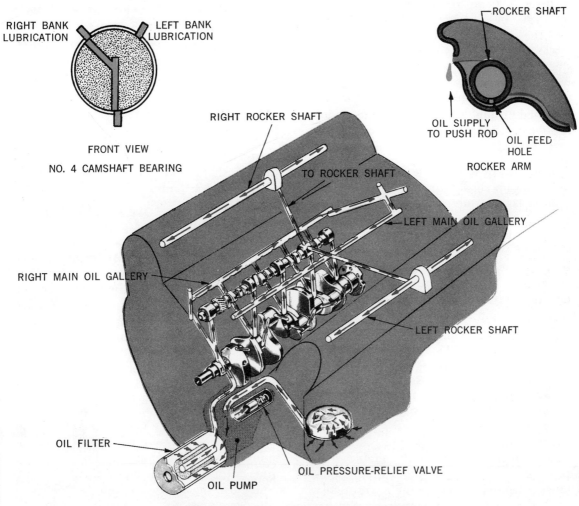

(C) PRESSURE LUBRICATING SYSTEM

Fig. 6-2   Engine Oiling System

Chrysler Canada Ltd.

To enable the oil to pass from the drilled passageways in the engine block to the rotating crankshaft, the main bearings must have oil feed holes or grooves that line up with the drilled holes in the crankshaft each time the crankshaft rotates. The same is true in the case of the connecting-rod bearings and the drilled passageways in the connecting rods. Since the oil in the passageways is under pressure, each time the drilled holes in the crankshaft and connecting rod line up with the holes in the bearings, the pressure forces the oil through these drilled passages into the crankshaft and connecting rod, lubricating their respective bearings.

After the oil has been forced to the area requiring lubrication, it falls back down into the oil pan ready to be picked up again and returned through the system. As the oil falls, it is frequently splashed by the moving parts onto some other part requiring lubrication.

The Splash System.   The splash system is used only on small four-stroke-cycle engines such as lawn mower engines. As the engine is operating, dippers on the ends of the connecting rods enter the oil supply, pick up sufficient oil to lubricate the connecting-rod bearing, and splash oil to the upper parts of the engine. The oil is thrown up as droplets, or fine spray, which lubricates the cylinder walls, piston pins, and valve mechanism. Frequently, small oil cups are used to catch the splashed oil in order to lubricate certain parts of the engine such as the crankshaft.

In two-cycle engines used on some lawn mowers and outboard engines, the proper amount of lubricating oil is added to the gasoline. The oil is atomized as it enters the air stream in the carburetor, forming a fine mist which circulates through the crankcase to provide the necessary lubrication. Sometimes, small oil cups or troughs are used to catch the condensed oil and direct it to particular points requiring lubrication.

UNITS OF THE ENGINE LUBRICATION SYSTEM

Oil Supply.   The oil supply is carried in the oil pan or lower half of the crankcase. It is poured into the case through the oil filler, and the amount is indicated by reading the graduated oil gauge rod or *dip stick.*

Since the oil absorbs some of the heat from the engine, this heat must be dissipated. The heat is conducted from the oil to the oil pan, which is exposed to the air stream under the car. The moving air picks up the heat and carries it away.

Oil Pump.   An oil pump is used to produce the pressure necessary to circulate the oil through the lubricating system. The oil pump may be mounted on the engine above the oil supply, but it is customary for it to be submerged in the oil supply, thus eliminating any need of priming. The pump is driven by a shaft which is usually geared to the camshaft. Two types of oil pump are used—the gear pump, and the rotor pump.

The gear pump (Figure 6-3A) depends upon a pair of meshing gears enclosed in a housing. As the gears rotate and unmesh, a partial vacuum is created. Atmospheric pressure on the oil in the oil pan forces the oil to enter the pump and fill the spaces between the gear teeth. The oil is then carried around between the casing and the gear teeth. As the teeth mesh again, the oil is forced out of the spaces between the teeth, through the pump outlet, and to the various parts of the engine.

The rotor pump (Figure 6-3B) uses an inner and an outer rotor. The inner rotor is attached to the oil-pump drive shaft, which is mounted off-centre in the housing. The inner rotor drives the outer rotor. As the two units turn, the spaces between the inner and outer rotors are first filled with oil. After 0.5 revolutions, the lobes of the inner rotor move

General Motors Products of Canada, Limited

(A) GEAR TYPE

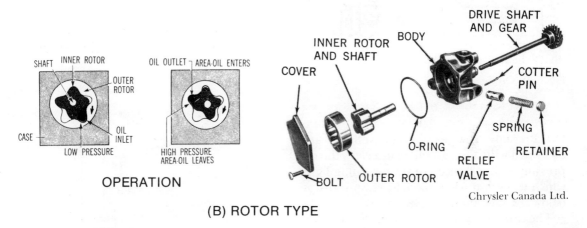

Chrysler Canada Ltd.

(B) ROTOR TYPE

Fig. 6-3   Oil Pumps

into the spaces of the outer rotor, forcing the oil out of the spaces, through the pump outlet, and to the various parts of the engine.

Oil Regulator and Relief Valve.   The pressure built up by the oil pump increases with the speed of the engine. The system includes a relief valve, which relieves any excess pressure at high engine speeds. The valve consists of either a ball and spring, or a plunger and spring, and is mounted in the housing on the oil outlet side of the oil pump. When the pressure produced by the pump is greater than the pressure of the oil relief-valve spring, this greater pressure causes the ball or plunger to move, compressing the spring and opening the port. The opening of the port permits the oil to flow back to the oil pan, thus reducing the pressure in the system. (See Figure 6-4).

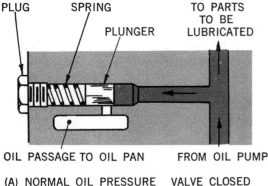

(A) NORMAL OIL PRESSURE   VALVE CLOSED

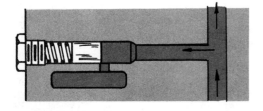

B) EXCESSIVE OIL PRESSURE   VALVE OPEN

Fig. 6-4   Oil Relief Valve

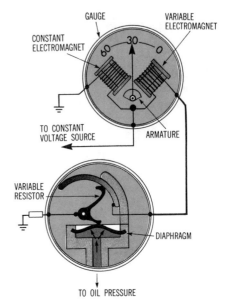

(A) TYPICAL ELECTROMAGNETIC TYPE
OIL PRESSURE GAUGE CIRCUIT

Oil Pressure Gauges. Motor vehicles are equipped with a gauge which indicates the oil pressure either directly or by a warning light which comes on when the oil pressure drops below the safe limit.

The gauge type consists of a *sending unit* and a *dash unit*. The sending unit contains a pressure diaphragm attached to the sliding contact of a variable resistance. As the oil pressure increases, the diaphragm moves inward, causing the contact to move along the resistance, thus increasing the resistance in the circuit.

In the balancing coil type of dash unit, the resistance changes in the sending unit alter the strength of one of the coils in the dash unit. The needle is attracted to the stronger magnetic field, thus indicating an increase in oil pressure.

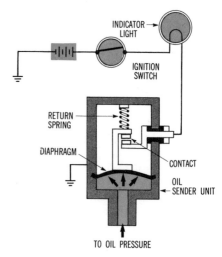

(B) TYPICAL OIL PRESSURE
INDICATOR LIGHT CIRCUIT

Fig. 6-5   Oil Pressure Indicators

When a warning light is used, the light is connected to a pressure-operated switch. When the oil pressure is above the setting of the switch, the electrical contact through the switch is broken and the light remains off. When the oil pressure falls below the setting of the switch, the electrical circuit is completed and the light goes on. This indicates that there is not sufficient oil pressure for safe operation of the engine (See Figure 6-5).

NOTE: Engine oil pressure is usually between 200 kPa and 350 kPa.

Strainer. A wire gauze strainer or screen is placed in the oil pan around the oil-pump inlet. This strainer or screen prevents any small solid matter, such as broken cotter pins, from entering the oil pump. In some engines the strainer floats near the top of the oil in the oil pan. Since dirt and metal particles are heavier than the oil, they sink to the bottom, leaving the cleanest oil at the top.

Oil Filters. Carbon particles, dust, and dirt become mixed with the lubricating oil during the operation of the engine. The heavier particles usually drop to the bottom of the oil pan, but some of the smaller particles may travel through the oil lines to the bearing surfaces, causing damage to the bearings and journals. To reduce the possibility of damage by these particles, many lubrication systems filter part or all of the oil. The filtering material traps the particles of foreign material but permits the oil to pass through. Filters are of two types: those that filter part of the oil from the pump, called *bypass* filters, and those that filter all of the oil in circulation, called *full-flow* filters (Figure 6-7). As the filter cartridges become clogged with foreign particles and impurities, their efficiency decreases.

In the bypass filter, as the cartridge becomes clogged, less and less oil passes through the filter, until finally the filter is

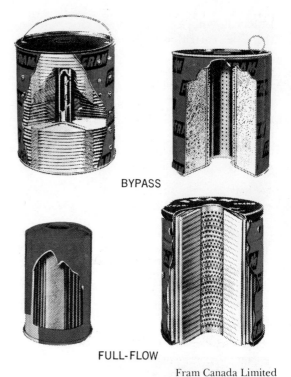

BYPASS

FULL-FLOW

Fram Canada Limited

(A) CARTRIDGES

FILTER PAPER

DIRTY OIL

DIRTY OIL

CLEAN FILTERED AIR

(B) OPERATION

Fig. 6-6 Oil Filters

practically inoperative. Before this happens, the filter cartridge or element should be replaced or cleaned, depending on the type of filter.

In the full-flow filter, the oil needed to lubricate the engine must pass through the filtering media. In a full-flow filter, the cartridge must have a flow rate ten to fifteen times as great as in the bypass type filter.

Therefore, all full-flow filters use coarser filtering media than the bypass type.

A filter relief valve that opens at a relatively low pressure must be provided around the filter. Otherwise, if the cartridge were to become plugged, the engine would be ruined through lack of lubrication. In cold weather, or after the cartridge has become partly plugged, a large part of the oil bypasses the filter, thus reducing its efficiency.

LUBRICATING GREASES

Grease is basically mineral oil thickened with metallic soap. The primary purpose of the soap is to make the oil adhere at the point of application. Thus the soap is the medium that traps the mineral oil, but the actual lubrication job is performed by the mineral oil in the grease. Greases are made of many varieties to suit different purposes. In automobile lubrication work, chassis grease and wheel-bearing grease are the most frequently used, although some older models require water-pump and cup grease.

Chassis Grease. Chassis grease is used in all pressure-gun fittings of the automobile. It is relatively soft in consistency and varies in tackiness. It is important that it be insoluble in water, so that it will not wash off when exposed to rain. Chassis grease should not dry out or oxidize.

With the addition of extended relubrication periods, such as 48 000 km, in many late-model automobiles, special chassis greases are required. These greases contain lithium-lead soap and molybdenum disulphide. The addition of these chemicals produces a chassis grease having the following advantages: a high melting point, better protection against rust and corrosion, improved load-carrying ability and shock resistance, better adhesion, and higher resistance to water washing. Special grease guns and adapters are required for this type of lubrication.

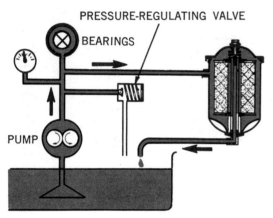

(A) BYPASS SYSTEM

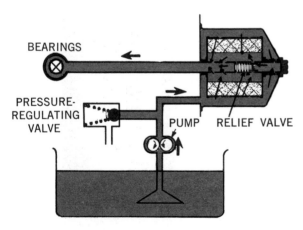

(B) FULL-FLOW SYSTEM

Fram Canada Ltd.

Fig. 6-7   Oil Filtering Systems

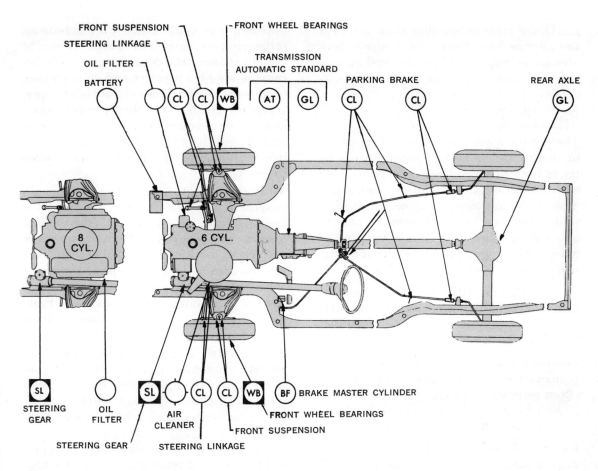

Fig. 6-8 Typical Lubrication Chart

General Motors Products of Canada Limited

LUBRICATE OR SERVICE EVERY 10 000 km

REPLACE EVERY 40 000 km

LUBRICATE EVERY 60 000 km

AT — Automatic Transmission Fluid
BF — Hydraulic Brake Fluid
SL — Steering Gear Lubricant
GL — Multi-purpose Gear Lubricant
WB — Wheel Bearing Lubricant
CL — Chassis Lubricant

Wheel-Bearing Grease. Since the automobile uses four-wheel brakes, there is a considerable amount of heat generated during brake application, and the proximity of the wheel-bearing lubricant to the braking mechanism makes it necessary to use only greases having a high melting point. Wheel-bearing greases generally have a sodium base, as sodium soaps impart high melting-point properties to the grease.

Special Greases. There are many other greases prepared for special applications. One such compound, used on rubber spring shackles, is made by blending an oil with a talc and asbestos fibre. Others are compounds of grease and graphite. These are used on rubber body mountings and door-lock assemblies.

GEAR LUBRICANTS

The correct application of gear lubricants is so vital to any lubrication program that refiners have developed several types of gear lubricants to meet different gear lubrication problems. These types may be classified as straight mineral oils, compounded mineral oils, extreme pressure oils, all-purpose or universal-type oils, and automatic transmission fluids.

Straight Mineral Oils. Straight mineral oils of highly treated, carefully refined materials are used for standard gear designs operating under normal conditions.

Compounded Mineral Oils. Compounded gear oils are blends of mineral oils and fatty oils or soaps with a sodium or lead base. Compounded gear lubricants are used principally in worm-gear units.

Extreme-Pressure Oils. In ordinary straight-tooth gear design, one gear tooth rolls across the surface of the other. This simple rolling action is comparatively easy to lubricate. However, since the drive shaft of the modern automobile has been lowered, it is no longer possible to use the *straight-cut spur gear* contact. Instead, *hypoid gears* are used. Hypoid gear teeth are cut on a curve, and not only having a rolling action, but also a wiping action which creates high pressures. These pressures can exceed 700 000 kilopascals and the wiping action or *slip* often reaches a speed of 27 600 metres per second (m/s). This pressure and sliding action could be described as a welding action, in which tiny irregularities on the surface of one gear tooth become so hot that they actually weld themselves to the opposing gear tooth. Under these conditions ordinary gear lubricants would either be wiped off the surfaces of the gear teeth because of the high pressure and sliding action, or be burned off because of the high temperatures present. To meet these conditions certain chemical compounds, such as chlorine and sulphur, have been added to prevent the lubricant from being removed from between the teeth.

All-Purpose or Universal-Type Oils. All-purpose or universal-type oils combine all the desirable features of straight mineral oils, compounded gear oils, and extreme-pressure oils. These lubricants are ideal because they are noncorrosive, stable, inexpensive, yet capable of meeting the lubrication requirements of most automotive applications. As a result, the all-purpose gear lubricants are the most popular.

Automatic Transmission Oils or Fluids. Automatic transmission fluids are combinations of high-quality base oils with special oxidization inhibitors, anti-wear additives, anti-foam agents, and detergent compounds.

An automatic transmission fluid must perform a variety of functions. In the fluid coupling or torque converter, it is the means of transmitting power and thus is exposed to very high temperatures. In the transmission it serves as a gear and bearing lubricant; controls the friction characteristics of the clutches and bands that provide the various gear ratios; transfers the pressures required to operate the clutches and bands; maintains cleanliness in the close fitting control valves; and prevents the drying out of the seals used in the transmission. This fluid is also used in power steering units.

SELECTION OF LUBRICANTS

The automobile and petroleum manufacturers provide lubrication charts which specify the type, grade, location, and frequency of lubrication required on all parts of the vehicle. Strict adherence to these recommendations is advised if satisfactory results are to be obtained.

PRACTICAL ASSIGNMENTS

a. Remove and Replace an Oil Filter Cartridge.

Procedure:
1. Remove the cover nut and cover.
2. Remove the used element.
3. Clean out the filter case.
4. Determine the type of filter unit required.
5. Have the instructor inspect your work.
6. Replace the element, checking whether the upper and lower seals seat properly.
7. Replace the cover gasket and cover-nut gasket.
8. Replace the cover and tighten.
9. Run the engine and check the filter for oil leaks.

b. Disassemble and Assemble an Oil Pump.
Procedure:
1. Remove the oil-pump gear cover.
2. Slide the gears out of the oil-pump housing.
3. Remove the cap nut which holds the pressure relief valve and spring in place.
4. Remove the oil relief valve and spring.
5. Study the pump construction and determine: (1) the direction in which the gears rotate, (2) the path of oil through the pump, (3) the operation of the pressure relief valve.
6. Replace the pressure relief valve, valve spring, and cap nut.
7. Replace the oil-pump gears.
8. Replace the gear cover.

c. Change Engine Oil.

Procedure:
1. Check the engine oil level 3 to 5 minutes after the engine has been stopped. This will permit the oil to drain down into the crankcase. The oil level should be between the *full* and *add* marks on the gauge rod. Do not fill above the *full mark*. The condition of the motor oil will determine whether the oil in the crankcase should be changed. Dirt, grit, and discolouration are good signs that the oil requires changing. Distance travelled is not a true indication, as some vehicles, depending on the way they are driven, require oil changes more often than others.
2. Place the car on the hoist and lift to a suitable height, or jack up the car and place on safety stands.
3. Remove the drain plug from the crankcase and drain the oil. (The engine should be at operating temperature.)
4. After all the oil has drained, replace the drain plug and install a new drain-plug gasket.
5. Lower the car to the floor.
6. Insert the proper grade and quantity of engine oil in the engine.

d. Lubricate Chassis.

Procedure:
1. Place the car on the hoist and lift to a suitable height, or jack up the car and place it on safety stands.
2. Wipe any dirt from the lubrication fittings, then apply, under pressure, a good grade of water-resistant chassis lubricant to the following points as required:
   (1) Lower control arms, inner and outer ends.
   (2) Upper pivot pins or ball joints.
   (3) Steering-knuckle bushings.

(4) Tie-rod ends, intermediate steering rods, and idler-arm support bushings.

(5) Clutch release mechanism.

(6) Brake-pedal and clutch-pedal shafts.

3. (a) *Standard Transmission.* Check the transmission grease level by cleaning around the area and removing the filler plug. The level should be maintained at the filler-plug opening. Fill to level with a suitable transmission lubricant. Replace the filler plug.

(b) *Automatic transmission* fluid levels are checked by removing the transmission dip stick, wiping it dry, replacing it, and removing it again to check the reading. It should read in the operating range.

NOTE: Check the manufacturer's recommendation regarding engine operation and gear position before checking the level.

4. Check the differential grease level by cleaning the area around the filler plug and slowly removing the filler plug to vent any pressure present. The level should be maintained at the height of the filler plug opening. Fill to this level with a suitable differential grease. Replace the filler plug.

5. Lower the car to the floor.

6. Inspect the fan belt for condition and adjustment.

7. Check the coolant level in the radiator when the engine is cold and, if required, add water to within 40 mm of the top of the tank.

8. (a) Check the standard steering-box oil level as follows. Clean the area adjacent to the filler plug and, if necessary, add lubricant to bring the level to the bottom of the filler plug opening. Replace the filler plug.

(b) Check power steering level according to manufacturer's specifications.

9. Service the battery.

10. Check the master-cylinder fluid level. First, clean the area adjacent to the filler plug; then remove the filler plug and, if necessary, add brake fluid to bring the level up to the bottom of the filler opening. Replace the filler plug.

11. Check the manifold valve shaft for free movement and lubricate it with engine oil.

12. Check and inflate the tires.

13. Lubricate the door locks and striker plates with special door grease.

14. Check the operation of the lights, horn, windshield wipers, and directional signals, and record the defects.

15. Record the odometer reading on a suitable sticker and stick it on an accessible place.

16. Wipe the steering wheel, door handles, control knobs, and fenders to remove any grease or dirt.

17. Have the instructor inspect your work.

REVIEW QUESTIONS

1. What is friction?
2. List four factors affecting friction.
3. How does a lubricant help to reduce friction?
4. Give four reasons for using lubricants in the automobile.
5. Explain the process of distillation.
6. Explain the process of fractionation.
7. What are the advantages of the cracking process?
8. After the cracking process, the manufacture of fuels and oils is divided into three sections. Explain each section.
9. Define the term viscosity.
10. State the purpose of the following tests: (a) cold test, (b) flash point test, (c) volatility test.

11. Why was it necessary to establish the SAE system of oil classification?
12. Explain the difference between the SAE system and the service rating system of oil classification.
13. What is the difference between SAE 10 oil and SAE 10W oil?
14. What is the difference between SAE 10W-30 oil and the three oils SAE 10, SAE 20, and SAE 30?
15. Describe heavy duty motor oil.
16. Name four grades of oil and state briefly the conditions under which each is used.
17. Name four substances which contaminate motor oil.
18. State how each of the four substances mentioned in question 17 gets into the oil and how it affects the oil.
19. Name six units of the lubricating system and state the purpose of each.
20. State the two methods of lubricating the connecting-rod bearings.
21. Why are oil filters necessary?
22. Name and give a brief description of two types of oil filters.
23. State the difference in the filtering elements of the two types of filters.
24. Write a complete report on the purpose and operation of the filter relief valve.
25. Describe the operation of one type of oil pressure gauge.
26. Why are soap compounds added to lubricants?
27. Why is it necessary to have special wheel-bearing grease?
28. Name the two important characteristics of chassis grease.
29. Why is it necessary to have special hypoid-gear lubricants?
30. Why is it important to use a gear lubricant that is designed for the job?
31. Why are special automatic-transmission fluids used?
32. Why should the engine be at operating temperature before draining the crankcase?
33. Should rubber spring bushings be lubricated? Why?
34. Why should grease fittings be wiped off before attaching the grease gun?

THE FUEL SYSTEM

7

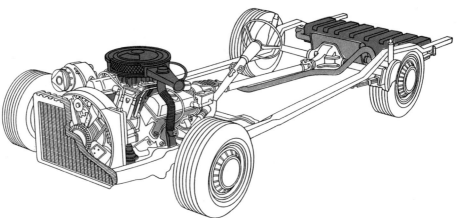

The fuel system (Figure 7-1) is used to carry the supply of gasoline in the automobile, so that the vehicle is a self-contained unit capable of travelling a considerable distance. The fuel system must also prepare the fuel for combustion in the cylinders and carry the exhaust gases to the rear of the vehicle.

GASOLINE

Gasoline is a blend of various types and proportions of fuel obtained from crude oil or petroleum. Fuel chemists prepare the best product for all round performance by compounding different types of gasoline. Several characteristics are considered in this compounding procedure, such as volatility, anti-knock value, and freedom from harmful chemicals and gum formations.

Volatility. Volatility refers to the ease with which gasoline or other liquids vaporize. For example, since alcohol vaporizes at a lower temperature than water, it is said to be more volatile. Gasoline is compounded of many kinds of hydrocarbons, each having a different volatility. This blending is done in order to obtain a fuel that will satisfactorily provide the following features: easy starting, speedy warmup, smooth acceleration, good economy, freedom from vapour lock, and freedom from crankcase dilution.

Highly volatile gasoline is known as *high-test gasoline*. It vaporizes easily and is the most desirable gasoline for starting cold engines. Unfortunately, it burns very rapidly when highly compressed and therefore its force would be spent before the piston has travelled very far down in the cylinder on the power stroke.

Low volatile gasoline is known as *low-test gasoline*. It does not evaporate easily, burns and expands at a slower rate, and makes starting a cold engine difficult.

Modern gasoline is a blend of low-test and high-test gasolines. The amount of low-test

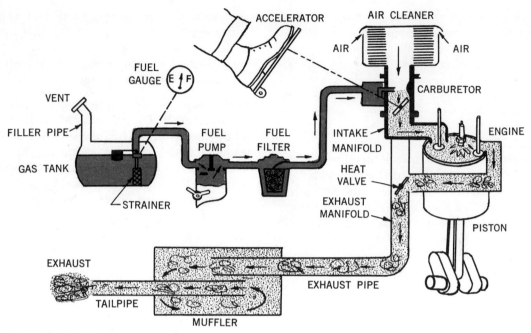

Fig. 7-1   The Fuel System

lead, or ethyl. The lower compression ratios and combustion temperatures of modern engines have reduced the need for high octane gasolines and practically eliminated the use of additives such as tetraethyl lead. and high-test gasoline in the blend depends upon the season of the year and the geographical location. The blend contains more high-test gasoline in winter than in summer. Gasoline sold during the winter time in northern areas contains more high-test gasoline than the gasoline sold in warmer areas at the same time. More low-test gasoline is used in the blend during the summer months.

Anti-Knock Value. When chemists were developing higher octane gasolines that would permit the building of higher-compression engines, various chemicals were employed. These chemicals, when added to the gasoline, reduce the rate of flame travel during combustion. This results in the prevention of excessive pressures which cause detonation, or *knocking*. One of the most successful of these chemicals is tetraethyl

In order to identify the anti-knock qualities of gasoline, an *octane rating* is used. This rating is determined in a special test engine. The gasoline to be tested is used to operate the test engine and the results are recorded. The engine is then operated on a mixture of iso-octane and heptane. Iso-octane is a fluid possessing high anti-knock properties and is rated at 100 octane. Heptane is a liquid possessing low anti-knock properties and rated at zero octane. The octane rating is determined by the amount of octane in the octane-heptane mixture that gives the same results as the gasoline tested. In other words, if the octane and heptane mixture requires 90% octane and 10% heptane to match the performance of the gasoline tested, then that gasoline would be given a 90 octane rating.

The research readings for modern gasolines are as follows: premium grade is rated at approximately 99; regular grade at approximately 95; non-leaded grade at approximately 90. The anti-knock ratings for premium and regular grade gasolines are obtained by adding varying amounts of tetraethyl lead compounds to the gasoline. The anti-knock rating for non-leaded gasoline is obtained by a special blending and refining process; no tetraethyl lead is added.

Non-leaded gasolines are required for use in vehicles equipped with catalytic converters in the exhaust system. This is because the continuous use of the lead salts contained in tetraethyl lead will destroy the catalyst in the converter unit, thus preventing the unit from eliminating certain pollutants in the exhaust gases.

Freedom from Harmful Chemicals and Gum Formations. As the gasoline-air mixture burns, the sulphur content of the gasoline tends to form sulphuric acid, which attacks and corrodes the metal parts in the engine, particularly the bearings. Gum formation is due to the presence of dissolved gum in the gasoline. The gum solidifies in the gasoline passages of the carburetor and the intake manifold, and on the valves and piston rings, causing premature failure of these parts. In manufacturing gasoline, every effort is made to keep these harmful substances to a minimum.

UNITS OF THE FUEL SYSTEM

The units of the fuel system include the gasoline storage tank, gasoline gauge, fuel pump, carburetor, air cleaner, intake manifold, and exhaust system (Figure 7-2).

Gasoline Storage Tank. The storage tank is usually located at the rear of the chassis and holds from 40 litres to 80 litres of gasoline. It must be vented to the atmosphere in order to maintain a constant pressure on the fuel in the tank. This pressure acts in conjunction with the vacuum produced in the fuel pump to deliver fuel. A gauge, usually of the electric type, is used to inform the operator of the amount of fuel in the storage tank.

Fuel Lines. Steel or copper tubing is used to transfer the fuel from the tank to the fuel pump and from the fuel pump to the carburetor. A short, flexible neoprene hose is usually placed at the fuel pump end of the line from the tank. This hose absorbs the vibration in the line between the engine and the car frame.

Fuel filters are frequently placed in the fuel line between the fuel pump and the carburetor. These filters contain paper, ceramic, or metallic elements which remove dirt, water, etc., from the gasoline.

The fuel lines must be placed away from the exhaust system to minimize the possibility of the fuel vaporizing in the line and creating what is known as a *vapour lock*.

FUEL PUMP

Some means must be provided for supplying the engine with gasoline. One method used is a *gravity feed* from a storage tank placed higher than the carburetor. Another system used is a *vacuum tank* operated by a vacuum taken from the engine manifold. This latter method creates an area of low pressure into which the fuel from the tank is forced. From there it runs by gravity to the carburetor. Modern automobiles use an *engine-operated* fuel pump, which pumps fuel through tubing from the storage tank to the carburetor (Figure 7-3).

The majority of mechanical fuel pumps operate in the following manner: As the highest part of a special fuel-pump-operating cam on the camshaft comes around, it pushes on the rocker arm which, through linkage, pulls the diaphragm down. As the diaphragm moves down, it creates a vacuum in the fuel

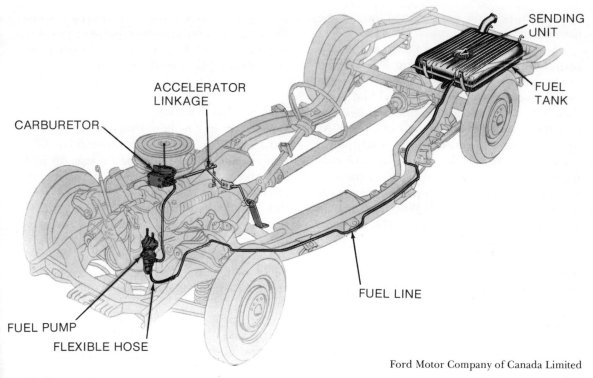

SENDING
UNIT

FUEL
TANK

ACCELERATOR
LINKAGE

CARBURETOR

FUEL LINE

FUEL PUMP

FLEXIBLE HOSE

Ford Motor Company of Canada Limited

Fig. 7-2   Typical Fuel System Installation

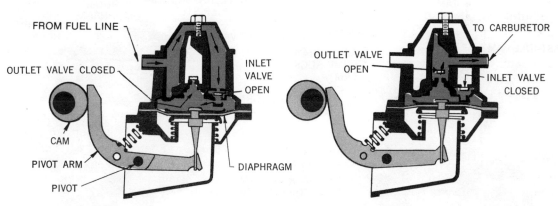

FROM FUEL LINE

OUTLET VALVE CLOSED

INLET
VALVE
OPEN

CAM

PIVOT ARM

PIVOT

DIAPHRAGM

TO CARBURETOR

OUTLET VALVE
OPEN

INLET VALVE
CLOSED

Fig. 7-3   Fuel Pump

chamber which opens the inlet valve and closes the outlet valve. Gasoline is forced into the chamber by atmospheric pressure on the fuel in the storage tank. As the lowest part of the cam on the camshaft comes around, the diaphragm return spring forces the diaphragm up, creating a pressure on the gasoline in the chamber. This closes the intake valve and opens the outlet valve, forcing the gasoline up the carburetor.

The needle valve in the float bowl of the carburetor maintains a constant level of fuel in the carburetor bowl. When this valve is closed, fuel cannot enter the bowl and pressure is built up in the fuel line between the carburetor and the fuel pump chamber. As the pressure increases in the fuel pump chamber, it resists the action of the diaphragm return spring and prevents the diaphragm from taking a complete stroke, thus reducing the flow of fuel. When the needle valve in the carburetor is open, the pressure in the line and chamber is reduced and gasoline is needed in the carburetor bowl. This reduced pressure allows the diaphragm to take longer strokes, thus increasing the flow of fuel.

Most fuel pumps include a fuel strainer, or filter, to remove from the gasoline any solid particles of foreign material before they can damage either the pump or carburetor. Some filtering elements are also capable of preventing water which may be in the gasoline from entering the pump or carburetor.

THE CARBURETOR

Gasoline in its raw liquid form will not burn satisfactorily to operate an internal-combustion engine. It must first be broken up into tiny particles, or *atomized*. After being atomized, the gasoline is vaporized and thoroughly mixed with air in proper proportions for combustion. While these proportions vary slightly for different makes of engines, one part of gasoline to fifteen parts of air by mass is the average mixture used. By volume that would amount to about 10 000:1 ratio.

The carburetor, therefore, is a device which automatically vaporizes and mixes the gasoline and air in the proper proportions

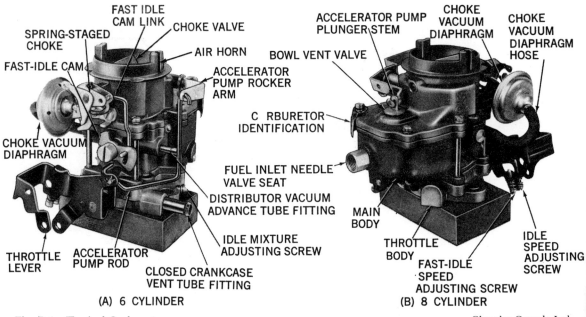

Fig. 7-4   Typical Carburetors

Chrysler Canada Ltd.

necessary for starting, idling, acceleration, and power at various speeds.

CARBURETOR PRINCIPLES

Fuel-Air Ratio. A mixture with more than fifteen parts of air to one part of gasoline is said to be *lean,* and is frequently used when the vehicle is cruising along a level road at reasonable speed. A mixture with less than fifteen parts of air to one of gasoline is said to be *rich,* and is used for high speed and heavy load conditions. The modern carburetor has a mixture range from a lean of 17:1 to a rich mixture of 12:1.

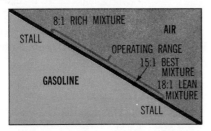

Fig. 7-5　Fuel-Air Ratio

The fuel-air ratio is controlled by *jets, air bleeds,* and *valves.*

Jet. A jet contains a calibrated hole. The size of the hole determines the amount of gasoline which can flow through the jet. The jet may be integral with the casting or a separate part fitted into a passageway in the casting. Each carburetor circuit has one or more jets to control the flow of fuel.

Air Bleeds. Air bleeds are small openings that conduct air from the air horn to the various carburetor circuits. By mixing air with the fuel, the fuel is partially atomized before it reaches the discharge point.

Valves. Valves of various types are used to control the flow of fuel and air. Needle or plunger type valves usually control the flow of the fuel, and butterfly type valves control the flow of air.

The Venturi. The venturi is a narrowed section of the carburetor air passageway. Its

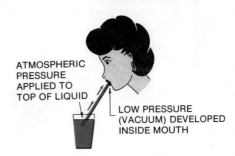

(A) VACUUM PRINCIPLE

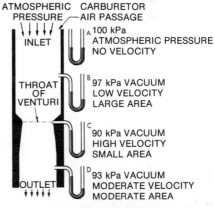

(B) VENTURI VACUUM

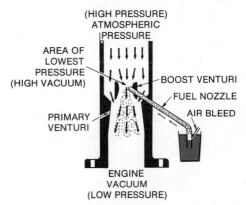

(C) VENTURI OPERATION

Fig. 7-6　Venturi Principle

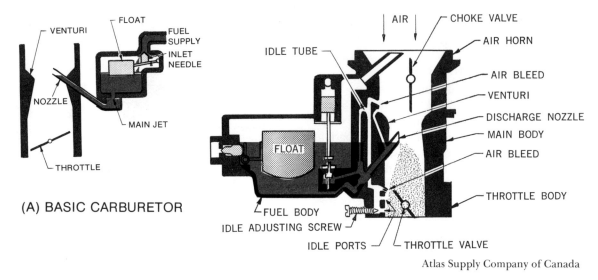

VENTURI

FLOAT

FUEL SUPPLY

INLET NEEDLE

NOZZLE

MAIN JET

THROTTLE

(A) BASIC CARBURETOR

IDLE TUBE

AIR

CHOKE VALVE

AIR HORN

AIR BLEED

VENTURI

DISCHARGE NOZZLE

MAIN BODY

AIR BLEED

FLOAT

THROTTLE BODY

FUEL BODY

IDLE ADJUSTING SCREW

IDLE PORTS

THROTTLE VALVE

Atlas Supply Company of Canada

(B) CARTER (BALL AND BALL) TYPE

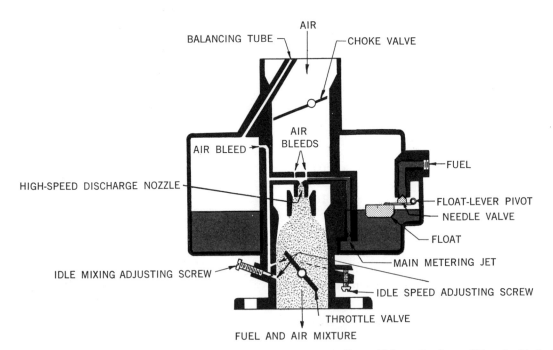

BALANCING TUBE

AIR

CHOKE VALVE

AIR BLEEDS

AIR BLEED

HIGH-SPEED DISCHARGE NOZZLE

FUEL

FLOAT-LEVER PIVOT

NEEDLE VALVE

FLOAT

MAIN METERING JET

IDLE MIXING ADJUSTING SCREW

IDLE SPEED ADJUSTING SCREW

THROTTLE VALVE

FUEL AND AIR MIXTURE

General Motors Products of Canada, Limited

(C) ROCHESTER TYPE

Fig. 7-7   Carburetors

purpose is to create a partial vacuum in the air passage. When the same amount of air moves through the venturi as through the rest of the passage, the velocity of the air will be greatest at the narrowest point. The greater the velocity, the lower the pressure. Therefore, air pressure is lowest at the narrowest point. This low pressure draws gasoline, in the form of a fine spray, through the discharge nozzle which is mounted in the narrowest part of the venturi. The faster the air passes through the venturi, the greater the amount of fuel that will be drawn out of the nozzle into the air stream. Frequently, dual and triple venturis are used to produce the low-pressure area in a desired place in the passageway (Figure 7-6).

CARBURETOR CONSTRUCTION

The carburetor usually consists of three separate castings: the upper, called the *air horn;* the centre, called the *main body and fuel bowl;* and the lower, called the *throttle body.* The passageway in the carburetor through which the air passes is called the *throat.*

The air horn, to which the air cleaner is attached and where the air enters the carburetor, includes the choke assembly. The main body includes the venturi and most of the carburetor circuits. The throttle body includes the throttle valve, the idle mixture and speed screws, and the parts which attach the carburetor to the manifold.

CARBURETOR CIRCUITS

The carburetor consists of six different circuits: the float, idle, high-speed, accelerating, power, and choke circuits.

Carburetor Float Circuit. The float circuit is the most important circuit because it controls the height of the gasoline level in the bowl and nozzle. A gasoline level that is too high or too low will cause trouble in the other circuits and make complaints difficult to

trace. The float bowl acts as a reservoir to hold a supply of gasoline throughout the entire range of engine performance. Gasoline is available at a fairly constant pressure from the fuel pump, and when the needle valve is off its seat, gasoline will flow into the float bowl. If gasoline enters more rapidly than it leaves, the bowl will tend to fill up, causing the float to rise. The float is connected to a lever and a pivot, and as the float rises, the lever bears against the lower end of the needle valve, causing it to be lifted upward into the needle-valve seat. This closes the inlet, preventing further delivery of gasoline into the float bowl until some of the gasoline is withdrawn through the carburetor circuits. When this happens, the float drops and releases the needle valve from its seat so that additional gasoline will be delivered into the bowl from the fuel pump. In actual operation, the gasoline is maintained at a practically constant level in the bowl. The float tends to hold the needle valve partly closed so that the incoming gasoline just balances the gasoline being drawn through the fuel passages in the carburetor. (See Figure 7-8).

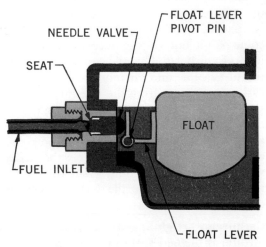

Atlas Supply Company of Canada

Fig. 7-8 Typical Float System

Carburetor Idle and Low-Speed Circuit. The idle and low-speed circuit completely controls the supply of gasoline to the engine during idle and no-load speeds up to 30 km/h and partially controls the supply of gasoline for no-load speeds between 30 km/h and 50 km/h. During idle and low-speed operation of the engine, the gasoline flows from the float bowl through the idle-speed jet to a point where it is combined with a stream of air coming in from the carburetor throat through the upper air bleed. The combining of the stream of air with the stream of gasoline tends to atomize the gasoline, or break it up into a vapour. This mixture of air and gasoline continues through the passage until it begins to pass the point where it is combined with a stream of air coming in through the lower air bleed. This further breaks up the gasoline particles into a finer vapour. The gasoline and air mixture that flows downward into the passage from the lower air bleed is still richer than required, but when it mixes with the air which has come past the throttle valve, it forms a combustible mixture of the right proportion for idling speed.

The idle port is made in a variety of slotted or round shapes so that, as the throttle valve is opened, it will not only allow more air to come past it, but will also uncover more of the idle port or ports. This allows a greater quantity of gasoline and air mixture to enter the carburetor throat from the idle mixture passage. The idle position of the throttle is such than an idling speed of approximately 15 km/h leaves enough of the slotted port covered to act as a reserve to supply the necessary mixture for the time when the carburetor changes from the idle to the high-speed circuit.

Carburetor High-Speed Circuit. As the throttle is opened sufficiently for a no-load speed of a little more than 30 km/h, the velocity of the air flowing down through the carburetor throat creates a pressure difference between the end of the nozzle and the float chamber. Since the gasoline in the float bowl is acted upon by atmospheric pressure, the difference in pressure between the two points causes the gasoline to flow from the fuel bowl, through the metering jet, and out the main nozzle into the throat of the carburetor. As the speed increases from 30 km/h the high-speed system continues to cut in more and more while the idle or low-speed system continues to cut out until the car reaches a speed of 50 km/h. At this point the high-speed system is carrying the entire load and the idle system ceases operation.

The idle or low-speed circuit ceases to function completely because the throttle valve has moved past the idle port openings. Now there is little or no difference in pressure between the upper and lower parts of the carburetor. (See Figure 7-9.)

Carburetor Power Circuit. Since a richer mixture is required for high speed or heavy load conditions, it is necessary to vary the fuel-air ratio automatically to meet these conditions. This is the job of the power circuit which is controlled by engine vacuum. When engine vacuum is high, the power valve is closed. When engine vacuum drops below a specified amount, the power valve starts to open. This allows additional fuel to enter the high-speed circuit to enrich the mixture in accordance with engine load or speed. This system provides for extra power when needed and for economy at other times.

Carburetor Accelerator Circuit. When the throttle is opened suddenly, it causes the engine vacuum to drop. Without sufficient vacuum in the throat of the carburetor, the gasoline flow through the high-speed circuit decreases. The result is a lean mixture reaching the cylinders and causing a drop in engine power. To prevent this, a *plunger-type pump,* operated by the throttle linkage, dis-

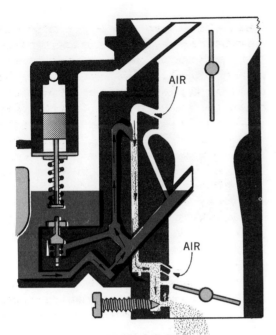

(A) IDLE CIRCUIT

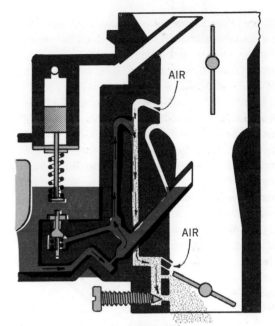

(B) LOW SPEED CIRCUIT

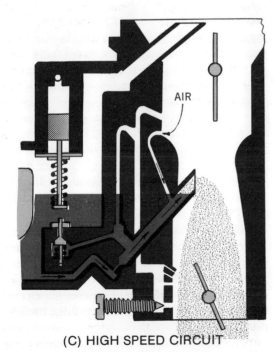

(C) HIGH SPEED CIRCUIT

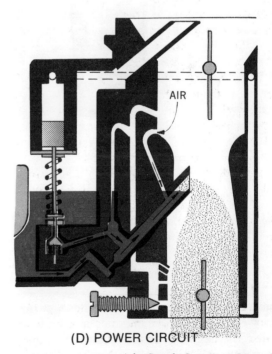

(D) POWER CIRCUIT

Fig. 7-9   Carburetor Circuits

Atlas Supply Company of Canada

charges a stream of gasoline into the air stream as the throttle is opened. The pump discharge maintains the proper fuel-air ratio during the initial acceleration period. (See Figure 7-10).

The pump consists of a *piston,* an *inlet* and an *outlet valve,* and a *discharge jet.* When the throttle is closed, the linkage lifts the pump piston, creating an area of low pressure beneath it. Fuel from the carburetor bowl enters by way of the inlet valve. When the throttle is opened, the piston is forced down, creating a pressure on the fuel beneath it. This pressure opens the outlet valve and forces the fuel out through the discharge jet.

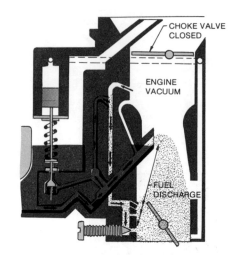

FUEL DISCHARGE WHEN
CHOKE VALVE IS CLOSED

Fig. 7-11   Carburetor Choke Circuit

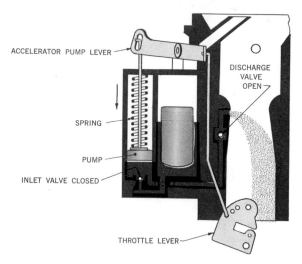

Fig. 7-10   Carburetor Accelerator Circuit

Carburetor Choke Circuit. The choke is used to provide the rich mixture needed for starting a cold engine. The choke valve controls the amount of air entering the air horn. It may be operated manually or automatically.

The rich starting mixture is required because the gasoline vapours condense when they contact the cold engine parts and because the engine produces a low vacuum at cranking speeds.

When the engine starts, the choke must be partially opened to prevent flooding. As the engine warms up, a leaner mixture is required. Therefore, the choke must be gradually opened to its full extent at normal engine operating temperatures to maintain the proper fuel-air ratio.

In an automatic choke, the various stages of choke-valve positioning are controlled by the combination of a temperature-operated thermostatic spring, the engine vacuum, and the air flow through the throat of the carburetor.

When the engine is stopped and cold, the choke valve is closed by the winding action of the thermostatic spring as the accelerator pedal is depressed. The instant the engine is started, engine vacuum is applied to a piston which is connected to the choke valve. As engine vacuum moves the piston, the choke valve is opened sufficiently to prevent flooding. In order to maintain the proper fuel-air ratio at higher engine speeds during the warm-up period, the choke valve is offset on its shaft. As the engine speed increases, the air flow opens the choke valve an additional amount to prevent high-speed flooding. When a heavy load is placed on the engine, the engine vacuum drops and its effect on the choke position decreases. This closes the choke valve, resulting in an enrichment in the fuel-air ratio. As the engine warms up to its normal operating temperature, the thermostatic spring expands due to the temperature change and opens the choke to its maximum position.

The positioning of the manual choke is controlled by the driver through a choke cable attached to a button mounted on the dash.

The fast idling device is incorporated with both types of choke-operating mechanisms. This device increases the throttle-valve opening in proportion to the position of the choke valve. The device provides for a faster idling speed during the warm-up period to prevent stalling.

TYPES OF CARBURETORS

Carburetors are typed according to the location of the fuel bowl. If the bowl is off to one side of the throat, the carburetor is classed as *eccentric*. If the bowl surrounds the throat, then the carburetor is classed as *concentric*.

When the carburetor is mounted below the intake manifold, it is classed as an *up-draft carburetor*. A *down-draft carburetor* is mounted above the intake manifold. Carburetors mounted in line and to the side of the manifold are classed as *side-draft carburetors*. Down-draft carburetors are the most common in use today.

Carburetors may have one, two, or four barrels. Multiple barrel carburetors have certain circuits duplicated in the additional barrels and use other circuits that are common to all barrels.

AIR CLEANERS

The air cleaner is mounted on the air horn of the carburetor and does three jobs: it re-

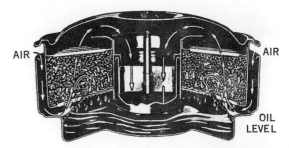

Chrysler Canada Ltd.

(A) OIL BATH TYPE

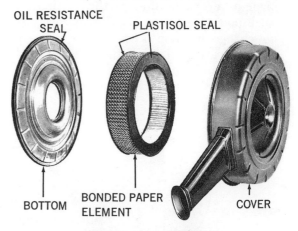

BONDED PAPER ELEMENT

POLYURETHANE ELEMENT

General Motors Products of Canada, Limited

(B) DRY TYPE

Fig. 7-12 Carburetor Air Circuit

moves dust particles from the air before they enter the carburetor; it muffles the noise of the air rushing into the engine; and it acts as a flame arrester, should the engine backfire through the carburetor (Figure 7-12).

Two types of air cleaner are used, the oil-bath type and the replaceable or washable cellulose fibre-element dry type.

Oil-Bath Cleaners. In the oil-bath cleaner, the air passing through the air cleaner is made to reverse its direction directly above a small pool of oil. Since the dust particles do not change direction as easily as air, many of the dust particles fall into the pool of oil instead of continuing in the air stream. The air then passes through a copper mesh or similar

filtering element to remove any remaining dust particles. Silencing pads, usually made of felt, muffle the hissing sound of the rushing air.

Dry-Air Cleaner. In the dry-air cleaner, the dust particles are trapped by a cellulose filtering element as the air passes through it. Silencing pads, usually made of felt, muffle the hissing sound of the rushing air.

MANIFOLDS AND THE EXHAUST SYSTEM

The Intake Manifold. An intake manifold is a passage that conveys the fuel and air mixture from the carburetor to the cylinders.

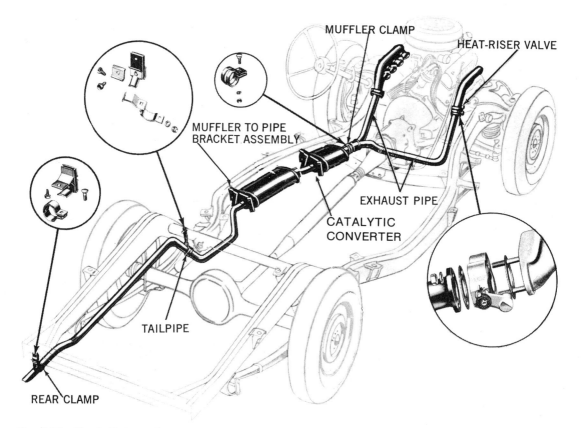

Fig. 7-13   Single Exhaust System

The Exhaust System. The burnt gases come out of the exhaust port with considerable noise. These gases are also poisonous. Therefore, they must be silenced and conveyed away from the passenger compartment to the rear of the vehicle. These functions are accomplished by the exhaust system (Figure 7-13) which consists of the *exhaust manifold, exhaust pipe, muffler,* and *tailpipe.*

The exhaust manifold, made of cast iron, is bolted over the exhaust ports of the engine, alongside the intake manifold pipe, and provides heat to the intake manifold. This heat

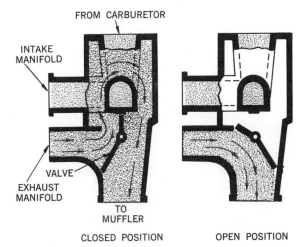

(A) MANIFOLD HEAT-CONTROL VALVE FOR 6-CYLINDER ENGINES

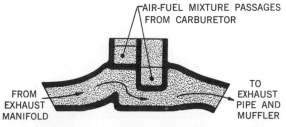

(B) EXHAUST FLOW THROUGH INTAKE MANIFOLD IN V8 ENGINE

Fig. 7-14   Manifold Heating Systems

further vaporizes the fuel in the intake manifold. Since the maximum amount of heat is required only during the warm-up period, a valve called the manifold heat-control valve, or heat-riser valve, is used to direct the exhaust gases through the passageways in the intake manifold or through special channels in the carburetor base.

The manifold heat-control valve is operated by a bimetal spring. When the engine is cold, the valve is in a position which directs the hot exhaust gases into the intake manifold or carburetor passageways. As the engine warms up, the bimetal spring gradually changes the position of the valve so that the exhaust gases go directly to the exhaust pipe.

On V8 engines, the manifold heat-control valve is mounted between the exhaust manifold and the cross-over pipe. When the valve is in the closed position, the exhaust gases are directed to the exhaust pipe through special passageways in the cylinder heads and the intake manifold, thus warming the intake manifold. In the open position, the exhaust gases pass through the cross-over pipe.

It should be mentioned that the use of thermostatic type air cleaners has eliminated the use of manifold heat control valves on many modern engines.

The exhaust pipe is a long pipe leading from the exhaust manifold to the muffler.

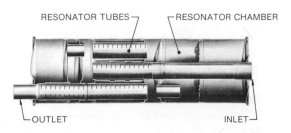

Fig. 7-15   Muffler Cross Section

The muffler reduces the noise of the exhaust. It does this by slowing down the speed of the escaping gases, and passing these gases through different passages before allowing them to escape through the tailpipe to the rear of the vehicle.

PRACTICAL ASSIGNMENTS

a. Disassemble, Assemble, and Test the Fuel Pump.

Procedure:
1. If the pump is dirty, wash it in a cleaning fluid (Varsol, kerosene, etc.).
2. Mark the diaphragm and pump chamber so that they can be assembled in their proper relation. A file can be used to put a light nick in each housing for line-up purposes.
3. Remove the screws holding the two housings together. In most cases the two housings will come apart easily. However, some will stick and the student will have to find a suitable means of separating them without causing damage to either part. These housings damage easily since they are made of a very soft metal.
4. After separating the two housings, take the valve chamber from the pump housing and remove the valves. These valves are located in different positions in various types of pumps. Sometimes they are held in by hexagonal nuts screwed on from the outside. In other cases they are fastened by means of a small plate on the inside of the housing. Care should be taken not to damage any part of this valve mechanism. The valve springs should be checked for bends, the fibre valves for roughness and wear, and the brass valve seat for scores and scratches.
5. Take a drift punch and drive out the rocker arm pivot. This will allow the removal of the rocker arm, linkage, and diaphragm assembly. The linkage should be

checked for wear and the diaphragm checked for cracks or porous condition. Particular attention should be paid to the linkage, for worn links or parts result in lost motion and poor fuel pump operation. The position of the linkage should be noted when the pump is disassembled, so that it can be assembled correctly.
6. When you have learned the names of the parts and the operating principles of the pump, ask your instructor to question you about them.
7. Reassemble the pump, being careful to see that all parts are placed in their correct position.
8. Check the pump with a vacuum and pressure gauge. If the pump is assembled correctly, it should have at least 20 kPa of vacuum and 120 kPa of pressure.
9. Have the instructor inspect your work.

b. Disassemble and Assemble a Single-Barrel Carburetor.

Procedure:
1. Disassemble the carburetor according to the instruction sheet.
2. Locate the following carburetor parts: (a) venturi, (b), air horn, (c) float, (d) needle valve, (e) throttle valve, (f) idle discharge port, (g) high-speed nozzle.
3. Assemble the carburetor, using the instruction sheet as a guide.
4. Have the assembled carburetor inspected by the instructor.

c. Adjust Carburetor to Idle. To set idle adjustment on late-model engines, it is necessary to use two pieces of test equipment, a *tachometer* and a *vacuum gauge*. Instruction on the use of the test equipment must be given by the instructor before this assignment is attempted.

The engine idle speed and mixture should be adjusted when a tune-up or any other motor work is done. There are two different adjustments to be made on the carburetor, one for idling mixture and the other for idling speed. Both of these adjustments should be made together after the engine has been thoroughly warmed up. Engines with two-barrel carburetors have two mixture-adjustment screws. Each screw must be adjusted to give the best idling-mixture setting.

Procedure:

1. Open the idle-mixture adjusting screw 1.5 to 2 turns from the fully closed position.
2. Turn the high-speed adjusting screw until it just touches its stop. Then turn it in 2 additional turns.
3. Start the engine and run it at idle speed until it is thoroughly warmed up.
4. With the engine idling, turn the mixture screw or screws from the basic position until the best setting is made (highest engine vacuum and highest r/min).
5. When the hand choke is closed or when the fast-idling device of the automatic choke is in its lowest position, set the throttle-lever stop screw so that the engine runs at idling speed (approximately 650 r/min).
6. Have the instructor inspect your work.

d. Remove, Clean, and Replace the Fuel Filter.

Procedure:

1. Locate the fuel filter bowl. It may be a part of the fuel pump or a separate unit mounted in the fuel line.
2. Loosen the fuel-bowl retaining nut and move the nut and bracket from under the bowl. Care must be exercised not to dislodge the bowl.
3. Grasp the bowl firmly and remove it with a light twisting action. Do not lose the gasket or filter screen.
4. Drain and wipe the bowl with a lint-free cloth. Clean the filter screen by blowing compressed air through it.

5. Replace the bowl, using a new gasket.
6. Put the retaining bracket in place and tighten the retaining nut sufficiently to prevent leaks.
7. Start the engine and allow it to run for a few minutes. Check for leaks and, if necessary, retighten the retaining nut.
8. Have the instructor inspect your work.

e. Remove, Clean, and Replace a Dry Carburetor Air Cleaner (Metal Gauze Type).

Procedure:

1. Loosen the thumbscrew and remove the cover from the air cleaner.
2. Remove the filtering element and wash it in kerosene.
3. Allow the element to dry. Do not use compressed air for drying, as this could damage the element.
4. Re-oil the element by dipping it in engine oil. Let the excess oil drain from the element before reassembly.
5. Clean the dirt from the element area of the air-cleaner shell.
6. Reassemble the air cleaner.
7. Have the instructor inspect your work.

f. Remove, Clean, and Replace an Oil-Bath Air Cleaner.

Procedure:

1. Loosen the air cleaner from the carburetor air horn. Some cleaners are held in position by a screw clamp between the base of the air cleaner and the carburetor air horn. Other types are held by a screw located in the centre of the cleaner and screwed into a bracket inside the air horn. Some large air cleaners have an additional bracket between the cleaner and the engine block. This bracket must be detached before the air cleaner can be removed.
2. Remove the air cleaner from the carburetor. Caution must be exercised to prevent the spilling of oil that is inside the air-cleaner unit.

3. Drain the oil reservoir and wash it out with kerosene. Wipe it dry with a lint-free wiper.
4. Clean the copper-mesh element with cleaning fluid and allow to drain. Do not oil the element.
5. Reassemble the air-cleaner shell to the carburetor.
6. Refill the oil reservoir to the proper level with the proper grade of engine oil.
7. Replace the filtering element and cover. Tighten all the nuts securely.
8. Have the instructor inspect your work.

REVIEW QUESTIONS

1. Name three characteristics which must be considered when compounding gasoline.
2. Define the terms (a) volatility, (b) octane rating.
3. What are the advantages of (a) high-volatility gasolines, (b) low-volatility gasolines?
4. What factors are considered when blending gasoline?
5. How is the octane rating of gasoline determined?
6. Why must the gasoline tank be vented to the atmosphere?
7. What is a *vapour lock?*
8. Name and describe three methods of bringing gasoline from the gasoline tank to the carburetor.
9. Describe the operation of a fuel pump.
10. What is the purpose of a carburetor?
11. State the purpose of a carburetor jet.
12. Why are air bleeds used in the carburetor?
13. What is the purpose of the venturi?
14. Name and give the purpose of the three main bodies of a carburetor.
15. What must be done to gasoline so that it will burn satisfactorily in an engine?
16. State the proportions of fuel and air required for proper combustion.
17. Why is a partial vacuum in the air horn necessary?
18. Explain the purpose and operation of the float circuit.
19. Explain the purpose and operation of the idle circuit.
20. Explain why the delivery of fuel to the air stream changes from one carburetor circuit to another when the engine is operating at road speeds ranging from 30 km/h to 50 km/h.
21. Describe the operation of the high-speed circuit.
22. Why is an accelerator circuit necessary?
23. What is the purpose of the power circuit?
24. Why is the choke necessary?
25. What three factors control the operation of an automatic choke?
26. What is a fast-idle device and why is it necessary?
27. Name three ways in which carburetors may be typed.
28. State three purposes of the air cleaner.
29. Explain how the muffler accomplishes its purpose.
30. Why are heat-riser valves used?
31. State the purpose of each of the adjustments made on a carburetor to set the correct idle.

THE ELECTRIC SYSTEM

8

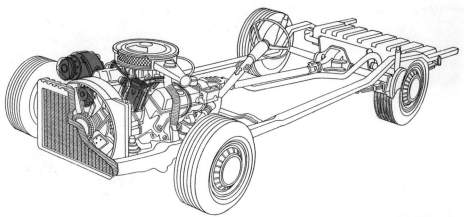

People have learned to control electricity, predict its reactions, and harness it in many ways. They have also observed the effects and powers of a force called magnetism. In fact, the effects of both forces have been observed for many centuries, and new information in these areas is being discovered and applied every day.

Electricity is known in many forms. One is *static electricity*. Static may be observed when dry hair is combed, or it may be seen in the form of lightning during a thunderstorm. Another form is *current electricity*, which can be produced by several methods. The two basic sources with which we are concerned are mechanical and chemical.

Current electricity is the type of electricity used to light our homes and operate our factories and motor vehicles. The electricity used in motor vehicles is produced both mechanically, by the generator or alternator, and chemically, by the battery.

The electrical system of the automobile consists of the battery and ignition, starting, charging, lighting, and accessory circuits. The basic principles of these circuits and their units are covered in this chapter.

THE ELECTRON THEORY

An accepted explanation of electricity is the electron theory. This theory is based on the concept that all matter may be divided into extremely small particles called *atoms*. An atom is not a solid particle but consists of a miniature *solar system* (Figure 8-1).

The centre of each atom is called its *nucleus*. A nucleus may consist of one or more particles that have positive electrical charges. These particles are called *protons*. In addition to protons some nuclei also contain particles which have no electrical charge. These are called *neutrons*.

Revolving around the nucleus, in much the same manner as the earth revolves around

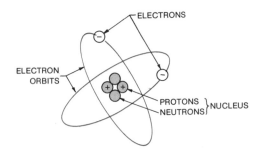

Fig. 8-1   Atomic Structure

the sun, are much lighter particles of matter that carry a negative electrical charge. These are *electrons*. A properly balanced atom always has exactly the same number of electrons as it has protons.

Atoms of different substances have different numbers of electrons; a hydrogen atom, for example, has only one electron, whereas a carbon atom has six (Figure 8-2).

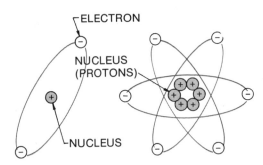

(A) HYDROGEN ATOM   (B) CARBON ATOM

Fig. 8-2   Atomic Structure of Materials

In some materials, such as copper, some of the electrons from one atom may gain enough energy to go into orbit around an adjacent atom. If an external source, such as a battery, is connected to a piece of copper wire, some electrons will *drift* from one atom to another. Because electrons each carry a negative charge, they repel each other. Thus, when one electron is repelled from the nega-

(A) USING BALLS

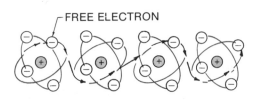

Fig. 8-3   Movement of Free Electrons

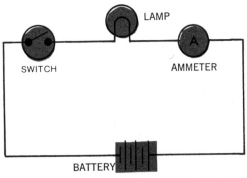

(A) AMMETER PROPERLY CONNECTED

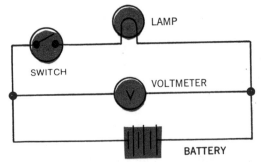

(B) VOLTMETER PROPERLY CONNECTED

Fig. 8-4   Connection of Ammeter and Voltmeter

tive terminal of the battery, it in turn repels another electron, and so on throughout the wire (Figure 8-3). This movement of electrons constitutes an electric current. The greater the number of electrons flowing, the larger is the current flow. Current is measured in *amperes;* it is necessary to have 6 280 000 000 000 000 000 electrons passing a given point in one second to have one ampere of electric current. Current is measured with an ammeter. An ammeter must always be placed in series with a load so that all of the electric current passes through the ammeter as well as through the load.

The electric pressure of the battery is measured in *volts,* with a voltmeter. A voltmeter must always be placed in *parallel* with the load (Figure 8-4) and is so designed that it does not draw very much current and so does not constitute an extra drain on the battery.

MAGNETISM

Magnetism is an elementary form of energy generated by the motion of electrons. It is believed that the orbiting of the electrons around the nucleus produces the magnetic effect. Each electron thus creates a weak magnetic field. In a piece of unmagnetized matter the electrons orbit in many directions and each magnetic field created is cancelled out by another. In a piece of magnetized material all of the orbits are arranged in one direction so that instead of the individual magnetic fields cancelling each other out, they add to each other, creating one strong magnetic field with a north pole at one end and a south pole at the other (Figure 8-5). When the orbits are correctly arranged in some types of iron, they remain in that position for a long period of time. These are called *permanent magnets.* In other types of iron the orbits will not remain in correct alignment unless some magnetizing force is present. These are called *temporary magnets.*

(A) MAGNETIC EFFECT OF ONE ELECTRON IN ORBIT

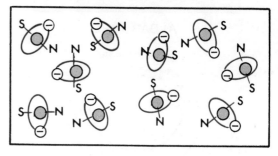

(B) NON-MAGNETIZED MATERIAL

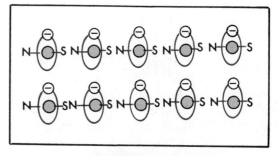

(C) MAGNETIZED MATERIAL

Fig. 8-5   Atomic Formation of Materials

MAGNETIC LINES OF FORCE

A *magnetic* field is the area around a magnet in which magnetism can be detected, and is made up of *magnetic lines of force* (Figure 8-6). These lines of force flow through magnetic material more readily than they do through air.

Magnetic lines of force converge at the poles of a magnet, and it is at the poles that the magnetic field is strongest. When the north pole of a magnet is brought in contact

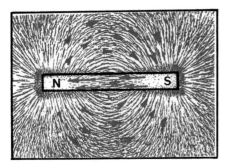

(A) BAR TYPE

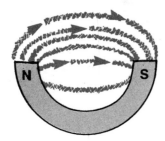

(B) U TYPE

(C) HORSESHOE TYPE

Fig. 8-6   Magnetic Field of a Permanent Magnet

(A) UNLIKE CHARGES ATTRACT

(B) LIKE CHARGES REPEL

Fig. 8-7   Law of Charges

passing through a conductor creates a magnetic field *around* the conductor, and when a conductor is passed through a magnetic field, a flow of electrons is set up *in* the conductor.

This relationship is the basis of operation for most of the automotive electrical devices,

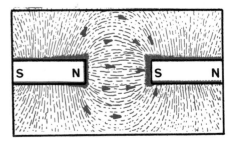

(A) FIELD BETWEEN UNLIKE POLES

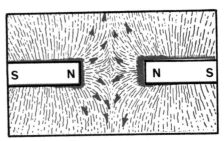

(B) FIELD BETWEEN LIKE POLES

Fig. 8-8   Magnetic Fields Between the Poles of Two Magnets

with the south pole of another magnet, the poles attract each other. On the other hand, if two north poles or two south poles are placed together, they will repel each other. In other words, *like poles repel, and unlike poles attract one another.*

There is a definite relationship between electrical current and magnetism: a current such as the starter motor, alternator, and ignition coil.

ELECTROMAGNETISM

Because there is a relationship between magnetism and electric current, it is possible to produce an electromagnet.

When a current passes through a conductor, there is a small magnetic field set up around the conductor. This magnetic field may be observed by putting the conductor through a piece of cardboard, which is placed in a horizontal position, and sprinkling iron filings on the cardboard around the conductor. When a current passes through the conductor, the iron filings will arrange themselves in a circular pattern around the conductor. The direction of travel of the magnetic field around the conductor may be determined by the use of a compass or by the left-hand rule for a conductor. This rule states that *if the thumb of the left hand points in the direction of current flow, the pointing of the fingers will indicate the direction in which the magnetic field circles the conductor.*

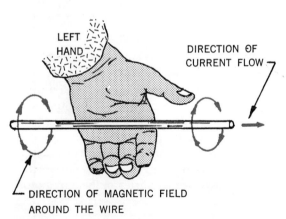

Fig. 8-9 The Left-hand Rule for a Conductor

Since there is a small magnetic field around every current-carrying conductor, it is only necessary to coil a conductor to unite the magnetic fields of each conductor into a stronger magnetic field. The combined field will have a north and south pole. The polarity of the coil may be determined by using a compass or by the left-hand rule for an electromagnet. This rule states that by *pointing the fingers of the left hand in the direction of current flow, the thumb will indicate the north pole* (Figure 8-10).

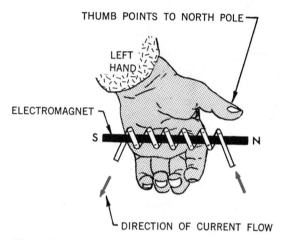

Fig. 8-10 The Left-hand Rule for an Electromagnet

The strength of this field will depend upon the number of turns of wire, the amount of current, and the type of core on which the coil is wound. Because magnetism flows more easily through magnetic material than through air, winding the coil around a soft iron core concentrates the magnetic field and increases the magnetic strength. As the strength of an electromagnet depends upon the amount of electric current flowing through the coil of wire, and since the electromagnet uses a soft iron core which does not retain magnetism, it is possible to control the strength of the magnetic field by increasing or decreasing the current or stopping it completely.

Electromagnets to which the current is switched either on or off are used to operate automotive electrical devices such as starter solenoids, horns, and light relays. Electromagnets to which the current is increased or decreased are used to operate the current and voltage units of a voltage regulator (Figure 8-11).

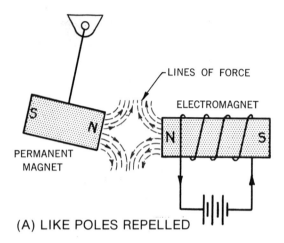

(A) LIKE POLES REPELLED

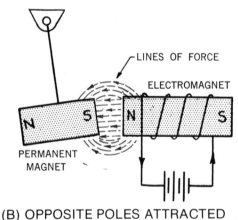

(B) OPPOSITE POLES ATTRACTED

Fig. 8-11 Electromagnetism

MAGNETIC INDUCTION

The relationship between electricity and magnetism is also used in another way—to induce a current to flow in a second conductor that is not connected to the first. When a magnetic field is set up, either by a perma-

nent magnet or by an electromagnet, and either an electrical conductor is passed through the field or the field is passed over the conductor, the movement of either induces a current in the conductor (Figure 8-12). The *moving conductor principle* is used in the generator, whereas the *moving field principle* is used in the alternator and ignition coil.

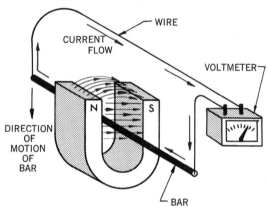

Fig. 8-12 Inducing Electromotive Force

The strength of the induced current depends upon:
1. The strength of the magnetic field
2. The speed of the movement
3. The number of conductors in the series

Similarly, when two current-carrying conductors are placed in close proximity, or a current-carrying conductor is placed in a magnetic field, a reaction results. If the magnetic fields set up are similar, then there is a repelling reaction, or if the fields are not similar, there is an attraction. This attraction and repulsion action can be used in electric motors, such as the starter or heater motors in vehicles.

ELECTRICAL TERMS

Electricity is a form of energy. It can be easily transmitted or converted to other forms, such as mechanical or heat energy. To transmit electricity, conductors such as copper, steel, carbon, or an electrolyte are used. Insulators such as rubber, procelain, or bakelite are used to prevent electrical leakage from conductors.

Materials such as silicon and germanium with minute quantities of other materials such as antimony or indium added produce what is known as a *semiconductor*. Semiconductors are used in the manufacture of solid state units such as diodes and transistors, which are used in certain electrical components of the automobile.

Figure 8-13 shows the special symbols which the mechanic should be able to recognize in order to work on automotive electrical circuits.

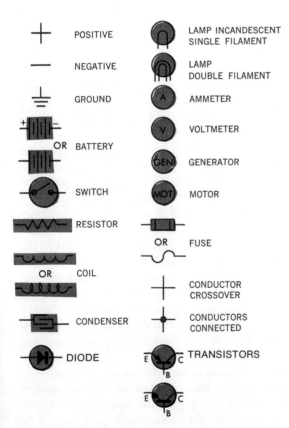

Fig. 8-13   Electrical Symbols

The units of electrical measurement are as follows: the *volt*, the unit of electrical pressure; the *ampere*, the unit of electrical current; and the *ohm*, the unit of electrical resistance. It requires the pressure of one volt to cause a current of one ampere to flow through one ohm of resistance. In order for a current to flow in an electrical circuit, the voltage or pressure must overcome the resistance in the circuit. The greater the pressure, the faster the current will flow.

Two types of current can be produced: *alternating current*, which flows first in one direction and then in the other; and *direct current*, which flows in one direction only. Until 1962, most motor vehicles were wholly operated by direct current (dc), the only exceptions being taxis, police cruisers, etc. These vehicles were equipped with an alternating current (ac) generator, or alternator. Most vehicles produced since 1962 have been equipped with alternators, which generate more current at lower speeds, enabling the battery to be recharged during slow city driving.

The ac current produced by the alternator is rectified (changed) to dc before entering the automotive electrical system.

ELECTRIC CIRCUITS

A circuit is an endless path formed by a conductor from a source of electrical supply to the control, through the load, and back to the source. There are various types of electrical circuits used in the modern automobile, among them the parallel, series, and ground-return circuits (Figure 8-14).

Series Circuit. In a series circuit there is only one path through which the current can flow. Should this path be broken, all of the equipment would cease to function.

Parallel Circuit. A parallel circuit consists of two or more paths through which the current may flow. A breakage in any one path

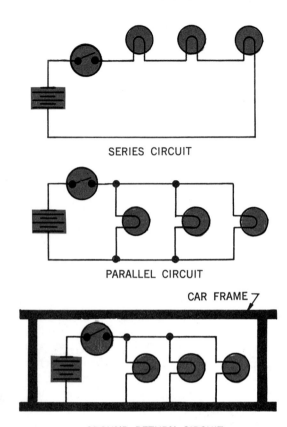

SERIES CIRCUIT

PARALLEL CIRCUIT

CAR FRAME

GROUND-RETURN CIRCUIT

Fig. 8-14   Electric Circuits

would not interfere with the operation of the remainder of the units in the circuit.

Ground-Return Circuit. A ground-return circuit uses the metal parts of the automobile as a common conductor for the return of the current to the source of supply. As a result, only half as much insulated electric wire is required.

Short Circuit. A short circuit occurs when the current takes a path of very low resistance back to the source, thereby bypassing the load. Examples are faulty insulation that allows a bare wire to touch ground, and faulty insulation between the turns of a coil, which reduces the number of turns used in the coil.

Unintentional Ground. The current goes to ground after passing through the load but without following the complete original path.

Open Circuit. There is a break in the complete circuit, because of either an open switch or a broken wire.

Closed Circuit. A closed circuit is a complete path from source to control to load and back to the source.

THE BATTERY

The storage battery is an electro-chemical generator and does not store electricity. The energy stored is *chemical energy,* which is transformed into *electric energy* when a circuit is completed across the terminals of the battery.

Battery Construction and Operation. A battery is made up of a number of cells. Each cell is normally enclosed in a hard rubber case which contains a number of positive and negative plates. The plates are held apart by separators and immersed in a liquid called an *electrolyte.* A *plate strap* is attached to each negative plate in a cell; while another strap at the opposite end of the cell is attached to each positive plate. Since each cell is capable of producing only 2.2 volts, the plate straps of each cell are connected in series by cell-connecting links. This means that the positive plate strap of the first cell is connected to the negative plate strap of the next cell in order to produce a battery of the required voltage. A six-volt battery consists of three cells; a twelve-volt battery consists of six cells.

To connect the battery to the electrical system of the vehicle, two terminal posts are provided. One post is connected to the positive plate strap, and the other post is connected to the negative plate strap at the opposite end of the battery. The positive and negative plates are made of different active materials. The active material of the positive plate is lead

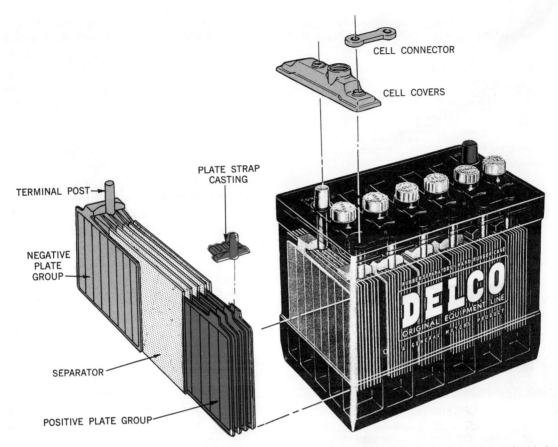

Fig. 8-15   Section View of a 12 Volt Battery   General Motors Products of Canada, Limited

peroxide and of the negative plate, lead oxide. These active materials are in paste form and are spread over lead grids to form complete plates. The separators are made of materials such as cedar wood or fibreglass. The electrolyte consists of distilled water and sulphuric acid mixed together to form a solution having a relative density of 1.300.

When an electric circuit is completed across the terminals of a battery, the sulphuric acid in the electrolyte attacks the active material of the plates. This chemical reaction between the active material on the plates and the electrolyte develops an electric pressure or *volt-*

age. A cell of this type is capable of producing a pressure or voltage of approximately two volts. When additional plates are added to a cell, it increases the *amperage,* that is, the current which a battery can deliver, or the length of time the battery can produce a given cur-

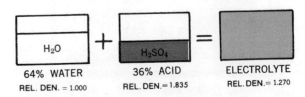

Fig. 8-16   Composition of Electrolyte

rent, or both. Between nine and twenty-one plates per cell are used in most automotive batteries.

The materials used in automotive batteries are such that not only can they produce electricity to flow in one direction, but when an electric current is applied in the opposite direction, the elements can be restored to their original condition ready to produce more electricity (Figure 8-17).

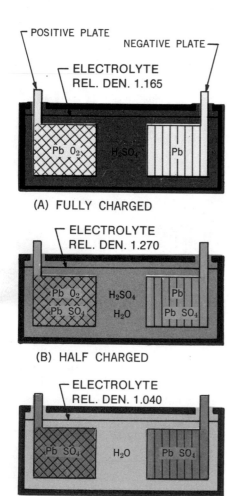

(A) FULLY CHARGED

(B) HALF CHARGED

(C) COMPLETELY DISCHARGED

Fig. 8-17   Chemical Action in Batteries

In a fully charged battery, there is sulphuric acid in the electrolyte, and the plates are in their basic state with lead peroxide for the positive plate and lead oxide for the negative plate. When the battery is producing electricity or being discharged, the electrolyte breaks up, or *ionizes.* Certain ions unite with the active material of the positive plate and at the same time drive out the oxygen from the active material to form water, which dilutes the electrolyte. Other ions attack the lead oxide of the negative plate to form a lead sulphate. When a battery is completely discharged, very little sulphuric acid is left in the electrolyte, and the plates are no longer different in composition. Both have been changed into lead sulphate. A cell in this condition will produce little or no electric energy.

When an external current, from either a battery charger or an alternator, is applied in the proper direction to the battery, the chemical process is reversed. The water is ionized and some of the ions return to the positive plate, driving out the sulphuric elements that were oxidizing the plate, thus returning the active material to its original form of lead peroxide. Some of the ions return to the negative plate, driving out the sulphuric elements and returning the plate to its original form—lead oxide. The sulphuric elements from both plates return to the electrolyte, thereby increasing its strength. The battery is once again capable of producing electric energy.

This charging and discharging process continues whenever the engine is in operation. The battery produces the electric energy required for starting and idling periods. The alternator, when it produces more electric energy than is required for ignition and the accessories in use, recharges the battery.

BATTERY RATINGS

The amount of current that a battery can deliver depends upon the size of each plate, the number of plates, and the amount and strength of the electrolyte. Two common methods of rating the capacity of batteries are the *20 ampere-hour* (A·H) *rate* and the *cold rate*.

The 20 ampere-hour rate is determined by the amount of electric current that a battery at 27°C can produce for 20 hours without the cell voltage dropping below 1.75 volts. A battery that could deliver 4 amperes for 20 hours before the cell voltage dropped below 1.75 would be rated as an 80 (4 × 20) ampere-hour battery.

The cold rate is determined by the number of minutes that a battery at −18°C will deliver 300 A before the cell voltage drops below 1.0 volt. This test indicates the battery's ability to crank an engine in cold weather. A 60 ampere-hour, 12-volt battery can supply 300 A for 4.4 minutes before the cell voltage drops below 1.0 volt.

These tests are frequently used in advertising battery capacity.

BATTERY SERVICE

Testing the Battery. The strength of the battery can be determined by the condition or strength of the electrolyte, which may be tested by means of a battery *hydrometer* (Figure 8-18), which measures the relative density of the battery fluid in comparison to pure water. This test is significant only when the battery is known to be in good mechanical condition. A second test using an accurate voltmeter, when the battery is under load, can determine the mechanical condition of the battery.

High or low relative density readings of the electrolyte indicate the amount of sulphuric acid in the electrolyte. The higher the reading is, the larger the amount of sulphuric acid

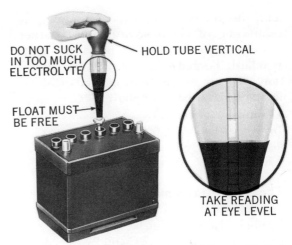

General Motors Products of Canada, Limited

Fig. 8-18   Testing the Relative Density of a Battery

in the electrolyte and therefore the higher the state of charge of the battery. The relative density readings shown in Figure 8-19 are an approximate guide to the condition of a battery charge.

RELATIVE DENSITY READINGS	BATTERY READINGS
1.265-1.290	Fully charged
1.250-1.265	Three-quarters charged
1.225-1.250	One-half charged
1.200-1.225	One-quarter charged
1.175-1.200	Barely operative

Fig. 8-19   Relative Density of Batteries

A battery with a relative density reading of less than 1.225 is not considered to be in a safe operating condition for the modern automobile.

Temperature changes the relative density of a liquid. As a liquid cools, it becomes thicker and gains gravity, and when heated it becomes thinner and loses gravity. Therefore, a correction must be made if the temperature varies from standard (Figure 8-20). During testing of the relative density of a battery, this correction involves the adding or subtracting of points according to whether the electrolyte is above or below the 27°C standard. To make the temperature correction, .004 points must be subtracted or added for every 5.6°C below or above 27°C.

Example: 1.250 at 50°C
Difference between 50°C and 27°C = 23°C
For every 5.6°C add

$$0.004 = \frac{23}{5.6} \times 0.004 = 0.016$$

The corrected reading is
    1.250 + 0.016 = 1.266
Example: 1.230 at −6.7°C
Difference between −6.7°C and 27°C = 33.7°C
For every 5.6°C subtract

$$0.004 = \frac{33.7}{5.6} \times 0.004 = 0.024$$

The corrected reading is
    1.230 − 0.024 = 1.206

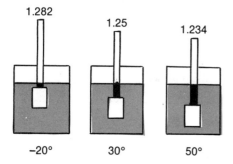

TEMPERATURE IN CELSIUS
Fig. 8-20   Temperature Compensation

Servicing the Battery. In order to obtain maximum battery life, it is necessary to inspect the battery periodically. These inspections should occur at regular intervals, depending on the number of kilometres driven, but the period between inspections should never be longer than one month. A great deal of preventive maintenance, which will reduce costly service calls, is part of proper battery service (Figure 8-21). Excessive water consumption indicates that the battery is being overcharged, and a low relative density read-

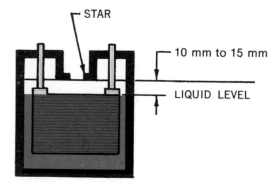

Fig. 8-21   Battery Liquid Level

ing on the hydrometer indicates that the battery is being undercharged. Both conditions indicate that either the alternator, the regulator, or the electric wiring of the car needs attention. The removal of corrosion around the battery terminals promotes longer life of both the terminal and battery cable.

Batteries that have remained in cars for some months may have corroded terminal clamps that are very difficult to loosen. Care must be exercised when these clamps are loosened, as the battery can be damaged. A strong solution of water and bicarbonate of soda may be applied to the terminal and post to eat away the corrosion, after which wrenches may be used to better advantage in removing the nuts from the clamp bolts. Care must be taken not to get the bicarbonate of soda solution in the battery, as this solution could neutralize the electrolyte. The use of a battery puller is recommended to remove the terminal clamp from the battery when a moderate twisting will not loosen it. An inspection should be made of the condition of the clamps, bolts, nuts, and cables. Badly corroded units should be replaced. It is possible to solder new clamps to existing cables, but complete replacement is recommended. The placing of a light coat of corrosion inhibitor over the exposed surface of the cable terminals and clamp bolts will reduce the future formation of corrosion.

RECHARGING BATTERIES

When a battery has become discharged to a point where it will no longer operate the starting motor, it is necessary to recharge the battery by some means other than the alternator. There are two methods of recharging a dead battery, the *slow-charge* and *fast-charge methods.*

The slow-charge method consists of removing the battery from the automobile and connecting it to a battery charger. If more than one battery is being charged, they are connected in series; that is, the positive post of the first battery is connected to the negative post of the second battery and so on for the number of batteries being charged. The negative line of the battery charger is connected to the negative post of the first battery, while the positive line of the battery charger is connected to the positive post of the last battery

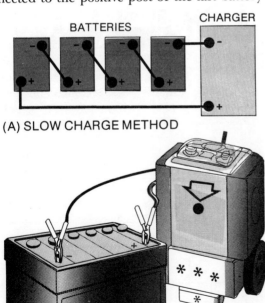

(A) SLOW CHARGE METHOD

(B) FAST CHARGE METHOD

Fig. 8-22   Recharging Batteries

to be charged (Figure 8-22).

The charging rate for any number of batteries should never exceed six amperes and the length of time required to recharge a battery to a state of good condition should never exceed 48 hours. If a longer period is necessary, then the battery is either highly sulphated or has been operated for a considerable period of time without having sufficient electrolyte to cover the plates. If these conditions exist, then the charging rate should be reduced to about two amperes.

Batteries which have been exposed to winter weather should not be charged at a high rate until the temperature of the electrolyte is up to 27°C. Excessive temperatures of the electrolyte also indicate a highly sulphated battery and the charging rate should be reduced to two amperes.

As the charging progresses, there will be a tendency for the battery to start gassing, and if charged at too high a rate, excessive gassing will be noticed. This gas is highly explosive and, if it is ignited by a spark from the battery charger, it may explode and scatter the battery case and the dangerous sulphuric acid. Batteries should never be charged with the filler caps in place. These caps must be removed in order to help dissipate the gases as they are formed.

When the battery shows no further rise in relative density after being on the charger for a period of five hours and being charged at a rate not exceeding five amperes, it will be considered as fully charged. The hydrometer reading, however, should not be less than 1.265. If it is less, then the battery is showing signs of sulphation or the acid has been lost due to spilling or boiling of the battery.

The fast-charge method does not require the battery to be removed from the vehicle, as most fast chargers are portable. This method is sometimes referred to as a *booster charge,* since it very rarely completely charges the battery. Its purpose is to recharge the battery sufficiently to allow the starting motor to start the engine. This is done in a short period of time, usually about one hour, and at a very high rate of charge, ranging from 60 to 100 amperes. The remaining recharging of the battery is done by the alternator when the engine is operating.

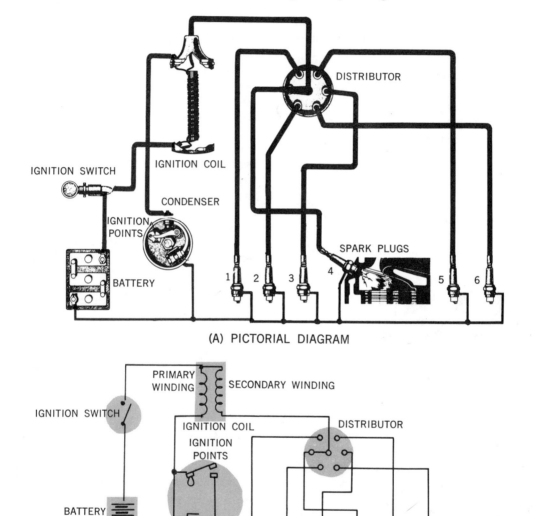

(A) PICTORIAL DIAGRAM

(B) ELEMENTARY DIAGRAM

Fig. 8-23   Ignition System

THE IGNITION SYSTEM

The purpose of the ignition system is to produce high voltage surges of current and deliver them to the right spark plug at the correct time. There are three types of ignition systems: the *battery ignition system*, the *magneto ignition system*, and the *electronic ignition system*. Only the battery and electronic types are in common use in automobiles. The magneto ignition system is most common in outboard, snowmobile, and lawn mower engines. Only the battery and electronic types, as related to the automobile, are covered in this text.

Ignition systems consist of two sections, the low-voltage or *primary circuit* (battery voltage of 6 or 12 volts), and the high-voltage or *secondary circuit* (of 15 000 to 25 000 volts in the battery type or 20 000 to 40 000 volts in the electronic type).

The primary circuit consists of the battery, ignition switch, ignition resistor, primary windings of the coil, ignition points or electronic triggering device, condenser, and the necessary connecting wire. The secondary circuit consists of the secondary windings of the ignition coil, the distributor cap and rotor, the spark plugs, and connecting wires.

BASIC IGNITION CIRCUIT OPERATION

When the ignition switch is turned on and the engine started, the ignition points or triggering device in the distributor are closed by the action of the distributor cam or rotating pole piece. Current flows through the primary windings of the ignition coil and creates a magnetic field. The rotation of the cam causes the ignition points of the timer to open or the rotating pole piece actuates the triggering device. As the ignition circuit is opened by either the ignition points or the triggering device the current in the primary windings stops, causing the magnetic field to collapse

quickly, and inducing a high voltage in the secondary windings. This high-voltage surge of current passes from the ignition coil through the high-tension lead to the centre of the distributor cap. The current passes from the centre tower of the cap to the distributor rotor. The rotor is opposite the outer tower terminal, which is connected to the spark plug. The cylinder in which the spark plug is located must be on the proper stroke for the igniting of the fuel. The current passes along this path and jumps across the spark-plug gap between the electrodes of the plug to ignite the fuel in the cylinder. This series of events takes place very rapidly. At 100 km/h, the ignition system of a six-cylinder engine must produce about 9000 sparks per minute.

UNITS OF THE BATTERY IGNITION CIRCUIT

The Battery.   The battery supplies the current for the ignition system.

The Ignition Switch.   The ignition switch is an electrical switch that turns the current off or on in the ignition circuit. It operates in the same manner as the light switches in your home. It is usually located on the instrument

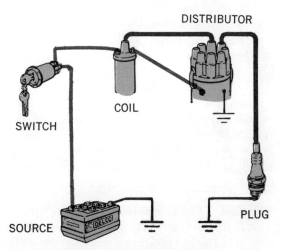

Fig. 8-24   Units of the Battery Ignition Circuit

panel and is operated by a key, so that only the person who has the key can turn on the switch.

The ignition switch, in addition to completing the ignition circuit, usually has additional terminals which complete the circuits to the instruments or warning lights, (fuel, temperature, oil pressure, and charging); to the accessories, (heater, radio, etc.); and to the starting motor.

The ignition, instrument, and accessories circuits are completed when the switch is turned to the *ignition position*. The instrument and the accessories circuits are connected when the switch is turned to the *accessories position*. Only the starting circuit is connected when the ignition switch is in the start position. The purpose of the multipurpose switch is to reduce the drain on the battery.

Ignition Resistor. Most ignition coils are designed to operate on less than 12 volts. Continuous operation on 12 volts would shorten coil life. Therefore, an ignition resistor which lowers the voltage is placed in the primary circuit between the ignition switch and the coil. Except during starting periods, all the current going to the ignition coil must pass through the ignition resistor, thus reducing the current flow through the primary windings of the coil.

When the key is turned to the start position, the resistor is bypassed and current flows directly from the starting circuit to the ignition coil. Since battery voltage drops during the starting period, the elimination of the resistor from the ignition circuit permits greater current flow through the primary windings of the ignition coil. This produces a better spark for starting purposes.

The Coil. The spark coil, or ignition coil, is a small transformer that uses magnetic induction principles to produce a new current with a very high pressure (voltage), which is re-

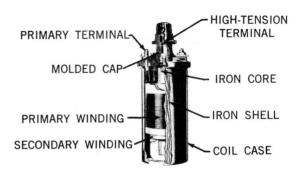

Fig. 8-25   Ignition Coil

quired to jump the space or gap of the sparkplug electrodes. The battery current is not strong enough to jump even a space the thickness of a paper.

The ignition coil is made up of primary and secondary windings, a laminated soft iron core, a protective case, connecting terminals, a bakelite sealing cap, and a cooling oil.

The *primary winding* consists of about 200 turns of a large wire capable of carrying the battery current. The *secondary winding* consists of about 20 000 turns of very fine wire in which the high voltage surges of current originate. The windings are wrapped around the core, and the core and windings are positioned and insulated from the bottom of the case by a porcelain insulator. Heavy paper insulation is wrapped around the outside of the primary windings to prevent them from touching the laminated liner placed inside the case. The ends of the primary winding are attached to their respective primary terminals. One end of the secondary winding is attached to the high-tension terminal; the other end is attached to one of the primary winding terminals. The sealing cap positions the terminals, keeps out moisture, and seals in the sealing oil which is used to help dissipate any heat produced by the primary windings.

When the ignition points are closed, the current flowing through the primary windings of the coil produces a magnetic field around both the primary and the secondary windings. When the ignition points open, the current in the primary winding stops flowing, quickly collapsing the magnetic field and inducing a high voltage in the secondary winding. This new voltage is in proportion to the number of turns in the secondary winding compared to the number of turns in the primary winding, plus the speed of collapse.

THE DISTRIBUTOR

The distributor includes units of the primary circuit (points and condenser); units of the secondary circuit (cap and rotor); and mechanisms required to advance the time the spark occurs at the spark plug in accordance with engine speed and load conditions.

Breaker Points, or Ignition Points. Breaker points, or ignition points, are used to open and close the primary circuit. When the points are closed, current flows through the primary circuit. When they are open, current cannot flow. The breaker-point contact faces are usually made of tungsten. One contact face is on the stationary breaker point. This point is attached to the breaker plate in such a manner that the point gap can be adjusted. It also usually includes a pivot pin for the breaker arm. The other contact face is attached to the breaker arm. This arm includes a fibre or nylon rubbing block which contacts the corners or lobes of the breaker cam. A breaker-point spring attached between the breaker arm and the primary distributor terminal conducts the primary current to the points and also returns the points to the closed position after they have been opened by the lobes of the cam.

The Breaker Cam. The breaker cam is used to open and close the breaker points. This cam has the same number of lobes as there are cylinders in the engine. The cam is ro-

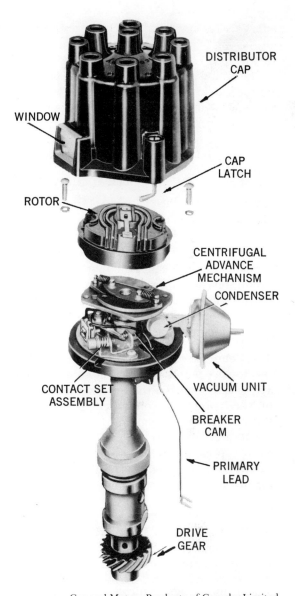

General Motors Products of Canada, Limited

Fig. 8-26   Distributor Assembly

tated by the distributor shaft, which in turn is geared to and driven by the camshaft. One revolution of the distributor shaft is equal to two revolutions of the crankshaft or one four-

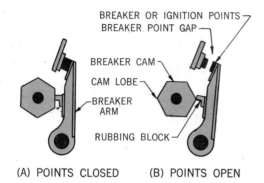

(A) POINTS CLOSED   (B) POINTS OPEN

General Motors Products of Canada, Limited

Fig. 8-27   Ignition Points and Housing

stroke cycle. The distributor drive shaft is so meshed with the camshaft that each time a piston reaches approximately TDC of the compression stroke, a lobe of the cam is in position to open the breaker points. This is called ignition timing.

The Condenser.   The continual breaking of the contact points tends to cause an electric arc, which results in the burning and pitting of the points. A condenser is placed or shunted across these points to reduce the arcing to a minimum and to temporarily store electric pressure. This stored electric pressure is then delivered back to the coil, resulting in a more efficient coil operation.

The Distributor Cap.   The distributor cap is made of bakelite and fits on top of the distributor housing. Around the perimeter of the cap are terminals for each spark-plug wire, and a centre terminal for the high-tension wire from the ignition coil. On the inside of the cap, the plug terminals have brass fingers extending down past the cap material. The centre terminal has either a spring-loaded or fixed carbon rod which contacts the centre of the rotor brush. The cap is properly positioned on the housing by placing the cap tongue, which is located on the lower edge, into a slot machined in the housing. Spring

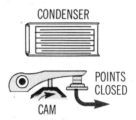

(A) POINTS CLOSED. CURRENT FLOWS THROUGH POINTS

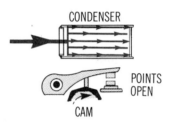

(B) POINTS OPEN. CURRENT FLOWS INTO CONDENSER

General Motors Products of Canada, Limited

Fig. 8-28   Condenser Action

clips, screw clips, or screws are used to seal the cap tightly to the housing to prevent the entrance of moisture or dirt.

The Rotor.   The rotor is used to carry the secondary voltage from the centre terminal of the cap to the plug terminals. It is attached to the top of the distributor shaft and rotates with the shaft. A tongue on the inner surface of the rotor fits into a groove on the shaft to maintain proper relationship between the rotor and the shaft. The outer edge of the rotor has a brass terminal that passes very close to the brass fingers on the plug terminals of the distributor cap. Attached to the rotor terminal is a spring that rubs against the carbon of the centre terminal. When a high-voltage surge from the coil arrives at the centre terminal of the cap, it travels down the carbon rod to the rotor spring, through the spring and rotor terminal, jumps the small gap between the rotor and the side terminal of the cap, and continues through the high-tension wire to the spark plug. The spark plug wires are arranged in the distributor cap according to the direction of rotation of the rotor and the firing order of the engine.

High-Tension Wires. High-tension wires carry the high-voltage surges from the ignition coil to the distributor cap and from the cap to the spark plugs. These wires must be well insulated to prevent the high voltage from escaping to ground before it reaches the spark plug. The insulation, usually rubber, must withstand heat and cold and must be impervious to gasoline, oil, and water. The electric conductor may be stranded copper wire, a linen thread impregnated with carbon, or a graphite-saturated fibreglass core. The latter two types, called *resistance wire,* are the most commonly used today because they eliminate radio and television interference. Suitable clips or wire ends are used to attach the wires to the cap and spark plug.

ELECTRONIC, OR TRANSISTORIZED, IGNITION SYSTEMS

The electronic ignition system makes use of a solid state transistor unit, called an *ignition pulse amplifier,* which is an electrically controlled switch. The amplifier consists of transistors, diodes, resistors, and capacitors mounted on to a printed circuit panel board. Since there are no moving parts, the control is a complete static assembly. It is a low-voltage unit with a current-carrying capacity superior to that of the conventional ignition breaker points. It provides immediate voltage build-up in the primary circuit, which results in higher voltage at the spark plug and maintains this higher voltage for longer periods of time.

The ignition pulse amplifier may be used in place of the conventional ignition breaker points when a *magnetic pulse pick-up* type of distributor is used, or it may be used in con-

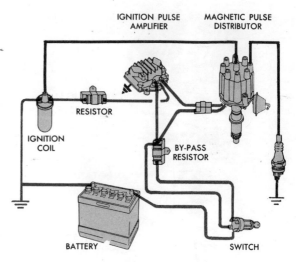

Fig. 8-29   Typical Electronic Ignition

junction with conventional ignition breaker points in other systems. The use of the transistor type ignition results in less frequent service to the ignition system. The ignition timing remains more accurately set for longer periods, thereby producing more complete combustion which results in lower pollution emissions.

General Motors Products of Canada, Limited

Fig. 8-30   Ignition Pulse Amplifier Unit

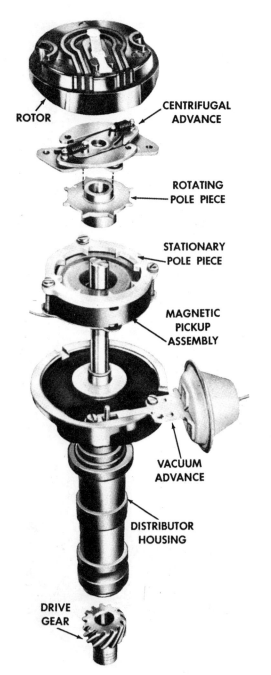

ROTOR

CENTRIFUGAL ADVANCE

ROTATING POLE PIECE

STATIONARY POLE PIECE

MAGNETIC PICKUP ASSEMBLY

VACUUM ADVANCE

DISTRIBUTOR HOUSING

DRIVE GEAR

General Motors Products of Canada, Limited

Fig. 8-31   Magnetic Pulse Type Distributor

High Energy Ignition Systems (HEI) are breakerless systems which eliminate the conventional ignition breaker points and condenser. All of the ignition components are contained within the distributor, including the ignition coil.

Except for its size, the ignition unit closely resembles a conventional distributor with one difference: the high-tension coil wire is missing. The ignition coil is built into the distributor cap and is located under a small cover on the top of the distributor cap. The diameter of the distributor cap has been increased to prevent arcing between the terminals, and the spark-plug wires are also larger in diameter.

This type of system is capable of producing secondary voltages in excess of 35 000 volts. The spark-plug gap used with this system may be 2 mm or more wide, thus producing a better spark within the combustion chamber to help reduce pollution emissions.

SPARK PLUGS

The spark plug is threaded into the cylinder head or cylinder block, with its lower end protruding into the combustion chamber.

The fuel in the cylinder is ignited by the spark produced by passing a high-voltage surge of current across an air gap between two electrodes. The spark plug provides these electrodes in the combustion chamber of the engine; it is built to withstand electrical surges of 10 000 to 40 000 volts, pressures up to 5600 kPa, and temperatures up to 2000°C.

A spark plug consists of a steel shell, threaded on one end so that it may be screwed into the threaded hole in the cylinder block or head. A porcelain insulator that will withstand high temperatures, pressures, and voltages is placed inside the steel shell. A centre electrode is fastened in the insulator with a terminal on top, and extends below the

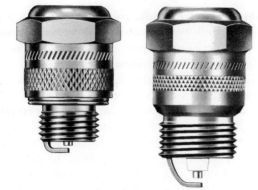

(A) CONVENTIONAL TIP (B) EXTENDED TIP

insulator at the bottom. The core and shell are assembled with suitable seals to prevent leakage of the gases in the cylinder and to aid in conducting heat. A ground electrode is welded to the shell (Figure 8-32).

The high-tension current produced by the coil passes down the centre electrode and jumps the gap to the ground electrode. The air gap, set to manufacturer's specifications, varies from 0.6 mm to 2 mm and can be adjusted by bending the ground electrode.

Spark-Plug Heat Ranges. The temperature at which the nose of the insulator operates determines the heat range of the spark plug. A hot plug operates at a higher temperature than a cold plug because the heat must travel farther before reaching the cooling cylinder-head water. Hot plugs are used when driving conditions or engine wear cause the plugs to become fouled with oil or soft carbon. Hot plugs are better able to burn off, or vaporize, these accumulations of oil. Where high-speed or heavy-load driving tends to burn the electrodes and insulators, a cold plug gives better service because it can carry off the heat faster (Figure 8-33).

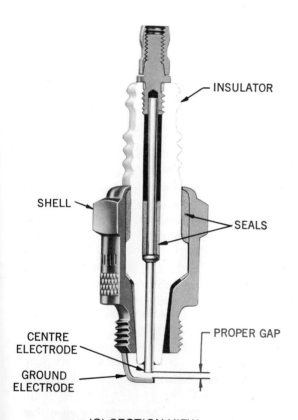

INSULATOR

SHELL

SEALS

CENTRE
ELECTRODE

GROUND
ELECTRODE

PROPER GAP

(C) SECTION VIEW

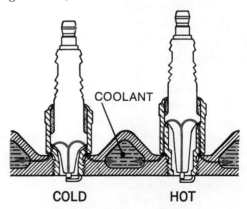

COOLANT

COLD   HOT

HEAT FLOW PATHS IN "HOT" AND
"COLD" TYPE PLUGS

Champion Spark Plug Company of Canada, Limited

Fig. 8-32 Spark Plug

Fig. 8-33 Spark-plug Heat Range

Extended-Nose or Thermal-Tip Spark Plugs. In late-model high-compression engines, where the spark plugs are required to run hotter at low speeds and colder at high speeds, special extended-nose or thermal-tip plugs are used. In this type of plug, the insulator tip extends beyond the lower end of the spark-plug shell. This places the firing tip deeper into the combustion chamber, which results in higher firing-tip temperatures at low speeds. The higher temperatures, plus the swirling of the exhaust gases around the firing tip, provide a self-cleaning action which tends to burn away combustion deposits that tend to form during low-speed operation.

At higher speeds, the fuel-air mixture entering the cylinder passes over and around the firing tip, providing additional cooling which results in lower tip temperatures.

Resistor-Type Spark Plugs. Resistor-type spark plugs are used to eliminate radio and TV interference when standard metallic conductor-type spark-plug wires are used. The resistor is placed inside the porcelain between the centre electrode and the spark-plug terminal.

Spark-Plug Sizes. Spark-plug sizes are determined by the size of the thread and the thread lengths or reaches. The popular types of threads used are 18 mm and 14 mm. The length of the thread or reach depends on the type of cylinder head used and the distance between the spark-plug seat in the head and the combustion chamber. The size is usually measured in millimetres.

Spark plugs may have flat seating surfaces that require a spark-plug gasket to assure a good seal between the plug and the engine head, or block. Other spark plugs have a tapered seat which provides adequate sealing without the use of gaskets.

Spark-Plug Failure. Spark-plug failure can be caused by a burnt insulator or electrode, incorrect heat range, engine overheating, lean fuel mixture, leakage between the electrode and the insulator, or improper installation of spark plugs. When spark plugs are installed, they should be torqued to the following scale:

THREAD SIZE	CAST IRON HEAD	ALUMINUM HEAD
14 mm	210 kPa	196 kPa
18 mm	238 kPa	224 kPa

If no torque wrench is available , screw the spark plug in finger-tight, then tighten it with a wrench according to the following table:

THREAD SIZE	NUMBER OF TURNS
14 mm	¾
18 mm	½ to ¾

Other causes of spark-plug failure are fouled or shorted spark plugs, incorrect heat range, excessive engine-oil consumption, defective ignition wiring, and loss of compression due to valve failure.

IGNITION TIMING

The opening of the ignition points by the distributor cam must be set so that the spark produced in the secondary winding of the ignition coil will occur when combustion can exert the maximum amount of pressure on the piston, the connecting rod, and the crankshaft, and when the throw of the crankshaft is in a position to utilize the pressure to the greatest advantage. This position of the crank throw is approximately 10° after top dead centre, regardless of engine speed. The entire distributor may be moved in order to set the time at which the spark should occur in relation to the position of the piston.

IGNITION ADVANCE MECHANISMS

In order to ensure the application of maximum combustion pressure on the piston, it is necessary to vary the times the spark occurs at

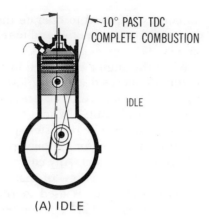

10° PAST TDC
COMPLETE COMBUSTION

IDLE

(A) IDLE

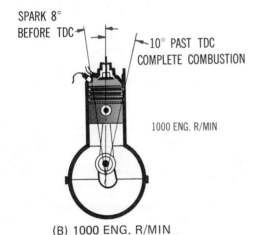

SPARK 8°
BEFORE TDC

10° PAST TDC
COMPLETE COMBUSTION

1000 ENG. R/MIN

(B) 1000 ENG. R/MIN

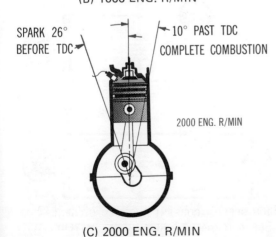

SPARK 26°
BEFORE TDC

10° PAST TDC
COMPLETE COMBUSTION

2000 ENG. R/MIN

(C) 2000 ENG. R/MIN

Fig. 8-34 Spark Advance and Engine Speed

the spark plug according to engine speed and load. This is accomplished through the use of *mechanical* and *vacuum advance units.*

Mechanical Advance. The mechanical governor controls the time at which the spark occurs according to engine speed. As the engine r/min increases, centrifugal force throws the governor masses outward. The higher the r/min, the greater the movement of the masses. As the masses move outward, they rotate the distributor cam a few degrees ahead of the distributor shaft. This rotation of the cam opens the breaker points sooner, thus advancing the spark.

Vacuum Advance. The vacuum advance unit controls the time at which the spark occurs, according to the engine load. This unit contains a *vacuum diaphragm,* which is connected by tubing to the intake manifold, and is connected by a linkage to the ignition point or breaker plate in the distributor housing. This plate is mounted in such a manner that it can be rotated a few degrees within the housing.

When the load on the engine is light, engine vaccum is high. This high engine vacuum attracts the vacuum diaphragm, compresses its return spring, and moves the linkage so as to rotate the point plate and points a few degrees in the opposite direction to distributor shaft rotation. This movement causes the cam to open the points sooner, thereby advancing the spark. As the load on the engine increases, engine vacuum drops. The lower vacuum has less effect on the diaphragm, and the spring expands to return the diaphragm to its normal position, thereby retarding the spark.

Some distributors use only a vacuum advance unit. The vacuum side of this unit is connected to the venturi area of the carburetor instead of to the intake manifold. The linkage of this unit is connected to the point plate in the usual manner. The amount of spark advance is controlled by the vacuum created by the volume of air rushing through the venturi. The volume of air passing through the venturi is in direct proportion to engine speed and load. Therefore, the vacuum created and applied to the diaphragm and the resulting movement can be used to advance the spark the correct amount.

THE CHARGING CIRCUIT

The charging circuit consists of: a *mechanical* device, either a generator or an alternator, which converts mechanical energy to electric energy; a *control* or *regulator* to regulate the amount of electrical current being produced in accordance with the amount being used and the state of charge of the battery; the *battery;* an *ammeter* or indicating device to indicate whether the charging circuit is operating properly; and the *wiring* to connect these various units.

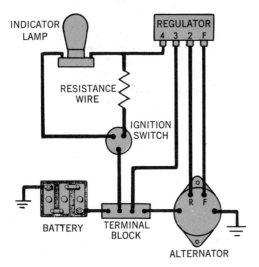

Fig. 8-35   Typical Charging Circuit

THE ALTERNATOR AND GENERATOR

The purpose of the alternator or generator is to convert mechanical energy into the electri-

cal energy required to operate the electrical devices in the automobile and to recharge the battery.

When the engine is cranked by the starting motor or operated at a very low speed, the battery is the source of electrical energy for the electrical units. When the engine is operating at off-idle or faster speeds, the alternator or generator supplies part or all of the required current. Any current produced by these units, in excess of that required by the electrical units, is used to recharge the battery. This recharging compensates the battery for the electric energy used during the starting or idling periods. The alternator or generator is usually located near the front of the engine, either to one side of or above the engine block. It is driven by a V-belt. In some automobiles, this belt also drives the water pump and fan.

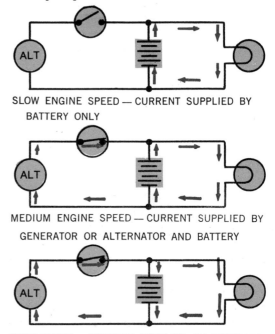

SLOW ENGINE SPEED — CURRENT SUPPLIED BY BATTERY ONLY

MEDIUM ENGINE SPEED — CURRENT SUPPLIED BY GENERATOR OR ALTERNATOR AND BATTERY

HIGH SPEED — CURRENT SUPPLIED BY GENERATOR OR ALTERNATOR — RECHARGING BATTERY

Fig. 8-36   Current Supplied by an Alternator—Recharging Circuit

THE ALTERNATOR **189**

OPERATING PRINCIPLES

The alternator or generator operates on the basic electrical theory that when a conductor is moved through a magnetic field, or a magnetic field is moved past a conductor, the movement of the field or the conductor will cause a current to flow in the conductor.

THE ALTERNATOR (DELCOTRON)

The alternator consists of:

1. A rotor made up of two multiple-fingered pole pieces assembled on a shaft over a coil of wire (an electromagnet), each end of which is attached to an insulated slip ring.
2. A set of brushes which carry battery current to the slip rings of the electromagnet of the rotor.
3. A stator assembled to the alternator frame, which consists of windings interconnected so that the current produced in the windings is added together.
4. A pulley which is attached to the rotor shaft and driven by the fan belt.
5. End frames and bearings which support the rotor in the frame.
6. Two sets of three diodes, which are used to convert the alternating current (ac) produced in the stator winding to direct current (dc) required by the electrical system.

When the ignition switch is turned on, the current from the battery is directed to the rotor windings through the control, brushes, and slip rings, producing a magnetic field in the rotor. The fingers of one pole piece act as the magnetic north pole and the fingers of the other pole piece act as the magnetic south pole. When the engine is started, the rotor rotates and the alternate north and south poles pass by the windings of the stator and induce an ac current in the stator windings. This current is directed through the proper set of diodes to produce dc current. Remember, the faster the engine speed, the greater the alternator output.

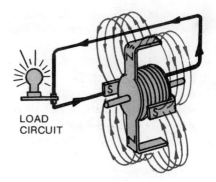

ROTATING MAGNETIC FIELD

(A) PRINCIPLES

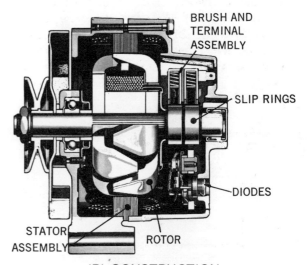

(B) CONSTRUCTION

Fig. 8-37   The Alternator

Alternator Regulator. An alternator regulator may contain one, two, or three units and be of the double contact or transistor type. Since the diodes in the alternator will only pass current in one direction, current cannot flow from the battery through the stator windings. The field current cannot flow through the ignition switch when the switch is in the off position, so the need of a cut-out is

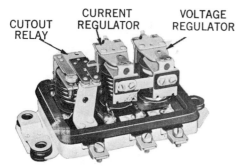

CUTOUT RELAY CURRENT REGULATOR VOLTAGE REGULATOR

(A) GENERATOR REGULATOR

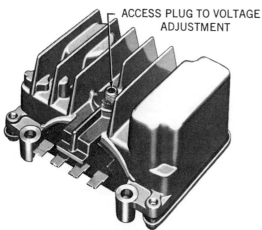

ACCESS PLUG TO VOLTAGE ADJUSTMENT

(B) TRANSISTOR-TYPE ALTERNATOR REGULATOR

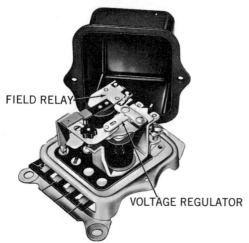

FIELD RELAY

VOLTAGE REGULATOR

(C) DOUBLE-CONTACT-TYPE ALTERNATOR REGULATOR

General Motors Products of Canada, Limited

Fig. 8-38   Alternator and Generator Regulators

eliminated. As the maximum current flowing through the rotor windings is limited by the resistance of the windings and battery voltage, the need for a current control is also eliminated.

The function of these regulators is to limit the alternator voltage to a preset value, thus reducing the output in accordance with the current usage and the state of charge of the battery. This is accomplished by the voltage control unit automatically connecting a resistor in series with the rotor current, thus reducing the current flow. The smaller the current flow, the weaker the field. The weaker the field, the smaller the alternator output.

Many alternator regulators have a *field relay* and an *indicator lamp relay*. Both are electromagnetic switches.

The field relay is used to reduce the amount of current passing through the ignition switch. A small amount of current from the ignition switch produces a magnetic field around the relay windings. This field closes a set of contacts which completes the circuit between the rotor windings and the battery.

The magnetic field of the indicator lamp relay is produced by current from the alternator. This current produces a magnetic field which attracts a contact arm to break the indicator-lamp circuit. The indicator lamp is connected in such a way that the lamp on the dash lights up when the ignition key is turned on and the engine is not running. When the engine is started and the alternator begins to charge, the indicator light goes out, showing that the charging circuit is operating satisfactorily.

Many late-model alternators use a solid-state type of regulator which functions electronically to perform the same operations as the older mechanical types. All of the regulator components are enclosed in a solid-state mould and are preset to the required voltage; most cannot be readjusted. These solid-state type units may be attached to the inside of the engine compartment or they may be mounted inside the slip ring end frame of the alternator.

THE GENERATOR

The generator consists of:

1. A set of field coils wrapped around the pole pieces and attached to the generator case or field frame.
2. An armature which consists of coils of wire that rotate in the magnetic field, causing a flow of electricity in the conductors or armature windings.
3. A commutator, which is basically a rotating switch, that is used to convert the alternating current (ac) produced in the armature to direct current (dc) used by the electrical system.

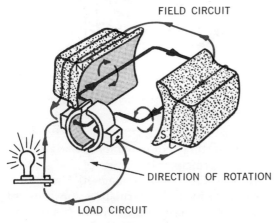

FIELD CIRCUIT

DIRECTION OF ROTATION

LOAD CIRCUIT

(A) PRINCIPLES

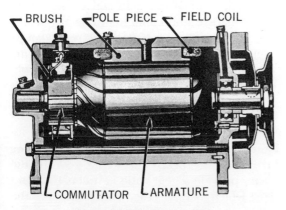

BRUSH ┌POLE PIECE ┌ FIELD COIL

COMMUTATOR ARMATURE

(B) CONSTRUCTION

General Motors Products of Canada, Limited

Fig. 8-39 The Generator

4. A set of brushes which contact the commutator to collect the current produced by the movement of the conductors or windings of the armature through the magnetic field.
5. A pulley which is attached to the armature shaft and driven by the fan belt.
6. The end frames and bearings which support the armature in the generator case.

When the engine is started, the armature is rotated in the weak magnetic field retained in the pole pieces. This creates a small amount of current in the armature. The current is first directed to the field windings to increase the strength of the magnetic field. The stronger field produces more current in the armature. As the speed of the armature and the strength of the fields increase, generator output increases. When this current and voltage is sufficient to operate the cut-out section of the regulator, the output of the generator is directed to the electrical system. The amount of current produced by the generator is controlled by the regulator unit.

REGULATORS

Generator Regulators. In order to control the output of the generator, a unit called the *voltage regulator* is used. The job of the voltage regulator for dc generators is threefold:

1. It connects the generator to the rest of the electrical system when the generator is producing a voltage greater than the battery voltage, and disconnects the generator from the electric circuit when the generator voltage is less than the battery voltage.
2. It prevents the generator from producing more electric current than the windings of the generator can safely carry.
3. It protects the battery and other units of the electrical system by limiting the maximum voltage the generator can produce.

Voltage regulators usually consist of the following units: the cut-out, the current control, and the voltage control.

The cut-out is used to connect and disconnect the generator to the electrical system.

The current control is used to limit the maximum output of the generator. This control automatically connects two resistors in parallel into the field circuit to reduce the amount of current flowing through the field windings of the generator. This weakens the field and therefore maintains the generator output within safe limits.

The voltage control automatically connects a single resistor in the field circuit to weaken the field strength considerably. Thus, the generator output is limited in accordance with the amount of current being used and the state of charge of the battery.

The current and voltage controls never work simultaneously. Either the current control is limiting the maximum output or the voltage control has reduced the output below the maximum and the current control is inoperative.

THE STARTING CIRCUIT

The starting circuit consists of the battery, starting motor, starting motor drive, solenoid switch, starter switch, and the wiring to connect these various units.

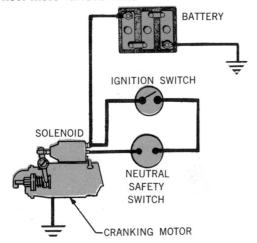

Fig. 8-40   Starting-motor Circuit

THE STARTING MOTOR

The starting motor is a device which converts electric energy into the mechanical energy required to crank the engine for starting purposes. The motor operates on the basic electrical theory that when a current-carrying conductor is placed in a magnetic field, movement of the conductor will result.

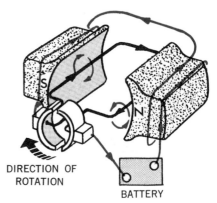

General Motors Products of Canada, Limited

Fig. 8-41   Starting-motor Principle

The starting motor is built in accordance with this principle. It consists of a set of field coils which produce a magnetic field of a given polarity and an armature consisting of current-carrying conductors which also produce a magnetic field. The magnetic field of the armature is such that it is repelled by the magnetic field of the field coils. This causes the armature and commutator to rotate. In order to maintain this magnetic repulsion, it is necessary to reverse the direction of current flow through the winding of the armature every 90°. This is accomplished by the commutator and the brushes.

STARTER DRIVES

Starter drives connect the starting motor drive gear to the flywheel ring gear. These gears provide a gear ratio between 10:1 and 16:1 which increases the turning effort of the starting motor. Two types of drive assemblies are in common use; the *Bendix drive* and the *overrunning clutch drive*.

The Bendix drive is mounted loosely on the armature shaft. It is a self-engaging pinion drive that is so designed that when the starter armature is rotated, the drive pinion stands still while a threaded sleeve rotates within the pinion. The rotating sleeve causes the pinion to move outward and mesh with the ring

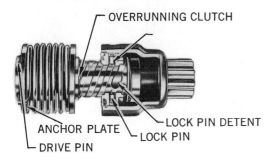

Ford Motor Company of Canada Limited

Fig. 8-42　Bendix Drive for Starting Motor

gear. When the pinion has reached the end of its travel, the turning sleeve causes the pinion to turn with it to start the engine. A heavy spring, connected between the pinion and the armature shaft, absorbs the sudden shock of pinion and flywheel engagement.

When the engine starts, the flywheel rotates the pinion faster than the armature shaft. This reverses the direction of pinion travel on the threaded sleeve and disengages the pinion from the flywheel.

Many Bendix drives include detent-pins which prevent the pinion from disengaging from the flywheel until the engine reaches a speed of 400 r/min. This prevents disengagement of the pinion when the engine false starts.

The overrunning clutch type of starter drive is not self-engaging. The drive pinion must be moved into mesh with the ring gear manually or by a mechanical linkage actuated by a solenoid before the electrical circuit to the starting motor is completed. The rotating

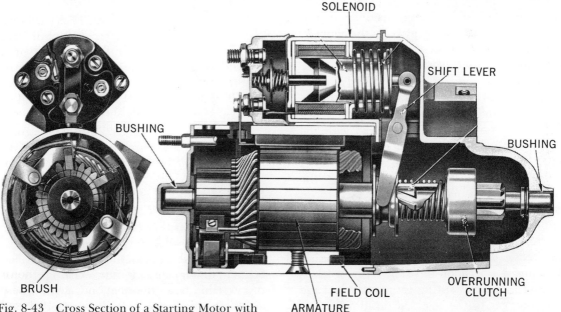

Fig. 8-43　Cross Section of a Starting Motor with
　　　　　Overrunning Clutch Drive

General Motors Products of Canada, Limited

motion of the armature is transmitted to the pinion gear through the locked position of the overrunning, or one-way, clutch.

When the engine starts, the flywheel drives the pinion faster than the armature shaft. The overrunning clutch unlocks the pinion from the armature shaft, and the pinion spins freely.

STARTING MOTOR CONTROLS

Since the starting motor draws several hundred amperes from the battery, heavy cables and special switches with large contacts are required. These switches may be of the magnetic-switch type mounted on the fender well, or the solenoid type mounted on the starter motor. Both are actuated by a separate dash switch or a separate switch position incorporated as part of the ignition switch.

The magnetic switch uses an electromagnet, controlled by the dash switch, to move a plunger and contact disc assembly against two contacts to complete the starter circuit. When the dash switch is released, the magnetic field collapses and the plunger return spring moves the contact disc away from the contacts to break the starter circuit. Magnetic switches can only be used with self-engaging type starter drives.

The solenoid control operates in a similar manner to the magnetic switch except that it moves the starter drive into mesh with the ring gear before completing the starter circuit. Solenoids contain two electromagnet windings, one called a *pull-in winding*, the other a *hold-in winding*. Both are used to do the mechanical work. As soon as the electric connection between the battery and the starter motor is completed, the pull-in winding ceases to function. The hold-in winding remains in operation until the dash switch is released. A heavy spring returns the linkage and plunger to the released position. Solenoid controls are required for overrunning-type starter drives.

THE LIGHTING AND SIGNAL SYSTEM

Various lighting and signaling devices are used in the automobile; headlights, parking lights, brake lights, back-up lights, dash lights, courtesy lights, and directional signals are common to most vehicles. All of these lights and signaling devices operate on a ground-return circuit. When more than one bulb is used in a circuit, the bulbs are connected in parallel. To protect the circuit from an overload, either a *fuse* or a *circuit breaker* is used; these devices are capable of carrying only a certain amount of current. The heat developed by additional current causes either the small strip of metal inside the fuse to melt and break the circuit, or the bimetal strip in the circuit breaker to move and separate the points, thus breaking the circuit. Both units prevent damage to the wiring or to the units in the circuit.

The wire used in the different circuits varies in size and current-carrying capacity; the current requirements of the circuit will determine the correct size of wire to be used. Stranded or flexible wire is used, covered with a suitable type and amount of insulation to prevent the possibility of a short circuit. Half-inch (12.7 mm) diameter wire is used on battery cables because of the large amount of current required for starter motor operation. Wires as small as 2 mm in diameter are used for dash and courtesy lights, which require very little current. In order to attach the wire to the different units in the electric system, a wide variety of clips and connectors are used. Switches of various types are used to control the electric circuits (Figure 8-44).

The Headlights. Each headlight consists of two electrical filaments placed between a highly polished reflector and a glass lens. The shape of the lens concentrates the light rays to give the best illumination of the road ahead. Today's automobile uses either two or four sealed-beam headlight units. A sealed-beam unit consists of a hermetically sealed,

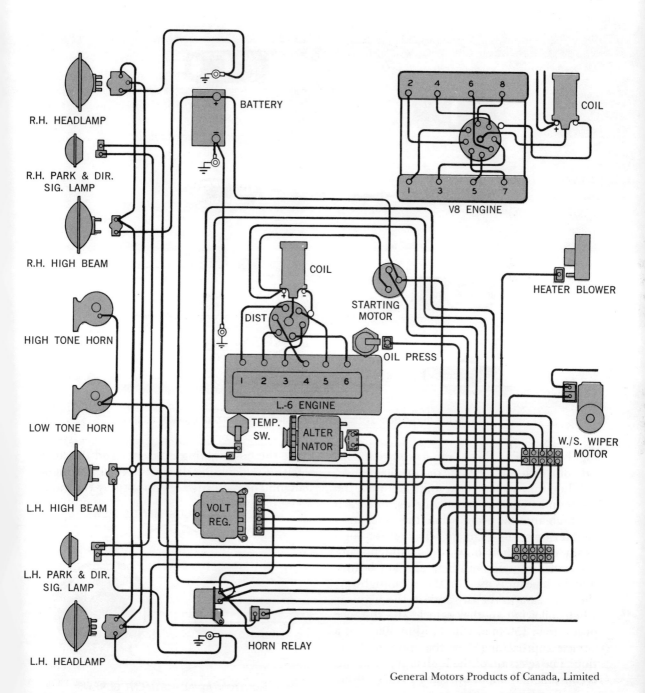

R.H. HEADLAMP

R.H. PARK & DIR.
SIG. LAMP

R.H. HIGH BEAM

HIGH TONE HORN

LOW TONE HORN

L.H. HIGH BEAM

L.H. PARK & DIR.
SIG. LAMP

L.H. HEADLAMP

BATTERY

COIL

V8 ENGINE

COIL

DIST

STARTING
MOTOR

OIL PRESS

HEATER BLOWER

L.-6 ENGINE

TEMP.
SW.

ALTER
NATOR

W./S. WIPER
MOTOR

VOLT
REG.

HORN RELAY

General Motors Products of Canada, Limited

Fig. 8-44   Electrical Diagram of Front Lighting
and Engine Compartment

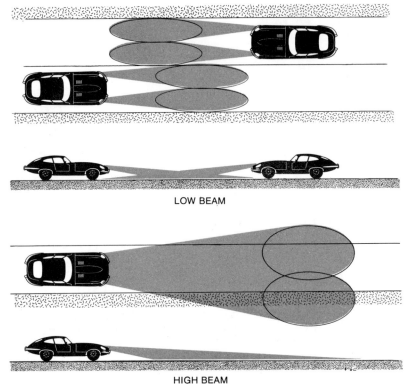

LOW BEAM

HIGH BEAM

Headlight Beams   General Motors Products of Canada, Limited

highly polished *reflector* and *lens assembly,* inside of which is placed one or two filaments.

When four sealed-beam units are used, the outer units contain two filaments, one each for high and low beam, while the inner ones contain only one filament which is for high beam only. When only two headlights are used, they contain both high and low beams. The high beam is used on the open highway; the low beam in the city and on the highway when following another vehicle at a distance of less than 150 m or when within 300 m of a vehicle approaching from the opposite direction. The selection of the high and low beams is controlled by a foot-operated switch. Often, a small red light on the dash indicates when the high beam is in use (Figure 8-46).

Headlights must be focussed or aligned to give the best lighting efficiency and the least glare to oncoming drivers. Special headlight alignment patterns are supplied by the auto-

VERTICAL ADJUSTMENT SCREWS

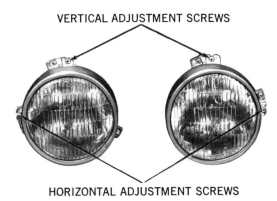

HORIZONTAL ADJUSTMENT SCREWS

Chrysler Canada Ltd.

Fig. 8-46   Headlight Adjusting Points

motive manufacturers, and the lamps must be adjusted to conform to these patterns.

PRACTICAL ASSIGNMENTS

a. Test a Battery With a Hydrometer.
CAUTION: Keep the electrolyte away from your hands, face, and clothing because it can cause serious burns. If electrolyte is splashed on hands, face, or clothing, douse the spot immediately with clear water to dilute the acid.
Procedure:
1. Wash the top of the battery with warm water to remove all loose dirt.
2. Remove the filler caps from all cells.
3. If the electrolyte covers the plates sufficiently, test the battery with a hydrometer.
4. If the electrolyte does not cover the plates sufficiently, add sufficient distilled water to cover the plates to the right depth. Place the battery on charge for approximately four hours to mix the added water thoroughly with the electrolyte, before taking the hydrometer readings.
5. Place the hydrometer vertically in the filler hole and draw in sufficient electrolyte to raise the float of the hydrometer. At eye level, read the number at the point where the float stem projects out of the electrolyte. This number indicates the relative density of the electrolyte.
6. Compare the reading with the chart to determine the state of charge of that cell.
7. Repeat steps (5) and (6) for the remaining cells of the battery.
8. Report your findings to the instructor.
9. Replace the filler caps in the filler holes.

b. Service a Battery.
CAUTION: Keep the electrolyte away from your hands, face, and clothing because it can cause serious burns. If electrolyte is splashed on hands, face, or clothing, douse the spot

immediately with clear water to dilute the acid.
Procedure:
1. Locate the position of the battery in the car, and remove the protective cover, if used.
2. Examine the condition of the battery terminals and remove any corrosion by using a solution of bicarbonate of soda and water. (Care must be exercised to prevent the bicarbonate of soda solution from entering the battery, as this solution could neutralize the electrolyte.) Rinse with clear water.
3. Remove any dirt from around the filler plug hole and test the battery with a hydrometer according to the procedure given in practical assignment a.
4. Add any water necessary to bring the electrolyte up to the proper level, which is approximately, 10 mm to 15 mm above the plate tops. The battery filler may be used to measure this height; fill only to the star in the bottom of the filler-plug hole. You may be able to judge with the eye after experience.
5. Remove any moisture from the top of the battery with a clean, dry cloth.
6. Check the terminal bolts and nuts to be sure they are tight.
7. Coat the terminals with a light coat of corrosion inhibitor.
8. Have the instructor inspect your work.
9. Replace the protective cover if used.

c. Remove and Replace a Battery.
CAUTION: Keep the electrolyte away from your hands, face, and clothing because it can cause serious burns. If electrolyte is splashed on hands, face, or clothing, douse the spot immediately with clear water to dilute the acid.
Procedure:
1. Locate the position of the battery in the

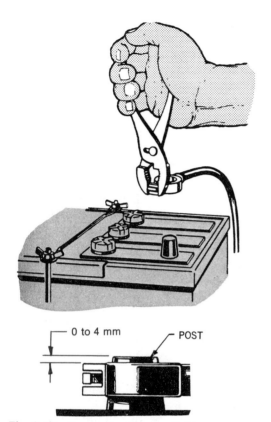

Fig. 8-47   Connecting Battery Cables

is in readiness; then lift it from the battery compartment, using the proper carrying strap.

6. Inspect the battery case or compartment to see that it is in good condition. Repair if necessary. The corrosion in the battery compartment may also be removed with a solution of bicarbonate of soda and water. Rinse with clear water.

7. Inspect and test the battery to be installed, to ensure satisfactory operation.

8. Determine the correct *polarity* of the electrical system of the automobile. This may be done from the specifications in the repair manual. The identity of the battery posts may be determined in the following ways: (1) the positive post is usually larger than the negative post; (2) the positive post is usually darker in colour than the negative post; (3) the positive post is marked with a plus (+) sign while the negative post is marked with a minus (−) sign.

9. Install the hold-down bracket and clamps.

10. Install the cable terminals and tighten the terminal screws.

11. Coat the terminals with a light coat of corrosion inhibitor.

12. Check the installation by operating the starter motor. If the battery has been installed correctly, the engine should turn over in a brisk manner. If the engine turns over slowly and the battery and starting motor are in good condition, a further inspection of the battery installation is necessary to see that all connections have been properly made.

13. Have the instructor inspect your work.

14. Install the protective cover if used.

d. Recharge a Battery.
Procedure:

1. Service and test the battery as outlined in practical assignments a and b.

car, and remove the protective cover, if used.

2. Inspect cable and clamp bolts, and remove any corrosion by using a solution of bicarbonate of soda and water. Rinse with clear water.

3. Loosen the nuts on the cable-clamp bolts and remove the cables. It is recommended that you remove the ground cable first, thus reducing the possibility of creating a short circuit which would damage the battery. The use of a battery-terminal puller is recommended for tight terminals.

4. Remove the nuts from the hold-down clamp bolts; lift off the clamps and hold-down bracket, and lay them aside.

5. Inspect the battery to see that everything

2. Connect the battery to the charger according to the instructions.

3. Have the instructor inspect your work and in his presence set the proper charging rate.

e. Ignition System. Using the model ignition system in the shop, study the location of all ignition system components. Trace the path of current through the primary and secondary circuits. Ask the instructor to question you.

f. Remove, Replace, and Set Ignition Points.

Procedure:

1. Remove ignition points and condenser from the distributor according to manufacturer's instructions.

2. Show the removed parts to the instructor.

3. Install the new points and condenser according to manufacturer's instructions.

4. Adjust the points to the proper gap opening, testing it with the proper size of feeler gauge.

5. Have the instructor inspect your work.

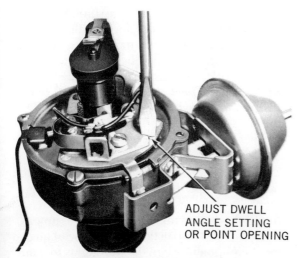

ADJUST DWELL
ANGLE SETTING
OR POINT OPENING

General Motors Products of Canada, Limited

Fig. 8-48 Setting the Distributor

g. Service Spark Plugs. After suitable instruction on the operation of the spark-plug cleaner, have the instructor assign to you an engine that requires spark-plug servicing.

Procedure:

1. Remove the spark-plug wires, noting the proper location of the wires for reinstallation.

2. Using a spark-plug socket wrench, loosen the spark plugs about half a turn.

3. Blow away any loose dirt.

4. Replace spark-plug wires and start the engine to blow out from the combustion chamber any carbon particles which were dislodged when the plugs were loosened.

5. Remove the spark-plug wires and plugs, and place plugs in the stand supplied.

6. Compare spark plugs to the spark-plug chart to determine whether the plugs are of the right heat range.

7. Wash the plugs in a suitable solvent. Air dry.

8. Clean the threads of the plugs with a wire brush.

9. Clean the inside of the plugs by sand-blasting them in the spark-plug cleaner.

10. Blow excess sand off the plugs.

11. Clean between the electrodes with a fine file. File the electrodes until they are flat.

12. Adjust the air gap by bending the ground electrode to the gap specified by the manufacturer.

13. Test the spark plugs by comparing the sparks with the spark of a new plug at pressures between 550 kPa and 850 kPa.

14. Test for air leaks between the insulator and the electrode, and between the insulator and shell, by dropping oil on the joints while the plug is under pressure.

15. Have the instructor check the clean spark plugs.

16. Install new gaskets and install the plugs in the motor finger-tight.

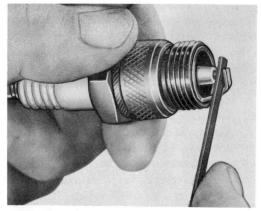

(A) CLEANING PLUG ELECTRODES

(B) CHECKING SPARK-PLUG GAP

Ford Motor Company of Canada Limited

Fig. 8-49   Servicing Spark Plugs

17. Using the proper wrench, tighten the plugs to the proper specifications.
18. Replace the spark-plug wires in their proper order.
19. Have the instructor inspect your work.

h. Disassemble and Assemble a Generator.

Procedure:
 1. Remove the through bolts attaching the end frames. Separate the commutator end frame and the field frame from the drive end frame.

 2. Disconnect the brush leads from the brush holders.
 3. Locate all the parts of the generator mentioned in this chapter.
 4. Assemble the generator by following the reverse of the procedure for disassembly.
 5. Have the instructor inspect your work.

i. Disassemble and Assemble a Starting Motor.

Procedure:
 1. Remove the cover band, and disconnect the brush leads.
 2. Remove the through bolts, and separate the drive housing, commutator end frame, and field frame.
 3. Locate all the starting motor parts mentioned in this chapter.
 4. Assemble the starting motor, following the reverse of the procedure for disassembly.
 5. Have the instructor inspect your work.

j. Wiring. On the demonstration wiring board, trace the circuits for headlights, taillights, brake lights, and dash lights. Ask the instructor to question you. Remove wiring as instructed by the instructor. Replace wiring on units and check their operation. Have the instructor inspect your work.

k. Align Headlights. After suitable instruction on the operation of the headlight alignment, have the instructor assign you to an automobile requiring headlight alignment. Following the instructions on the use of alignment equipment, align the headlights to manufacturer's specifications. Have the instructor inspect your work (Figure 8-50).

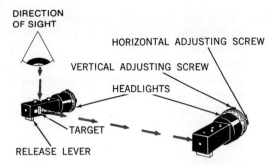

Chrysler Canada Ltd.

Fig. 8-50   Aligning Headlights

REVIEW QUESTIONS

1. Name and describe two types of electricity.
2. Name and define the three units which make up an atom.
3. Which unit of question 2 moves from one atom to another and what causes it to move?
4. Which has more electrons, a positive or a negative electric charge?
5. Define a free electron.
6. Explain, by using simple electron theory, how a current passes through a conductor.
7. Discuss briefly the theory of magnetism.
8. Compare the relationship of the atoms of an unmagnetized material with those of a magnetized material.
9. Name five characteristics of magnetic lines of force.
10. State the difference between an electromagnet and a permanent magnet.
11. Name three factors which control the strength of an electromagnet.
12. What is meant by magnetic induction?
13. Name three factors which control the strength of an induced current.
14. Which three units of the automobile operate on the electromagnetic principle?

15. State the rules for determining (a) the direction of the magnetic field around a conductor, (b) the polarity of an electromagnet.
16. Define the following terms: (a) conductor, (b) electric circuit, (c) volt, (d) ampere, (e) short circuit, (f) open circuit.
17. Explain the difference between a series and a parallel circuit.
18. Describe a ground-return circuit.
19. Name the two plates used in battery construction and state the type of active material on each.
20. What is an electrolyte? What substance is used as an electrolyte in automobile batteries?
21. Explain the chemical reaction that takes place when a battery is being discharged.
22. Describe the construction of a battery cell.
23. Explain how batteries are rated.
24. Explain why a relative density reading of the electrolyte gives an indication of a battery's state of charge.
25. What is the relative density reading of (a) a fully charged battery, (b) a half-charged battery, and (c) a discharged battery?
26. How often is battery service required?
27. What is the advantage of applying an inhibitor to the battery terminal connection?
28. Why must care be exercised to prevent the bicarbonate of soda solution from entering the battery?
29. Name three methods of determining the identity of a positive battery post.
30. What causes batteries to gas?
31. What care must be taken to dissipate battery acid gas?
32. What causes batteries to overheat while recharging?
33. How are the terminals of a battery charger identified?
34. State the purpose of the ignition system.

35. Trace the electrical path through (a) the primary circuit, (b) the secondary circuit.
36. Describe briefly ignition circuit operation.
37. Why is a multipurpose ignition switch used?
38. What is the purpose of the ignition resistor?
39. Describe the construction of an ignition coil.
40. Name the units of the distributor which form part of (a) the primary circuit, (b) the secondary circuit.
41. What is the purpose of the ignition points?
42. How is the distributor shaft driven?
43. Why is a condenser used?
44. Why are the distributor cap and rotor necessary?
45. What type of high-tension wire is most commonly used today? Why?
46. List four advantages of electronic, or transistorized, ignition systems.
47. What replaces the ignition points in a breakerless ignition system?
48. What is a transistor?
49. What is the purpose of a spark plug?
50. What is meant by (a) a cold spark plug, (b) a hot spark plug? Explain why the different heat ranges are necessary.
51. Why are extended nose spark plugs used?
52. How are spark-plug sizes determined?
53. Explain what is meant by fouling of a spark plug.
54. Explain the effects of (a) over-tightening, (b) under-tightening a spark plug.
55. What is meant by the term "ignition timing"?
56. Why are advance mechanisms necessary in the ignition system?
57. Name the two types of advance mechanisms used and state the conditions under which each operates.
58. Name the units of the charging circuit.
59. What is the purpose of the generator or alternator?
60. State the basic electrical principle governing the operation of a generator or alternator.
61. Name and state the purpose of the components of an alternator.
62. How are the rotor windings of an alternator energized?
63. Why does an alternator not require (a) a cut-out unit, (b) a current-control unit, in its regulator?
64. Explain the purpose of (a) the field relay, (b) the indicator relay, as used in an alternator regulator.
65. Name and state the purpose of the components of a generator.
66. How are the field windings of a generator energized?
67. State the three purposes of a generator regulator.
68. What is a starting motor?
69. State the basic electrical principle governing the operation of a starting motor.
70. What is the purpose of the commutator in a starting motor?
71. Name and describe two types of starter motor drives.
72. Name two types of starter motor controls, state the difference between them, and name the type of starter drive each requires.
73. Why are various sizes of wire used in automotive wiring circuits?
74. Name and describe the operation of two types of circuit protectors used in automotive electric circuits.
75. Describe the construction of a sealed-beam headlight unit.
76. Why must headlights be aligned, or focused?
77. When should the (a) high, (b) low beams of headlights be used?

AIR POLLUTION AND EMISSION CONTROL 9

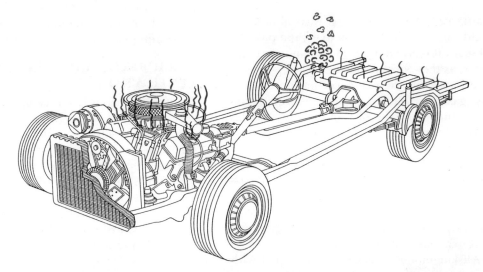

Many modern processes and machines can contribute to air pollution, the modern automobile being one such device. There are four areas in the automobile which may cause air pollution: the crankcase, carburetor, gasoline tank, and exhaust system.

The automobile engine and fuel system release into the atmosphere a variety of gaseous compounds such as: unburnt hydrocarbons, carbon monoxide, nitrogen oxides, and unburnt particulates.

In 1963 a government program for the control of motor vehicle emissions was begun. By 1980 these emissions are to be reduced by the following amounts in comparison to the original 1963 levels: hydrocarbons by 97%, carbon monoxide by 94%, nitrogen oxides by 93%, and exhaust particulates by 90%.

To meet these requirements, two different approaches to the problem have been fol-

lowed by the automotive manufacturers: first, reduction of the formation of emissions in the engine by raising combustion efficiency; secondly, destroying pollutants after they have been formed by using catalytic-type or flame-type afterburners which burn the discharged hydrocarbons after they leave the combustion chamber. The designing engineers have redesigned the ventilating systems of the crankcase, carburetor, and gasoline tank; and they are increasing combustion efficiency by altering the combustion chambers, fuel system, cooling system, exhaust system, and ignition system.

CRANKCASE VENTILATION

The crankcase must be ventilated for several reasons. There is always a certain amount of pressurized gases leaking from the combustion chamber past the rings and into the

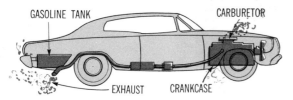

Fig. 9-1   Sources of Motor Vehicle Air Pollution

crankcase. If this pressure was allowed to build up, it would force oil to escape past the oil seals. It is also important to eliminate these gases, as they form moisture and deposit sulphuric acid in the oil. A certain amount of raw gasoline will also escape past the piston rings and enter the oil. As the oil becomes heated, the water and gasoline evaporate, forming gases which must be eliminated.

The crankcase ventilating system provides for a constant stream of fresh air to pass through the valve chamber and crankcase. This stream of fresh air relieves the excess gas pressure and carries away the gasoline, water vapours, and oil fumes.

All late-model vehicles are equipped with positive crankcase ventilating (PCV) systems. With this type of system, the crankcase fumes and vapours are burnt in the cylinders instead of being deposited in the atmosphere.

To operate this system, a *vacuum line* from the intake manifold is attached to the crank-

case ventilating-system outlet breather. A second line is attached between the carburetor air cleaner and the ventilating-system inlet. When the engine is started, engine vacuum pulls filtered air through the engine and the fumes are burnt in the cylinder. The residue is expelled through the exhaust system. A special crankcase ventilating (PCV) valve is inserted in the vacuum line to maintain proper engine operating vacuum.

CARBURETOR AND FUEL TANK VENTILATION

Evaporation losses from the gasoline and carburetor account for 10% to 15% of the hydrocarbons discharged into the atmosphere. To reduce this emission, gasoline tanks and carburetors are no longer vented to the atmosphere. Instead, the vent of the fuel tank and the carburetor are connected to the crankcase ventilating system so that the vapours will be drawn by way of the intake manifold into the combustion chamber for burning.

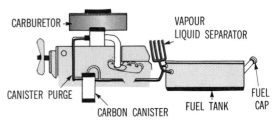

Fig. 9-3   Evaporation Control System

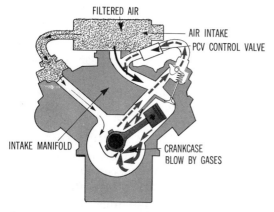

Fig. 9-2   Positive Crankcase Ventilating System

The system includes a special fuel tank and filler cap, liquid-vapour separator, carbon canister, canister purge hoses, and carburetor modifications. Fuel vapour which would otherwise escape to the atmosphere is directed into the carbon canister. The carbon absorbs the vapour and stores it. The vapour is removed from the canister during periods of engine operation as manifold vacuum draws the vapour into the engine and burns it.

RAISING COMBUSTION EFFICIENCY

ENGINE DESIGN CHANGES

One of the major changes in engine design is the lowering of the compression ratio from approximately 10.5:1 in 1969 to 8.5:1 in 1976. This has been done in order for the engine to operate satisfactorily on non-leaded or low lead gasoline. The lead compounds in gasoline caused damage to the catalyst used in catalytic-type mufflers.

Combustion chambers have been redesigned to reduce the cool areas around the chamber, thus improving complete combustion of the fuel-air mixture.

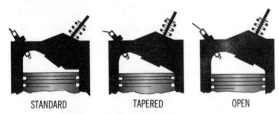

(A) COMBUSTION CHAMBER QUENCH AREAS

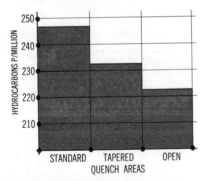

(B) RELATIONSHIP BETWEEN COMBUSTION CHAMBER AND HYDROCARBONS P/MILLION

Fig. 9-4   Combustion Chamber Design and Exhaust Emissions

COOLING SYSTEM CHANGES

Many cooling systems are now equipped with thermostats which open at temperatures up to 94°C. The higher engine operating tem-

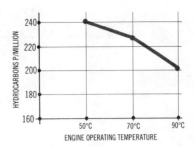

Fig. 9-5   Relationship Between Engine Operating Temperature and Exhaust Emissions

peratures increase the temperature of the metal surrounding the combustion chamber. This helps to reduce the cool areas around the chamber which tend to reduce complete combustion of the fuel-air mixture, thus producing unburnt hydrocarbons.

FUEL SYSTEM CHANGES

The Carburetor. Carburetor changes include higher idling speeds and methods of preventing mechanics from adjusting and producing an idle mixture which is too rich.

Thermostatically Controlled Air Cleaners. This type of air cleaner is designed to improve carburetor operation and engine warm-up characteristics. It accomplishes this by maintaining the temperature of the air entering the carburetor at a minimum of 29°C to 40°C. The thermostatically controlled valve selects warmed air from a heat stove attached to the exhaust manifold and/or cooler air from the engine compartment.

The system includes a *temperature sensor,* a *vacuum motor,* and a *control damper* (all of which are mounted in the air cleaner), a *manifold-mounted heat stove,* and the necessary *vacuum* and *heat hoses.*

When the temperature of the air entering the carburetor throat is below 40°C, the sensor control admits engine vacuum to the vacuum motor. The motor moves the control

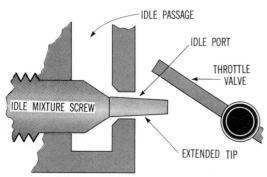

(A) EXTENDED TIP TYPE IDLE MIXTURE ADJUSTING SCREW

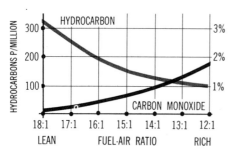

(B) IDLE MIXTURES AND EMISSIONS

Fig. 9-6   Idle Mixtures and Exhaust Emissions

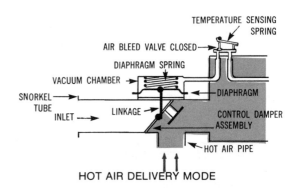

HOT AIR DELIVERY MODE

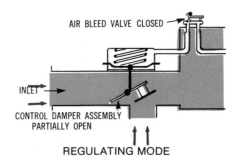

REGULATING MODE

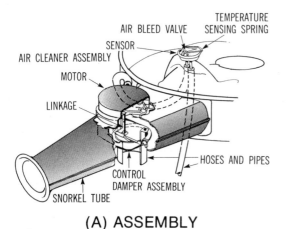

(A) ASSEMBLY

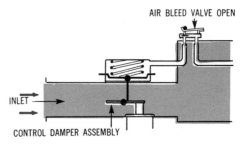

COLD AIR DELIVERY MODE

(B) OPERATION

Fig. 9-7   Thermostatically Controlled Air Cleaner

damper to the position which permits only the air which has been warmed by passing through the heat stove to enter the carburetor. When the temperature of the air reaches approximately 38°C, the sensor control reduces the amount of vacuum reaching the vacuum motor. Then the damper is moved to regulate the flow of under-the-hood air and the warm air from the exhaust-manifold heat stove, maintaining the minimum temperature required. Eventually, the temperature of the under-the-hood air will be high enough so that the sensor will close, stopping the vacuum from reaching the vacuum motor; the damper will be in a position to admit only air from under the hood. (See Figure 9-7).

IGNITION SYSTEM CHANGES

IGNITION TIMING

The ignition timing has been retarded at idling speeds to improve complete combustion of the fuel-air mixture. Mechanical advance curves have been modified to provide greater spark advance, so that the timing pro-

duces the most efficient engine operation at normal driving speeds.

In some emission control systems, the vacuum advance unit may not operate under certain driving conditions, such as before the transmission is shifted into high gear, or on deceleration, thus helping to reduce emissions during these periods of engine operation.

COMMON EMISSION CONTROL SYSTEMS

Various combinations of the previously mentioned factors are used by various motor vehicle manufacturers and classified under various trade names such as CAS, Cleaner Air System (Chrysler); CCS, Combustion Control System (General Motors); CCC, Climatic Combustion Control (General Motors); IMCO, Improved Combustion Exhaust Emission Control System (Ford); EMS, Engine Mod System (American Motors).

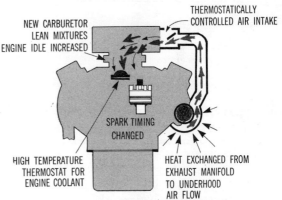

Fig. 9-9   Controlled Combustion System

Each different size of engine and transmission and rear axle combination to which it is connected can require different components in the emission control system. It is advisable to refer to the owner's operation manual to determine the systems and components used on any particular vehicle.

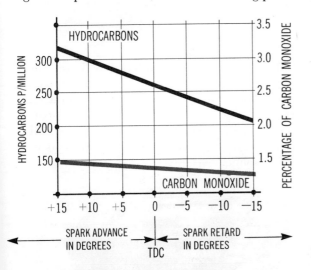

Fig. 9-8   The Effect of Spark Timing on Exhaust Emission at Idle

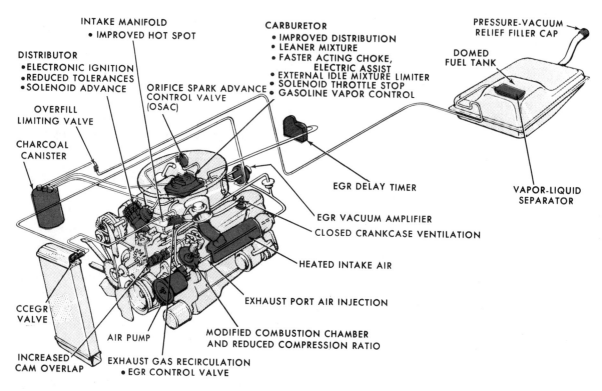

Fig. 9-10   Typical Pollution Control System

Chrysler Canada Ltd.

DESTROYING POLLUTANTS AFTER THEY HAVE BEEN FORMED

Catalytic-type after-burners, sometimes referred to as catalytic mufflers, use a chemical reaction to consume hydrocarbons. The unit is a muffler-like canister installed in the exhaust system, but it does not replace the conventional system muffler. The unit contains chemically coated plastic pellets arranged so that the heat of the exhaust gases activates the pellets, promoting oxidization of the unburnt hydrocarbons. A minimum temperature of 250°C is required to activate the pellets. The resulting chemical action converts the un-burnt hydrocarbons into harmless water vapour and carbon dioxide. Any carbon build-up on the pellets is prevented by the flow of exhaust gases agitating the pellets. Unfortunately, the catalytic material is expensive and deteriorates rapidly in reaction with lead in the gasoline.

Fig. 9-11   Catalytic-type After-burner

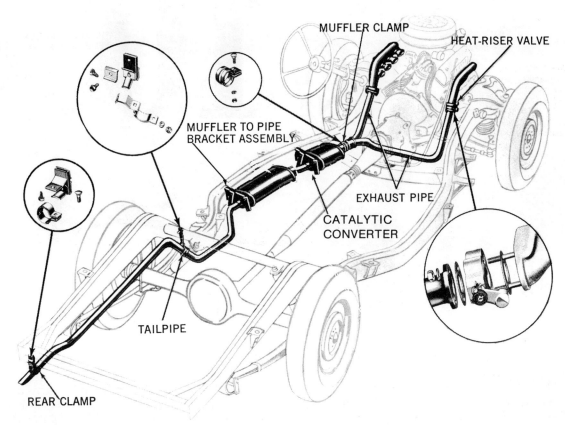

MUFFLER CLAMP

HEAT-RISER VALVE

MUFFLER TO PIPE
BRACKET ASSEMBLY

EXHAUST PIPE

CATALYTIC
CONVERTER

TAILPIPE

REAR CLAMP

Fig. 9-12   Single Exhaust System

PRACTICAL ASSIGNMENTS

a. On a shop vehicle trace the (a) fuel vapour control system, (b) crankcase ventilating system, and be able to identify all components.

b. Using the manufacturer's service manual, (a) determine the types of emission control systems used; (b) identify the components of those systems.

REVIEW QUESTIONS

1. List four possible sources of pollution found in the automobile.
2. State briefly the two approaches that have been used by automobile manufacturers to reduce pollution.
3. List the changes that have been made to increase engine combustion efficiency.
4. Give three reasons which make the crankcase ventilating system necessary.
5. How are the vapours from the carburetor and fuel tank prevented from escaping to the atmosphere?
6. Why have the compression ratios been lowered in late model automobiles?
7. Why are thermostatically controlled air cleaners used?
8. Describe the operation of a thermostatically controlled air cleaner.
9. Explain how a catalytic-type muffler reduces pollutants.

THE DRIVE LINE 10

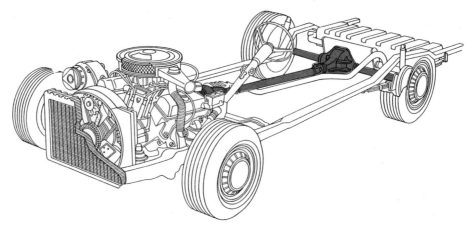

The drive line consists of several mechanisms that carry the engine power to the rear wheels. These are the clutch, transmission, propeller shaft differential, and rear axles.

THE CLUTCH

The clutch is a friction-type uncoupling device. It is linked to a clutch pedal in the driver's compartment. The clutch assembly is divided into four main parts: the flywheel, the clutch plate, the pressure-plate assembly, and the control pedal and linkage.

The single plate, dry-disc clutch is the mechanical connection between the engine and the gears that drive the car. The engine imparts a rotary motion to the flywheel on the end of the crankshaft. After the flywheel has reached a certain speed, its turning effort must be transferred to the transmission shaft. This transfer is accomplished through a *friction* or *dry* disc, which is pressed and held

against the turning flywheel until it turns as a unit with the flywheel. Because the disc is splined to the main drive pinion shaft of the transmission, the rotary motion of the crankshaft is thus transferred to the transmission gears.

The clutch disc is moved and held against the turning flywheel by a pressure plate. When the driver has his foot off the clutch pedal, the clutch is engaged, that is to say, the clutch disc is tightly pressed between the flywheel and the pressure plate. When the driver presses down on the clutch pedal, the release bearing moves forward against the clutch-release levers or fingers, and by leverage pulls back the pressure plate, thus compressing the springs. When this spring pressure is removed, the clutch disc is thrown off by the revolving flywheel and soon coasts to a stop between the pressure plate and the flywheel. When the driver again takes his foot off the clutch pedal, the release bearing

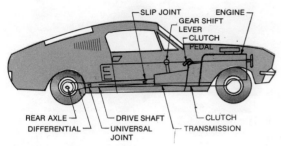

Fig. 10-1   The Drive Line

moves back, causing the release levers to slacken their leverage on the pressure plate. The springs once again force out on the pressure plate to sandwich the disc against the flywheel.

This system is simple but effective. The driver, by pressure of his foot, can regulate very minutely the rate of engagement of the clutch, and can move the release bearing slowly enough to engage the clutch smoothly and evenly.

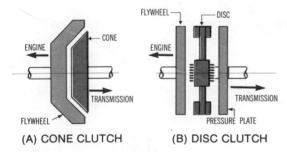

Fig. 10-2   Mechanical Clutches

CLUTCH PRESSURE-PLATE ASSEMBLIES

There are two types of clutch pressure-plate assemblies used in automobiles, the *coil pressure-spring type,* and the *diaphragm-spring type.*

Coil Pressure-Spring Type.   The coil pressure-spring type of pressure-plate assembly is made up of coil springs, a pressure plate, release levers, and a cover (Figure 10-3A). The parts are assembled inside the cover, which is in turn attached by bolts to the flywheel. The assembly rotates with the fly-wheel. When the clutch is engaged, the pressure springs push the pressure plate forward, forcing the clutch disc firmly against the flywheel. Consequently, these springs must be strong enough to hold the pressure disc against the flywheel and transmit the engine power at speeds up to 5000 r/mm. The pressure plate requires over 6900 kPa of pressure to hold the clutch disc against the flywheel. Insufficient pressure in these springs would cause loss of power, since all the power would not be picked up by the clutch and carried to the transmission. It would also cause a slipping clutch, which could overheat, resulting in possible failure.

To disconnect the transmission from the engine, it is necessary to move the clutch disc away from the flywheel. Pressure on the pressure plate must first be relieved so that the clutch disc no longer revolves with the flywheel. Depressing the clutch pedal causes the release bearing to push the inner end of the levers (near the centre of the assembly) toward the flywheel. Through the leverage action, the outer ends of these levers pull back the pressure plate from the clutch disc. This compresses the springs in the pressure plate and thereby relieves the pressure which is forcing the clutch disc against the flywheel. Then the clutch disc is able to spin freely without transmitting any power to the engine; that is, it is then disengaged. In order to overcome the great pressure of the pressure-plate springs, the fulcrum of the clutch-release levers is at a point which would produce a 6:1 ratio. Therefore, the inner end of the lever must be moved 10 mm to pull back the pressure plate 2 mm. This, along with the mechanical advantage of the clutch-pedal linkage, enables the driver to disengage the motor from the transmission with a minimum of physical effort.

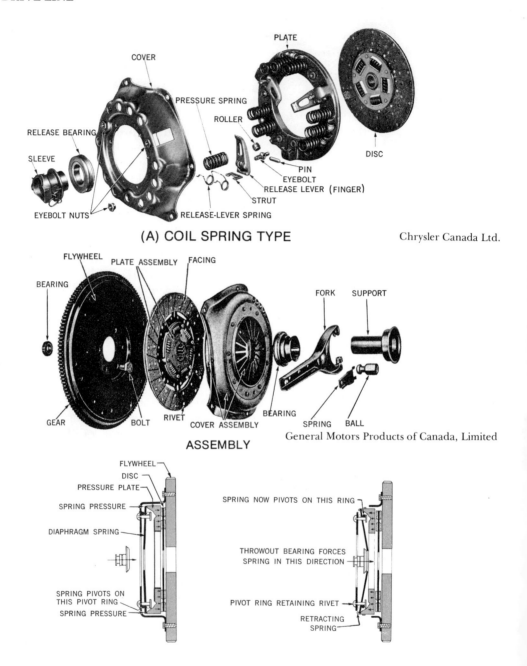

(A) COIL SPRING TYPE

Chrysler Canada Ltd.

ASSEMBLY

General Motors Products of Canada, Limited

OPERATION

(B) DIAPHRAGM SPRING TYPE

Fig. 10-3   Clutch Pressure-plate Assemblies

Diaphragm-Spring Type. The diaphragm type of clutch (Figure 10-3B) incorporates a diaphragm spring that not only provides the spring pressure required to hold the clutch disc against the flywheel, but also acts as the release lever to release the spring pressure when the clutch is disengaged. The diaphragm spring is a solid ring on the outer diameter, having a series of tapered fingers pointed inward toward the centre of the clutch. In the engaged position, the diaphragm spring is slightly dished, with the tapered fingers pointed away from the flywheel. In the disengaged position, the diaphragm spring is dished in the opposite direction. The flexing action is similar to the action of an oil can when the bottom is depressed. Because the diaphragm is pivoted near the outer circumference, it acts as a first-class lever. In the engaged position, the dished design of the spring places pressure around the entire circumference of the pressure plate. This pressure is sufficient to transmit the driving power of the engine.

In the disengaged position, the throwout bearing is moved inward against the spring fingers. The spring is forced to pivot around the inner pivot ring, causing the plate to dish in the opposite direction. The outer circumference of the diaphragm spring now lifts the pressure plate away through a series of retracting springs located around the circumference of the pressure plate. This allows the clutch disc to spin freely, and the connection between the motor and the transmission is broken.

CLUTCH DISC

When the clutch is engaged, the clutch disc is forced to revolve as a unit with the flywheel and the pressure-plate assembly. All the power developed by the engine is transmitted through the clutch disc to the transmission front shaft. The power is picked up by the lined faces of the clutch disc and transmitted through the steel hub, which is splined to the transmission front shaft.

The clutch-disc facings are of two main types, *moulded* and *woven*. The moulded facings are made of short asbestos fibres and a binder, moulded to size under pressure and cured at high temperatures. The surfaces are then ground flat and parallel. Some moulded linings have brass chips in the mixture to add to lining life.

Woven linings are made from sheets of long-fibre asbestos and copper wire, encased in a binder. The facings are wound into a flat ring and moulded to size under high pressure and cured at high temperatures.

The hub to which the linings or facings are attached includes a cushioning device and a torsional vibration-dampening unit. The cushioning device, between the two facings, is necessary to permit smooth engagement of the clutch and eliminate clutch chatter. The torsional device is located near the centre of the hub. This device absorbs the torsional vibrations of the crankshaft, thus preventing such vibrations from reaching the transmission. The centre of the hub is fitted with splines to transmit the power of the engine to the transmission front shaft (Figure 10-3).

CLUTCH PEDAL AND LINKAGE

The clutch pedal is connected through its linkage to the release bearing so that pressure on the pedal moves the bearing in against the release levers to disengage the clutch. The proper clutch pedal free travel is necessary to compensate for wear on the clutch facings and to avoid slippage. It ensures proper clearance between the clutch-release bearing and the clutch-release levers. When wear of the facings has caused the release levers to move back against the release bearing, adjustment is necessary. An adjustment of 25 mm free play at the pedal will move back the re-

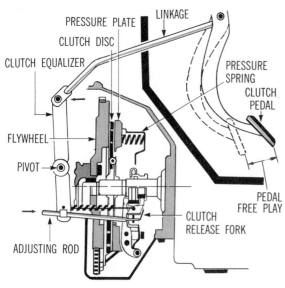

General Motors Products of Canada, Limited

Fig. 10-4   Clutch Pedal and Linkage

lease bearing approximately 3 mm and thus make allowance for facing wear.

The release bearing is pressed on the release-bearing sleeve, so that the inner race is stationary while the outer race can revolve when it makes contact with the rotating release fingers. These are fastened to the clutch cover.

As the facings wear, the pressure plate moves in towards the flywheel and the inner ends of the pivoted release levers move out towards the release bearing. When the adjustment is to be made, set the bearing back as far as practical from the lever noses by adjusting the pedal linkage. Do not set it so far back that it will not push in sufficiently to release the clutch, and do not set it so close that facing wear will cause the levers to rise and contact the bearing (Figure 10-4).

In general, the rule for clutch pedal adjustment is to allow as much clearance between the levers and the release bearing as possible and still provide full release of the clutch.

Improper pedal adjustment causes erratic clutch action, excessive wear, overheating, and eventual clutch failure. The purpose of adjusting the clutch pedal is twofold: (1) to provide full release of the clutch, and (2) to allow for full wear of the clutch-disc facings. These clearances are required for quick, easy gear shifting, without gear clash, and circulation of air over the flywheel and pressure-plate surfaces to dissipate heat.

FLUID COUPLING AND TORQUE CONVERTORS

Fluid couplings and torque convertors replace the friction-disc type of clutch when an automatic transmission is used. The main advantage of this type of unit is that the engine can run slowly without turning the rear wheels while the unit is connected. As the engine speed is increased, the unit will gradually take hold until finally the engine is driving the rear wheels at engine speed with practically no slippage.

The fluid coupling is a doughnut-shaped unit containing a vaned pump, or driving unit, and a vaned turbine, or driven unit. The pump is attached to the engine crankshaft and the turbine is connected to the transmission input shaft. Both units are partially filled with automatic transmission fluid.

When the pump is driven, centrifugal force causes the fluid to be forced out of the pump around its rim. The fluid strikes the vanes of the turbine, causing it to turn. The fluid returns to the pump via the centre section of the turbine.

The torque convertor is similar in construction to the fluid coupling except that a third unit called a *stator* is placed in the path of the returning oil between the turbine and the pump. This stator is attached to the transmission case through a one-way clutch. When there is a difference in speed between the pump and turbine, the stator is held station-

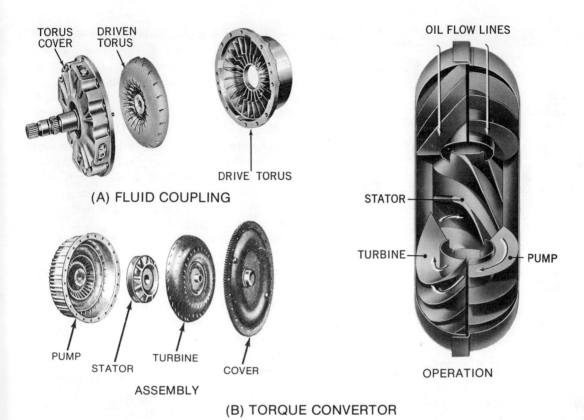

TORUS COVER   DRIVEN TORUS

DRIVE TORUS

(A) FLUID COUPLING

PUMP
STATOR
TURBINE
COVER

ASSEMBLY

(B) TORQUE CONVERTOR

OIL FLOW LINES

STATOR

TURBINE   PUMP

OPERATION

Fig. 10-5   Fluid Drives

General Motors Products of Canada, Limited

ary by the one-way clutch, which changes the direction of the returning oil to a direction which will assist in the rotation effort of the pump. When the pump and turbine are rotating at the same speed, the returning oil strikes the back side of the stator blades and the stator rotates freely on the one-way clutch in the same direction as the pump and turbine.

The *torque convertor* increases torque, while the fluid coupling does not. As a result, a torque convertor is used in conjunction with a two-speed or three-speed automatic transmission, while the fluid coupling is used with a four-speed transmission.

MECHANICAL ADVANTAGE

Mechanical advantage, or leverage greater than one, results when a gravity acting on a mass in one place lifts a heavier mass in another place, or a force applied at one point on a lever produces a greater force at another point. Two simple machines that give a mechanical advantage greater than one are the teeter-totter and the winch.

The teeter-totter shows how mechanical advantage can be applied using gravity. If a one kilogram mass is on one end and a two kilogram mass is on the other, then the one kilogram mass goes up and the two kilogram

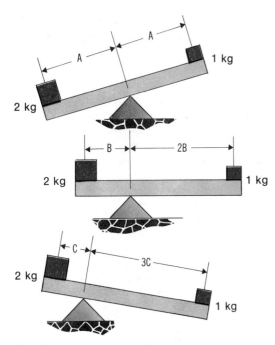

Fig. 10-6   Mechanical Advantage

torque. The shaft with the largest gear will have the greatest torque. The same rule applies as in levers, namely, what is gained in torque is lost in speed. If the diameter of the one gear is twice the diameter of the other, then one gear must have twice as many teeth as the other. For example, if the small driving gear has twelve teeth, and the large driven gear has twenty-four teeth, then one revolution of the driving gear would mesh with twelve teeth of the large gear or rotate in one-half a revolution. As the speed is decreased, the torque is increased.

A means of producing a mechanical advantage is usually called a *machine*. There are five basic machines: the lever, pulley, wheel and axle, inclined plane (wedge), and screw. All machinery is designed from any one or a combination of the five basic machines. The automobile is no exception; it uses all five types in various combinations.

mass goes down when both are equal distances from the fulcrum. If the fulcrum is moved so that the distance from the fulcrum to the one kilogram mass is twice the distance between the fulcrum and the two kilogram mass, then the two masses remain balanced. If the fulcrum is moved still closer to the two kilogram mass, then the one kilogram mass goes down and the two kilogram mass goes up (Figure 10-6).

The wheel and axle is usually just a wheel fastened to a rod. A force applied to the outside of a large wheel produces a greater twisting force on the small rod than if the rod itself were twisted. The wheel-and-axle principle is used in the winch, with a crank, or handle, taking the place of the large wheel.

The wheel and axle principle also applies to gears. A force applied at the outside of a gear will exert a twist, or torque, on its shaft. The bigger the gear, the greater will be the

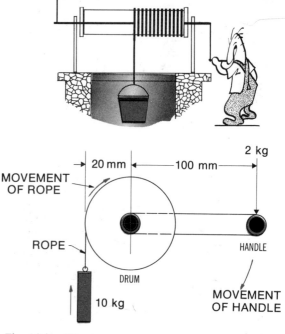

Fig. 10-7   Winch

GEARS

A gear is a wheel with projections on it called *teeth*. These teeth may be on the edge, on the side, or halfway between. A gear is usually fastened to a shaft, either turning and applying torque to the shaft, or turned by the shaft.

Spur Gear. The spur gear, the simplest and most common type of gear, has teeth cut straight across the edge. Spur gears are used to connect parallel shafts which rotate in opposite directions. The *starting-motor* gear and the *flywheel ring* gear are examples of spur gears. Because this type of gear is inclined to be noisy in its operation, other types of gears have become more popular in the transportation field.

Helical Gear. The helical gear is similar to the spur gear, except that its teeth are cut at an angle on its edge. The teeth of the gear it meshes with must be cut on the same angle if the shafts are parallel. It is quieter when operating than the ordinary spur gear, and for this reason is usually preferred. *Herringbone* gears are used for the same reason. They are like two helical gears fastened together side by side with the teeth angled toward the centre.

Bevel Gear. The bevel gear is used when the power must change direction. The teeth on this type of gear are cut on an angle. There are two types of bevel gears: one whose teeth are cut in a straight line across the corner; and the *spiral bevel gear*, whose

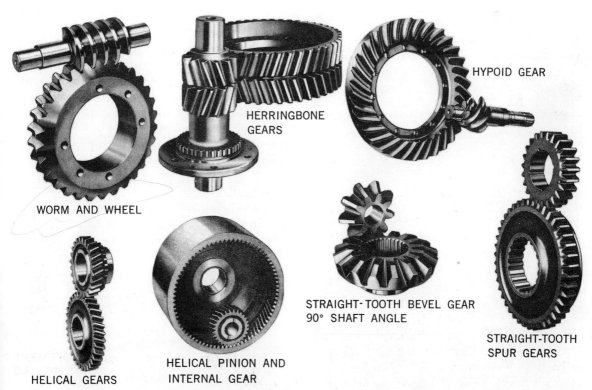

HERRINGBONE GEARS

HYPOID GEAR

WORM AND WHEEL

STRAIGHT-TOOTH BEVEL GEAR 90° SHAFT ANGLE

STRAIGHT-TOOTH SPUR GEARS

HELICAL GEARS

HELICAL PINION AND INTERNAL GEAR

Fig. 10-8 Gears

General Motors Products of Canada, Limited

teeth are cut on an angle similar to the helical gear. The spiral-bevel gear, like the helical gear, is much quieter in its operation.

Hypoid Gear.   Hypoid gears join shafts that are neither parallel nor intersecting. Their design allows the pinion shaft to be placed below or above the shaft of the other gear. For example, the centre line of the drive shaft of the automobile does not intersect with the centre line of the rear axle shaft, and therefore hypoid gears are used in the differential unit.

Internal Gear.   The internal gear is not as widely used as the external gear, but is used extensively in the automatic transmission. An internal gear is simply a ring with teeth cut on the inside instead of the outside. To mesh with it, an external gear of a smaller size is used.

Worm and Wheel Gear.   The worm and wheel, which is often called the worm and worm gear, is used to connect shafts that are not parallel. Worm and spherical gears will transmit very heavy loads, and are used when the gear ratio requirements are high. A sector of the worm wheel and a worm are used in the steering boxes of many automobiles.

Planetary Gears.   A planetary gear set is essentially a set of three helical-type gears. There is a sun gear in the centre, three or four planetary gears meshing with it, and around the outside an internal ring gear which meshes with the planetary gears. The planetary gears are fastened together by a planetary carrier which holds them in place but allows them to rotate individually. How these gears are fastened to the input and the output shafts depends upon what is required of the mechanism. The mechanism can be used to produce reduction or overdrive in either forward or reverse direction.

In order for the planetary gear set to transmit power, one gear is driven, one gear is

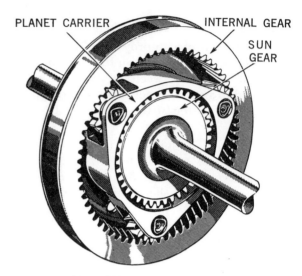

General Motors Products of Canada, Limited

Fig. 10-9   Planetary Gears

held stationary, while the third gear becomes the output member. A common method of obtaining forward reduction is to drive the sun gear and hold the ring gear. The planetary gear then becomes the output member.

Planetary gears are used extensively in automatic transmissions because it is not necessary to move these gears in or out of mesh in order to obtain different gear ratios.

GEAR RATIOS

Transmission speed changes (high, low, second, and reverse) are made by connecting driving and driven gears to form a gear train. When several gears are combined to give this ratio, it is not necessary to consider the speeds of each pair of gears (Figure 10-10).

The formula for determining gear ratio is as follows:

$$\frac{\text{Product of the teeth on all the driven gears}}{\text{Product of the teeth on all the driving gears}} = \text{Ratio}$$

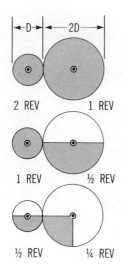

2 REV   1 REV

1 REV   ½ REV

½ REV   ¼ REV

Fig. 10-10   Gear Ratios

For example:

A transmission has a clutch gear with 14 teeth connected to a countershaft drive gear with 24 teeth. The low-speed countershaft gear has 18 teeth and the low-reverse sliding gear has 27 teeth. What is the ratio between the engine and the rear wheels in low gear?

Solution:

$$\text{Ratio in low gear} = \frac{24 \times 27}{14 \times 18}$$

$$= \frac{2.57}{1}$$

or 2.57 to 1 ratio

TRANSMISSIONS

A great deal more power is required to get an automobile from rest to motion than is required to keep it in motion. Considerably more power is necessary to propel a vehicle up a hill than along a level road. By means of the transmission, the engine obtains the necessary mechanical advantage over the rear wheels to get the automobile into action and

to take it up steep hills. The transmission provides a reverse gear for backing up. It also provides a means of disconnecting the motor from the rear wheels so that the engine may be operated with the vehicle parked and no operator at the controls.

The transmission consists of a number of gears of different size which may be meshed as required by moving the gear shift lever. There are usually three forward speeds or ratios in the transmission which are obtained by engaging different sizes of gears when in different gear shift positions (Figure 10-11).

Ford Motor Company of Canada Limited

Fig. 10-11   Three-speed Transmission

Neutral Gear. Neutral gear position is obtained by moving two sliding gears to a position in which they are not in mesh with the other gears. The connection between the engine and rear wheels is broken, thus allowing the engine to run without driving the rear wheels.

Low or First-Speed Gear. In low or first speed, a set of gears is required which will allow the engine to run at high r/min while the automobile runs very slowly. When the operator shifts the gear-shift lever into the low-gear position, the mechanism moves the low-reverse sliding sleeve into mesh with the rear main shaft low-speed gear. The main shaft low-speed gear has a greater number of teeth than the countershaft low-speed gear. Therefore, the rear wheels turn at a slower speed but with increased power. The countershaft revolves when the engine is running, because its large drive gear is always in mesh

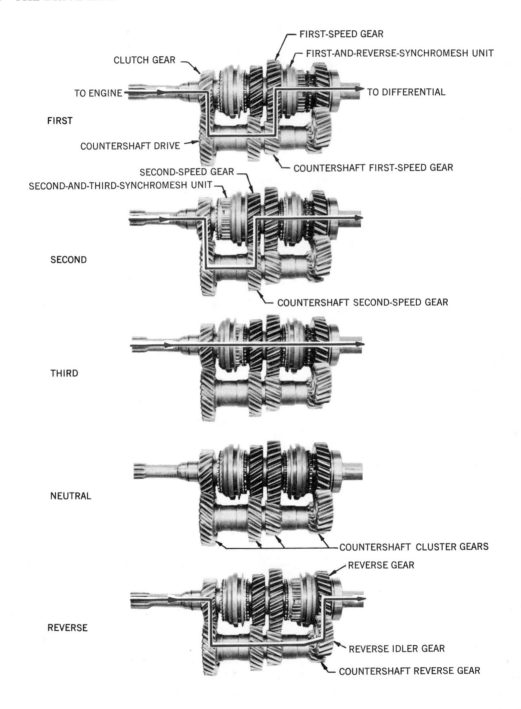

Fig. 10-12   Power Flow in Transmission   General Motors Products of Canada, Limited

with the smaller clutch-shaft gear. Since the driving gear of this set has fewer teeth than the driven gear of the countershaft, the countershaft revolves at a slower speed but with more torque than the engine crankshaft. The two sets of gears give a combined ratio of approximately 3 to 1.

Intermediate or Second Gear. When the operator shifts the gear lever from low to second-speed position, the shifter mechanism moves the low-reverse sliding sleeve to the neutral position and engages the synchromesh unit with the second-speed gear on the rear main shaft. The second-speed gear is always in mesh with the countershaft second-speed gear. These two gears have approximately the same number of teeth and their gear ratio is very low. Therefore, in second gear, the gear ratio is equal to the products of the gear ratio between the clutch-gear and countershaft-gear and the ratio between the countershaft second-speed gear and the main shaft second-speed gear. This total ratio is approximately 2 to 1.

High or Third-Speed Gear. When the operator shifts from second gear to high gear, the synchromesh unit disengages from the rear main shaft second-speed gear and meshes with a spline on the clutch-shaft gear. Since the clutch-shaft gear is revolving at engine speed and the synchromesh unit connects this gear directly to the rear transmission shaft, no reduction gears are in operation. The speed of the output shaft of the transmission is the same as that of the input shaft and there is no increase in torque or decrease in speed. Therefore, high gear ratio is 1 to 1.

Reverse Gear. When the operator shifts to reverse gear, the synchromesh unit is placed in the netural position and the low-reverse sliding sleeve meshes with the rear main shaft reverse gear, which is in constant mesh with the countershaft reverse gear through the reverse idler gear. Since this puts an extra set of gears in the gear train, opposite direction in rotation is achieved. Because the same gear is used in reverse as is used in low gear, both have the same approximate gear ratio of 3 to 1.

It will be seen that the gears in the transmission may be used to allow the engine to turn at higher speeds than the drive shaft and at the same time deliver more power. Thus the vehicle may start up smoothly and slowly without stalling the engine. Although transmissions vary in construction, most transmissions produce a gear ratio of approximately 3 to 1 for low gear, 2 to 1 for second gear, and 1 to 1 for high gear.

Various types of shifter mechanism are used, but the shift pattern of all American and Canadian cars is the same. European vehicles may vary this shifter pattern to suit the type of transmission used in the vehicle.

SYNCHROMESH UNIT

When gears were shifted in the older types of transmission, they frequently clashed, and broken or damaged gears resulted. The synchromesh unit (Figure 10-13) was designed to do away with this trouble. Synchromesh is the combination of two words—synchronize and mesh. *Synchronize* means to cause to happen at the same time, and *mesh* means to interlace or join. The synchromesh unit in the transmission does these two things. It synchronizes the speed of the clutch shaft with the main shaft by the use of friction cones, and in doing so it quietly meshes the two gears.

A synchromesh unit consists of a hub, mounted in the centre of a sliding sleeve, and two blocker rings mounted at each end of the hub. The blocker rings have cone-shaped inner surfaces. This cone shape matches a similar cone attached to each gear on the main shaft.

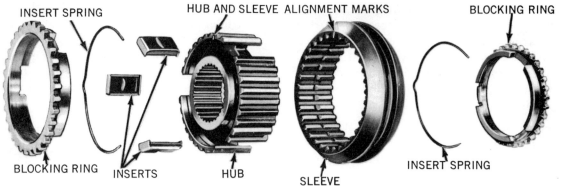

INSERT SPRING   HUB AND SLEEVE ALIGNMENT MARKS   BLOCKING RING

BLOCKING RING   INSERTS   HUB   SLEEVE   INSERT SPRING

Fig. 10-13   Synchromesh Unit   Ford Motor Company of Canada Limited

Before shifting, the gears are turning at different speeds. When the shifter lever is moved, the sliding sleeve and the blocker rings of the synchromesh unit move as a unit, until the blocker rings come in contact with the cones on the gears. This combined sliding action is caused by the pressure of the synchronizing balls and springs. As the shift lever is moved farther, the blocker ring is held against the gear cone, thus synchronizing the speeds of the gear and the blocker ring. The sliding sleeve then compresses the synchronizing balls and slides onto the gear, locking it to the rear transmission shaft.

AUTOMATIC TRANSMISSIONS

An automatic transmission is a transmission that will automatically change the gear ratios between the engine and the rear wheels without the driver changing gears. Mechanical governors, engine vacuum operated valves, and additional throttle linkage are used to select the proper gear ratio in accordance with vehicle speed, engine speed, and load conditions.

Two, three, and four speed automatic transmissions are made up of various combinations of planetary gear sets. To select the proper gear ratio, the coupling of the driving unit or the holding of the held unit of the planetary gear set is accomplished through hydraulically operated friction clutches or by brake bands. The valves which direct the automatic transmission fluid to these units are controlled by engine vacuum, engine speed, throttle linkage, or the manual control lever.

The manual valve-control lever, mounted on the steering column or the floor, permits the driver to select any of the drive positions [Park, Reverse, Neutral, Drive (Drive-one or Drive-two on some models), or Low range].

In drive range, the transmission upshifts or downshifts automatically. In low range, the transmission does not upshift on most models and remains in this gear ratio until the driver shifts the manual control to drive position. *NOTE:* High speed in low range is harmful to the engine.

Some sport-model cars have a control lever set in the floor which allows the driver to select all gear ratios manually or automatically. In manual operation, the driver shifts the lever to different drive positions; in automatic operation, the transmission shifts itself up to the highest gear selected by the driver.

When the driver wishes additional acceleration for passing, he may force the transmission to downshift from its highest gear ratio by depressing the accelerator pedal hard against the floor. This causes the transmission to downshift to the next lowest gear ratio.

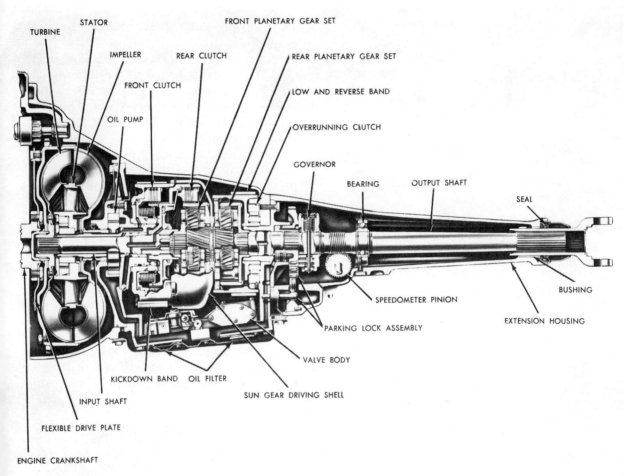

Fig. 10-14   Automatic Transmission   Chrysler Canada Ltd.

DRIVE SHAFTS

In order to connect the transmission to the differential, a drive shaft must be used. There are two popular types: the *torque-tube type,* or closed drive shaft type, and the *Hotchkiss,* or open drive shaft type. In order to compensate for the up-and-down motion of the differential and rear axle as the wheels encounter irregularities in the road, the drive shaft must be connected to the transmission or differential by at least one flexible or universal joint. The torque-tube type uses only one flexible joint, whereas two are used on the Hotchkiss type.

Since the drive shaft transmits torque through the differential to the rear wheels, causing them to rotate and drive the car, a reaction called *rear-end torque* is set up. This is the tendency of the drive shaft to rotate around the rear axle in the opposite direction to the axle shaft and wheel. In order to prevent this movement, several methods of bracing are used.

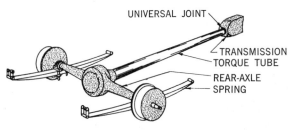

(A) TORQUE-TUBE DRIVE SHAFT

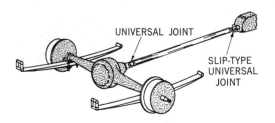

(B) HOTCHKISS DRIVE SHAFT

Fig. 10-15   Drive Lines

The Torque-Tube Drive Shaft. In the torque-tube drive shaft (Figure 10-15), the propeller shaft is enclosed in a hollow steel tube. This tube is bolted to the differential housing and attached to the transmission case by a flexible or universal joint. The universal joint is free to slide on the propeller shaft to compensate for the changes in length as well as changes in angle between the drive shaft and differential housing as the rear wheels encounter irregularities in the road. The torque tube absorbs the rear-end torque action and transfers this action through the transmission, motor, and motor mounts to the frame.

The Hotchkiss Drive Shaft. The Hotchkiss drive shaft (Figure 10-15) is a hollow steel tube with a universal or flexible joint attached to each end. The shaft is not encased in any cover, hence the term, *open drive shaft.* One universal joint, usually the front, is designed to compensate for changes of length in the drive shaft. Both universal joints are

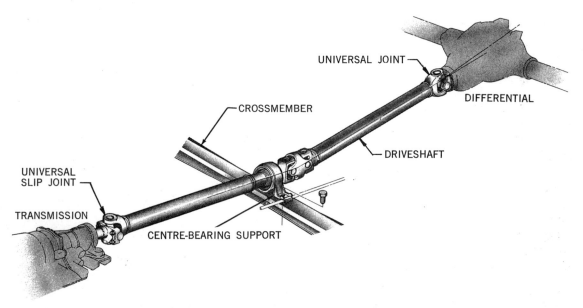

Fig. 10-16   Drive Shaft   General Motors Products of Canada, Limited

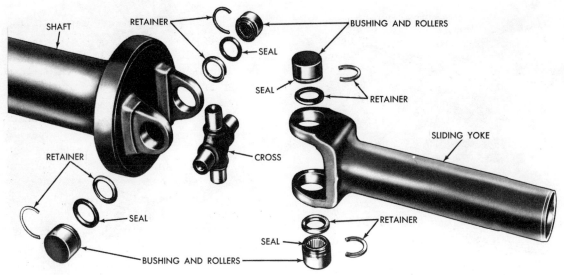

Fig. 10-17   Universal Joints

Chrysler Canada Ltd.

used to compensate for the changes in the drive-shaft angle as the wheel encounters irregularities in the road. This type of drive shaft is not designed to absorb any rear-end action. Instead, this action is transferred to the frame through the rear-spring front shackle and the rear springs.

Universal Joint.   A universal joint is basically a double-hinged joint (Figure 10-17). It consists of two yokes and a cross-shaped centre joint. The yokes are attached to the driving and driven units and are connected together by the centre joint. The drive is transferred from the first yoke to the cross-shaped piece or spider and then to the second yoke. Small roller bearings are usually placed between the arms or *trunions* of the spider and the yokes. These bearings not only transmit the drive, but also permit the yokes to turn freely on the spider as the joint rotates when the driving shaft is at a different angle to the driven shaft.

Universal slip joints   are universal joints in which one yoke is not rigidly attached to one

of the rotating members. Instead, it is attached to the shaft by means of a spline. A *spline* is like an internal and external gear set. The outside splines are cut on the shaft, whereas the internal splines are cut in the mating hollow section of the universal joint. The splines are cut long enough to permit the shaft to change its length as required by the spring action without coming out of mesh and stopping the rotating action. One end of the drive shaft, usually the transmission end, is always equipped with the slip-joint type of universal.

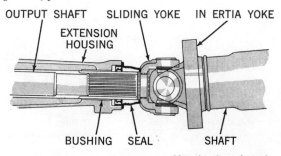

Chrysler Canada Ltd.

Fig. 10-18   Universal Slip Joint

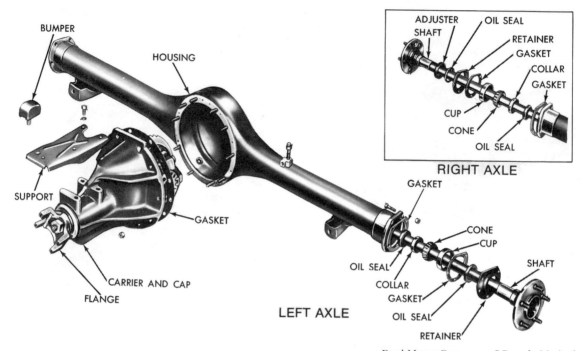

(A) SEPARATE CARRIER TYPE

(B) INTEGRAL CARRIER TYPE

Fig. 10-19   Rear Axle Assemblies

REAR AXLE ASSEMBLY

The rear axle assembly is made up of the axle housing, the axle shafts and bearings, and the differential. The assembly supports the rear of the car, transmits the propelling force to the rear wheels, and assists in transferring the reacting force (rear-end torque) to the frame. The final gear reduction takes place in the differential. The drive pinion (the smaller of the two gears) and the ring gear provide a gear ratio of from approximately 2.75 to 1 to 3.75 to 1.

The assembly will be divided into differential and rear axle sections for study purposes.

THE DIFFERENTIAL

If a car were to be driven in a straight line without having to make turns, then no differential would be necessary. However, when a car makes a turn, the outer wheel must travel farther than the inner wheel. If the drive shaft were geared rigidly to both rear wheels so that they had to rotate together, then one wheel would have to skid when the car was going around a turn. To prevent this condition, a *differential* (Figure 10-20) is installed between the two rear-axle shafts. The differential allows the wheels to rotate at different speeds when turns are made.

In the rear axle of the automobile, there are attached to the inner ends of the axles two small bevel bears known as differential or *side gears*. These two gears face each other and mesh with smaller bevel gears called *spider gears* or differential *pinion gears*. The spider gears are attached to a shaft mounted in the differential case. This case surrounds the spider and side gears and keeps the four gears in constant mesh. It is also attached to the *crown* or *ring gears,* which drive the assembly. The case is supported in the axle

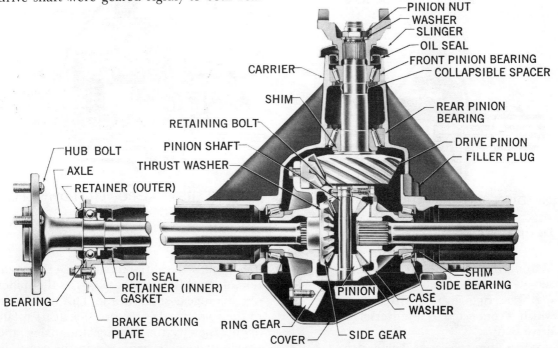

Fig. 10-20   Differential Assembly   General Motors Products of Canada, Limited

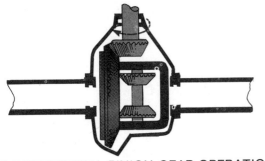

(A) DIFFERENTIAL PINION-GEAR OPERATION

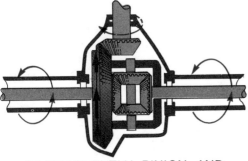

(B) DIFFERENTIAL PINION- AND
SIDE-GEAR OPERATION

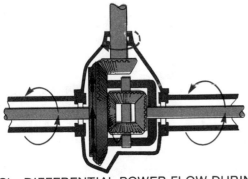

(C)   DIFFERENTIAL POWER FLOW DURING
STRAIGHT-AHEAD TRAVEL

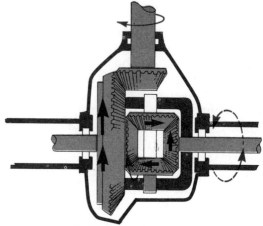

(D) DIFFERENTIAL POWER FLOW WITH
ONE WHEEL STATIONARY

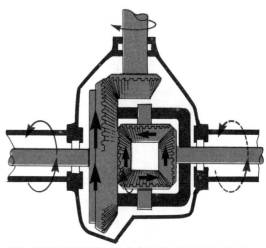

(E) DIFFERENTIAL POWER FLOW WHILE
CORNERING

Fig. 10-21   Differential Operation

housing by two bearings, to permit the assembly to rotate freely inside the axle housing. The ring gear is driven by a pinion, which is connected by a universal joint to the drive shaft.

When the vehicle is being driven in a straight line, the ring gear, driven by its pin-ion, rotates the differential case. The rotation of the differential case carries the spider or pinion-gear shaft with it. This movement of the spider makes the two side gears rotate about their axis, rotating the axles and wheels at equal speeds and in the same direction as the rotation of the differential case. When the vehicle is being driven in a straight line, the spider gears act only as a connection between the two rear axles.

When a vehicle turns a corner, the outside rear wheel must rotate faster than the inside one. Therefore, the side gears must rotate at different speeds. Since the differential case is rotated by the ring gear, and the spider gears no longer act as a solid connection between the two axle shafts, the spider gears must start to walk about the slower axle side gear and therefore rotate on their own axis. The other axle is forced to rotate at a speed equal to the sum of the speeds of the differential case and the spider gears. The action of the gears provides the difference in speed of the rear wheels and the necessary driving power.

LIMITED SLIP DIFFERENTIAL (POSI TRACTION)

This type of differential allows the wheels to rotate at different speeds when the vehicle rounds a curve. However, when the traction of one wheel is less than traction of the other and one wheel spins freely, as when the vehicle is stuck in snow or mud, the differential

locks up and transmits driving torque to the wheel having the greater traction.

The locking of the differential is accomplished by placing small multiple-disc clutches between the axle side gears and the differential case. One set of these clutch plates is attached to the axle and the other is attached to the differential case. These clutches slip when rounding a curve or transmit driving torque to the nonspinning wheel when the vehicle is stuck.

TYPES OF REAR AXLES

Axles may be divided into two types, the dead axle in which the axle is stationary and the wheel rotates, and the live axle in which both the axle shaft and the wheel rotate as a unit. The front wheels of an automobile are mounted on dead axles while the rear wheels are mounted on live axles. There are three types of live axles—*semi-floating, three-quarter floating,* and *full floating* (Figure 10-23). Each type is identified by the manner in which the outer end of the axle is supported in the axle housing. The inner ends of all axles are attached to the differential or side gears by means of a spline.

Semi-Floating Axle. This type is used in most automobiles. The outer or wheel end of the axle is supported in the axle housing by a single bearing mounted about six inches from the outer end of the axle. With this type of axle, the axle shaft not only transmits the driving torque, but also resists the bending moments caused by the forward motion of the car and the side thrusts imposed when the vehicle makes a turn. It must carry the entire weight (the force of gravity acting on vehicle mass) of the vehicle. As a result, a great stress is set up in the axle shaft of the semi-floating rear axle.

Three-Quarter Floating Axle. This type of axle is used on light trucks. In this type of axle, the single bearing used to support the outer end of the axle shaft is placed between the outside of the axle housing and the wheel

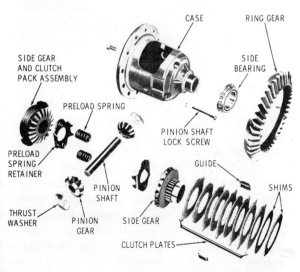

CASE   RING GEAR

SIDE GEAR AND CLUTCH PACK ASSEMBLY

SIDE BEARING

PRELOAD SPRING

PINION SHAFT LOCK SCREW

PRELOAD SPRING RETAINER

GUIDE

PINION SHAFT

SHIMS

THRUST WASHER

PINION GEAR

SIDE GEAR

CLUTCH PLATES

Chrysler Canada Ltd.

Fig. 10-22   Limited Slip Differential

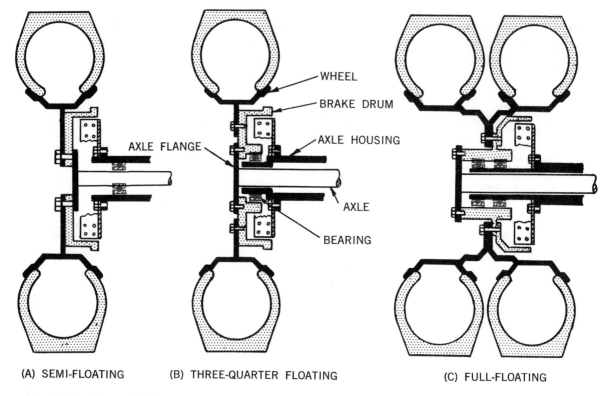

(A) SEMI-FLOATING   (B) THREE-QUARTER FLOATING   (C) FULL-FLOATING

WHEEL

BRAKE DRUM

AXLE HOUSING

AXLE FLANGE

AXLE

BEARING

Fig. 10-23   Rear Axle Types

hub. In this location, about 75% of the weight goes directly from the axle housing to the wheel; thus the axle shaft supports only about 25% of the vehicle's weight. However, it must still resist the bending moments of the vehicle's forward movement and the side thrusts when turns are made and transmit the driving torque. Because the shaft has been relieved of some of the vehicle's weight, heavier loads may be carried without the danger of axle breakage.

Full-Floating Axle.   The full-floating axle is used in all large trucks. In this type, two tapered roller bearings are used to support the outer end of the axle. These bearings are placed between the outside of the axle housing and the wheel hub, one on the inner and one on the outer edge of the hub. The wheel is mounted on the axle housing in a manner similar to the mounting of a wheel on a dead axle. The weight of the vehicle, the bending moment of the forward motion, and all side thrusts are transferred from the wheel directly to the axle housing through the tapered roller bearings. The axle shaft has only to transmit the driving torque to the wheels. Only on this type of axle arrangement may the axle shaft be removed without first jacking up the vehicle and removing the wheel. This is a convenient feature for the truck operator.

PRACTICAL ASSIGNMENTS

a. Remove and Replace a Clutch Assembly. Obtain the necessary manufacturer's overhaul instruction material.

Procedure:

1. Remove the transmission and linkage according to the manufacturer's instructions.
2. Disconnect the clutch linkage as instructed.
3. Remove the clutch assembly as instructed.
4. Locate the following clutch parts and identify as to type: (a) pressure plate (b) clutch disc (c) release bearing (d) clutch fork (e) clutch disc spline.
5. Replace the clutch assembly as instructed.
6. Have the instructor inspect your work.
7. Replace the transmission and linkage.
8. Connect the clutch pedal linkage.

b. Adjust Clutch Pedal Free Play. Obtain the manufacturer's adjustment instructions.

Procedure:

1. Adjust the clutch to the manufacturer's specifications according to instructions.
2. Have the instructor inspect your work.

c. Transmission Operation. Identify all the gears on a model or cut-away transmission. Be prepared to set the transmission gears in any one of the five possible gear selections and to trace the path of the power through each gear.

d. Disassemble and Assemble a Transmission. Obtain the manufacturer's overhaul instructions for operation.

Procedure:

1. Disassemble the transmission according to the manufacturer's instructions.
2. Identify all the gears and shafts. Be prepared to demonstrate the operation of the synchromesh unit.

3. Assemble the transmission according to manufacturer's instructions.
4. Have the instructor inspect your work.

e. Identification of Drive Shaft Types. In two or three automobiles, identify the type of drive shaft used on each. Report your information to the instructor.

f. Disassemble and Assemble a Semi-Floating Rear Axle, Removable Carrier Type.

NOTE: Be sure that the axle housing is supported by a suitable stand.

Procedure:

1. Remove the nuts holding the brake drum to the axle flange and remove the brake drum.
2. Remove the nuts securing the backing plate and the bearing-retainer plate to the axle housing. (See Figure 10-24.)

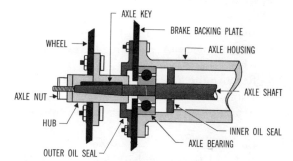

(A) TAPERED AXLE

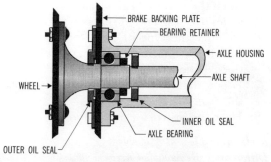

(B) FLANGED AXLE

Fig. 10-24 Methods of Attaching Wheels and Hubs

3. Using a suitable puller, pull the axle shaft from the housing. Be careful not to damage the oil seals when removing the axle shaft.
4. Install a nut to hold the backing plate in position.
5. Identify the type of axle and trace the path of weight transfer from the wheel to the axle housing.
6. Follow the reverse procedure to assemble the axle.
7. Have the instructor inspect your work.

g. Disassemble and Assemble a Full-Floating Rear Axle.
NOTE: Be sure that the axle housing is supported by a suitable stand.
Procedure:
1. Remove the nuts holding the axle flange to the wheel hub and remove the axle shaft.
2. Insert the correct size of socket wrench in the end of the axle housing to remove the wheel-bearing lock nut.
3. Remove the lock nut and plate.
4. Using the same wrench, remove the bearing-adjusting nut and tongue washer.
5. Loosen off the brake shoe adjustment and slide the brake drum and hub off the end of the axle housing. Be prepared to catch the outer wheel bearing as the hub slides over the end of the axle housing.
6. Identify the type of axle and trace the path of weight transfer from the wheel to the axle housing.
7. Follow the reverse procedure to assemble the axle.
8. Have the instructor inspect your work.

h. Disassemble and Assemble a Differential, Removable Carrier Type.
Procedure:
1. Place the differential housing in a vise. Mark the bearing-adjusting nuts and caps so that their relationship will be established.

2. Remove the adjusting lock nut, loosen the cap screws, and unscrew the adjusting nuts to relieve the bearing load.
3. Remove the bearing-cap screws and caps.
4. Lift out the differential case and ring-gear assembly.
5. Press out the pinion-gear shaft lock pin and take out the shaft. The gears will now come free.
6. Call the instructor and be prepared to identify all the parts.
7. Reassemble by reversing the procedure above.
8. Before installing the adjusting lock nuts, adjust the bearings for bearing preload. To adjust the bearing preload tension, leave the cap screws slightly loose. Set the left bearing-adjusting nut in approximately the correct position, as indicated by the marks on the adjusting nuts and caps as in step (a). Tighten the right nut with sufficient force to seat the bearing races. Tap the caps with a plastic hammer during this action to ensure alignment of the parts. The bearing tension is correct when there is a slight drag on the ring gear.
9. Check the *backlash* between the ring gear and its pinion after the bearing tension is adjusted. There should be approximately 0.3 mm free movement in the ring gear. If there is more than 0.3 mm movement, reduce the backlash by moving the differential case assembly to the right by backing out the right bearing-adjusting nut and turning in the left adjusting nut. Both nuts must be turned exactly the same amount in order to maintain the proper bearing tension. To increase the backlash, move the differential case to the left in the same manner.
10. Tighten securely the cap screws attaching the bearing caps, and install the adjusting nut locks.
11. Have the instructor inspect your work.

REVIEW QUESTIONS

1. What is the purpose of a clutch?
2. Explain how the pressure is released from the clutch disc when (a) a spring-type, (b) a diaphragm-type of pressure plate is used.
3. State the purpose of the (a) torsion, (b) cushion springs of the clutch disc.
4. What function do each of the following parts perform in the operation of the clutch: (a) the flywheel, (b) the clutch disc, (c) the pressure plate, (d) the release bearing, (e) the pedal and linkage?
5. List in order the parts that move when the driver presses his foot down on the clutch pedal.
6. When are fluid couplings or torque convertors used?
7. What is the main advantage of using a fluid coupling or torque convertor?
8. List two advantages of the torque convertor over the fluid coupling.
9. What is mechanical advantage?
10. How is torque increased through the use of gears?
11. What is the relationship between speed and torque when the input is the same?
12. Name the five basic machines used in automobiles and state where each is used.
13. What is a gear?
14. Describe a spiral-bevel gear.
15. Why are helical gears superior to spur gears?
16. Make a sketch of a planetary gear set and label all parts.
17. How are different gear ratios obtained through the use of a planetary gear set?
18. Determine the gear ratio for the first, second, and third gear of a transmission using the following gears: clutch gear 15 teeth, countershaft drive gear 30 teeth, countershaft low gear 16 teeth, second-speed gear 21 teeth, low-reverse sliding gear 29 teeth, countershaft second gear 24 teeth.
19. State the purpose and operation of a synchromesh unit.
20. State three reasons why a transmission is necessary.
21. How are the gears in the transmission arranged to obtain (a) neutral position, (b) reverse gear, (c) high gear?
22. What is the purpose of the reverse idler gear?
23. Make a sketch to illustrate the position of the gear-shift lever in each of the five gear-shift positions.
24. What is the main advantage of an automatic transmission?
25. How is the shifting of an automatic transmission controlled when the manual lever is in drive position?
26. What control does the driver have of an automatic transmission?
27. Give a definition of rear-end torque.
28. What is (a) a universal joint, (b) a slip joint?
29. Which type of drive requires two universal joints?
30. What absorbs rear-end torque in the (a) torque-tube type, (b) Hotchkiss type drive shaft?
31. What is the purpose of the differential?
32. Make a sketch of the differential assembly and label all parts.
33. What is the advantage of using hypoid gears in the differential?
34. Explain the difference in operation of the gears in the differential when driving straight ahead and when turning a corner.
35. One of the spider gears in a differential has two badly chipped teeth. When would the noise made by these damaged teeth be most noticeable to the driver?
36. Name and describe two basic types of axles.
37. Make a chart to show the different types of stress or loads that the axle shaft must support in each type of rear axle.

VEHICLE MAINTENANCE

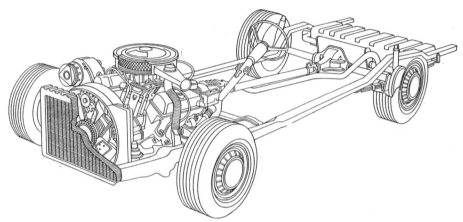

Protecting a vehicle against unsafe mechanical conditions, premature wear, and poor fuel economy are the reasons for establishing an efficient maintenance program. The establishing of a regular vehicle service program results in a saving of time and money and reduces the possibility of inconvenience due to mechanical failure. The best guide for the care and preventive maintenance of a vehicle is to follow the recommendations prescribed by the manufacturer as outlined in the owner's manual.

The service requirements for a vehicle can be divided into two general classifications: *preventive maintenance* and *periodic inspections and adjustments*.

PREVENTIVE MAINTENANCE

Preventive maintenance can be easily performed by the vehicle owner or by service station personnel when the vehicle is being refueled, and should include the following:

Gasoline. Buy only the grade of fuel recommended by the vehicle manufacturer. Using premium-grade fuel in a low compression engine does not improve performance or economy. Using regular-grade fuel in a high compression engine will cause "pinging," "carbon build-up," loss of power, and possible mechanical damage to the engine's moving parts. The use of other than unleaded gaso-

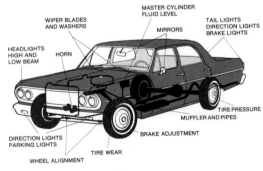

Fig. 11-1 Typical Safety Maintenance Checks

TIME OR DISTANCE TRAVELLED (USE INTERVAL WHICH OCCURS FIRST)

SERVICE	TIME	OR	6/4	12/8	20/12	26/16	30/18	32/20	38/24	45/28	50/32	60/36	64/40	70/44	76/48	84/52	88/54	90/56	96/60
Engine Oil — Change	every 3 months	OR	●	●	●	●		●	●	●	●	●	●	●	●	●		●	●
Engine Oil Filter — Change	every 2nd oil change	OR		●		●			●		●		●		●			●	
Manifold Heat Control Valve (6 cyl. only) — Apply Solvent	every 6 months (time interval only)																		
Carburetor Choke Shaft — Apply Solvent	every 6 months (time interval only)																		
Fast Idle Cam & Pivot Pin — Apply Solvent	every 6 months (time interval only)																		
Check Drive Belts — Adjust or replace if necessary	every 12 months	OR			●				●			●			●				●
Carburetor Air Filter — Clean (Replace every 2 years)	every 12 months	OR			●				●			●			●				●
Engine Idle Speed, Ignition Timing & Idle Mixture — Check & adjust as required	every 12 months	OR			●				●			●			●				●
PCV Valve — Check operation (Replace every 2 years or 40 000 km)	every 12 months	OR			●				●			●			●				●
Filter Element (in vapor storage canister) — Replace	every 12 months	OR			●				●			●			●				●
Crankcase Inlet Air Cleaner — Check	every 12 months	OR			●				●			●			●				●
Exhaust Gas Recirculation System — Check operation	every 12 months	OR			●				●			●			●				●
Spark Plugs - (Inspect Ignition Cables) — Replace	every 30 000 km (distance interval only)						●					●					●		
Orifice Spark Advance Control (OSAC) Valve — Inspect	every 24 months	OR							●						●				
Fuel Filter — replace	every 24 months	OR							●						●				
Choke — Check & adjust as required	every 24 months	OR							●						●				
Power Steering — check fluid level	every 3 months	OR	●	●	●	●		●	●	●	●	●	●	●	●	●		●	●
Tires — inspect for wear	every 3 months	OR	●	●	●	●		●	●	●	●	●	●	●	●	●		●	●
Tires — rotate	every 2nd oil change	OR		●		●			●		●		●		●			●	
Exhaust System — check for leaks, missing or damaged parts	every 6 months	OR		●		●			●		●		●		●			●	
Headlight aiming — check	every 6 months	OR		●		●			●		●		●		●			●	
Brake Master Cylinder, Transmission & Rear Axle — inspect fluid level	every 6 months	OR		●		●			●		●		●		●			●	
Brake & Power Steering Hoses — check for deterioration or leaks	every 6 months	OR		●		●			●		●		●		●			●	
Cooling System & Anti-Freeze — check	every 6 months	OR		●		●			●		●		●		●			●	
Air Conditioned Cars — check belts, sight glass & operation of controls	every 6 months	OR		●		●			●		●		●		●			●	
Suspension Ball Joints, Steering Linkage Pivots & Universal Joints — inspect seals	every 6 months	OR		●		●			●		●		●		●			●	
Body Mechanisms-hood, door & deck lid hinges, striker & latches — lubricate	every 6 months	OR		●		●			●		●		●		●			●	
Brake Linings — inspect	every 12 months	OR			●				●			●			●				●
Front Wheel Bearings — inspect	every 24 months★	OR							●						●				
Automatic Transmission — change fluid and filter (severe usage only)	every 40 000 km (distance interval only)								●						●				
Front Suspension Ball Joints & Tie Rod Ends — lubricate	every 3 years	OR										●							●

KILOMETRES IN THOUSANDS / MILEAGE IN THOUSANDS

NOTE: Refer to Vehicle Manufacturers Handbook for Service Intervals for your Vehicle.

Local driving conditions or special equipment such as high performance, heavy-duty, or trailer towing options may require special service recommendations.

★Inspect front wheel bearings whenever brake rotors are removed.

Fig. 11-2 Typical Maintenance Service Chart

line in vehicles equipped with catalytic-type mufflers will render the pollution-eliminating elements useless, thereby increasing air pollution.

Also, it is wise to keep the fuel tank above the one-quarter level to prevent water from condensing in the gasoline.

Oil. The engine oil level should be checked each time gasoline is purchased. Before checking the oil level, allow the engine to stand (not running) for a few minutes to allow all the oil being circulated through the engine to return to the oil pan. Add oil only when the oil dip stick indicates that the oil level is at or near the "add oil" mark. It is good policy to add only oil of the same type as is already in the engine.

Coolant. The maintaining of the proper coolant level in the radiator or reservoir tank is an important factor in maintaining proper engine operating temperatures. Should the level be low, check the cooling system for leaks, and repair as required. All modern vehicles require the use of an antifreeze solution all year round. Diluting the solution with water could reduce the effectiveness of the cooling system.

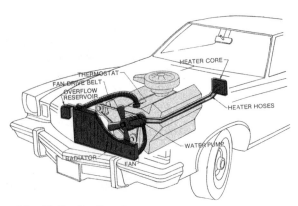

Fig. 11-3   Cooling System Components

Drive Belts. The condition of the fan, alternator, power-steering, and air-conditioner

drive belts should be checked regularly. Worn, frayed or cracked belts should be replaced. Loose belts should be properly adjusted so they will drive their units at the proper speed without slipping. See Figure 5-16, page 129.

Battery. The battery liquid level should be maintained properly to prevent serious damage and premature failure of the battery. If the battery uses excessive amounts of water, check it for leakage and check the charging circuit for too high a charging rate. See Figure 8-21, page 176.

Windshield Washer Liquid. Maintain sufficient liquid in the reservoir to assure washer operation when required.

Brake Master Cylinder. Maintain the proper liquid level in the reservoir. Add only the proper type of brake fluid as recommended by the manufacturer. If the level is down frequently, have the brake system checked for leaks and repaired immediately.

Power Steering and Automatic Transmission. Maintain the proper level in the reservoir, adding fluid only when the level reaches the "add oil" mark. Add only the recommended type of fluid.

Tires. Maintain the proper tire pressure according to manufacturer's specifications for tire size, load, and driving conditions. Tire pressures must be checked when the tires are cool, in order to get the proper pressure readings. Tire wear patterns and tread depth should be checked regularly. If the tread depth is less than 2 mm or the tread wear indicators are showing, (Figure 3-31) the tire should be replaced. If the front tires are indicating wear on the edges of the tread, the cause may be either excessive under-inflation, or that the front wheels need to be realigned (Figure 3-30). Excessive wear in the centre of the tread indicates over-inflation. Cupping in certain areas of the tread indicates defective shock absorbers.

Lights. Check all lights and signal systems for operation. Replace burnt-out bulbs and defective flashers immediately. Light bulbs can burn out at any time; check them frequently.

Windshield Wipers. Check wiper operation, and replace wiper blades that do not wipe the windshield clear or that leave streaks or smears.

PERIODIC INSPECTIONS AND ADJUSTMENTS

Periodic inspections and adjustments can be performed by the vehicle owner, but are usually more conveniently done by a qualified automotive serviceman. They are more complicated and frequently require the use of specialized tools and equipment. Some of the common service operations are listed below.

Engine Oil and Filter. Regular engine oil changes are required for proper engine operation. As a general rule the engine oil should be changed every three months or every 6000 km, whichever occurs first. Severe operating conditions, such as frequent use on dusty roads or in sandy areas, or a great deal of short-trip driving particularly in cold weather, may require more frequent oil changes. As a general rule, the oil filter cartridge should be changed with every second oil change.

Lubrication. Most modern vehicles have extended chassis and front suspension lubrication intervals. These intervals range up to 40 000 to 55 000 km. However, the suspension and steering joint seals should be inspected for damage or leakage every six months. Damaged seals can result in loss or contamination of the lubricant. Standard transmission and differential lubricant levels should be checked at least every six months and topped-up with the proper type of lubricant. Front-wheel bearings should be inspected and lubricated every 40 000 km. Light lubrication of the hinges and locks of doors, hood, and trunk every three months will help reduce rust, prevent seizing, and promote smooth operation.

Tires. Some manufacturers suggest that the tires should be rotated at least every 13 000 km or every second oil change, and should be in correct balance to obtain the most uniform tread wear. Tires should be inspected for cuts, cracks, and irregular tread wear at every oil change. If irregular tread wear has developed, the tires should be rotated (or replaced). Consult your service mechanic to determine the cause of irregular tread wear. Be sure to adjust tire pressures after rotating.

Engine Tune-up. An engine tune-up is a necessity, and it must cover all of the engine auxiliary systems to assure continued efficient and economical engine operation. For vehicles equipped with pollution-control systems, the efficient operation of those devices should be included in an engine tune-up.

Generally speaking, a complete engine tune-up should include the following: compression test; remove, inspect, and lubricate distributor; replace ignition points and condenser if necessary; set ignition timing; test ignition coil output; test fuel pump pressure

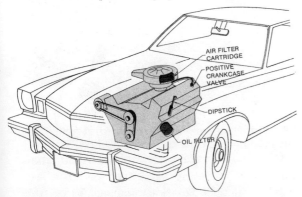

Fig. 11-4 Lubrication System Components

and volume; replace fuel filter(s); replace carburetor air filter element; test PCV system; adjust carburetor speed and mixture; check emission-control system; check heat-riser valve; test cooling system; test battery; check charging-circuit output; check cranking-motor current draw; check and adjust automatic transmission linkage; inspect the engine for oil leaks; road test for proper operation under all operating conditions.

All manufacturers include in the owner's manual a suggested maintenance chart. Figure 11-2 shows such a chart.

COMMON AUTOMOTIVE PROBLEMS

One of the most frustrating things that can confront a motorist is the sudden failure of his or her vehicle to operate or to operate properly. If the vehicle has been running fairly well before its sudden failure, the problem should not be too difficult to diagnose. The word "diagnose" is used instead of "repair," because you must find out what the problem is before it can be corrected. Once the problem has been diagnosed you can then decide whether you can repair it or whether it requires the services of a trained mechanic. The following are some of the more common problems that occur, along with probable symptoms and causes. As soon as trouble develops, the following items should be checked first: (a) Has the ignition key been turned off accidentally? (b) Is the fuel tank empty? (c) Is the cooling system overheated? Has the temperature indicator light lit up or is the temperature gauge reading hot? (d) Is the lubricating system working properly? Has the oil indicator light on the dash lit up?

PROBLEM A

The engine does not crank over or cranks slowly, or the starter just "clicks" or keeps "clicking" continuously.

Procedure:

1. Turn on the headlights. If the headlights burn brightly and stay fairly bright when the key is turned to the start position, proceed to step 2.

If the headlights are dim or go dim while cranking, then the battery is in a low state of charge or is discharged, or one of the battery cables is loose or corroded. Check both ends of the battery cables, and clean and tighten them as required. If the battery cables are clean and tight, then "jump" the battery with

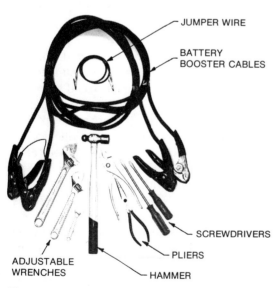

Fig. 11-5   Typical Emergency Tool Kit

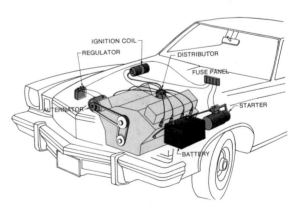

Fig. 11-6   Engine Electrical Components

Fig. 11-7   Temporary Tightening for a Battery Connection

(A) GENERAL MOTORS AND CHRYSLER

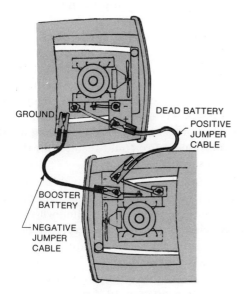

GROUND

DEAD BATTERY

POSITIVE JUMPER CABLE

BOOSTER BATTERY

NEGATIVE JUMPER CABLE

Fig. 11-8   Starting a Vehicle with Jumper Cables

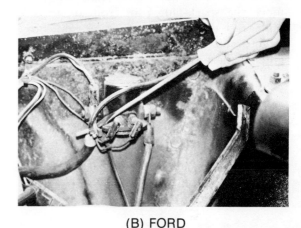

(B) FORD

Fig. 11-9   Jumping the Starter Solenoid

a booster battery and cables to start the engine. If the starter still just clicks or does not crank the engine properly when the battery is jumped, the problem is probably a defective starter motor or starter solenoid switch.

2. If the headlights burn brightly and stay bright when the key is turned to the "start" position, but the cranking motor does not operate, probably the electrical circuit be-

tween the starter switch and the starting motor solenoid has not been completed. If the vehicle is equipped with a seat-belt-ignition interlock system, check for unfastened seat belts or a package on the passenger's seat. Check for a faulty or improperly adjusted transmission neutral safety switch by moving the transmission selector to "N" or "P" (automatic transmissions), depress the clutch pedal (standard transmissions), and move the shift lever back and forth while holding the ignition switch in the start position. If the engine does not crank, probably the ignition switch is defective. Place the transmission in neutral and the ignition switch in the "on" position and bypass the ignition switch by jumping the starter solenoid (see Figure 11-9). If the engine cranks, the ignition switch or wiring to the solenoid is defective. Failure to crank indicates a defective starter solenoid or cranking motor.

PROBLEM B

The engine cranks over at normal speed but will not start.
Procedure:
1. To check for a spark at the spark plug: Remove the spark-plug wire from one spark plug, rest the bare end about 5 mm away from a suitable ground, and crank the engine. If there is a healthy spark, proceed to problem C.

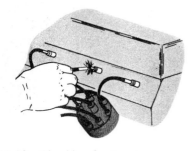

Fig. 11-10   Checking for Spark

2. If no spark can be seen, remove the high-tension-coil wire from the centre of the distributor cap, rest the bare end 5 mm from a suitable ground, and crank the engine. If there is no spark, proceed to step 3.

If there is a healthy spark, the problem is most likely in the distributor cap or rotor, since it is most unlikely that all spark-plug wires would become defective simultaneously. Remove the distributor cap, position the ignition-coil high-tension lead about 5 mm away from the centre of the rotor, and crank the engine. If a spark jumps to the rotor, the rotor is grounded to the distributor shaft and must be cleaned or replaced.

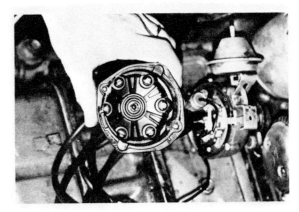

Fig. 11-11   Checking Distributor Rotor and Cap

If a spark does not jump to the rotor, wipe the rotor and distributor cap dry of any moisture and clean thoroughly. Replace the coil high-tension lead into the centre tower of the distributor cap, and crank the engine. A spark should not be seen. If a spark jumps to one or more spark-plug towers, check carefully for small cracks in the distributor cap.
Note: Do not use gasoline as a cleaning agent; an explosion or fire could result after the engine has started.

3. If no spark was seen when the high-tension-coil wire was placed 5 mm from ground and the engine was cranked, then with the ignition switch on, check for current to the positive (+) side of the coil by quickly *arcing* a jumper wire between the + terminal of the coil and a suitable ground. If there is no spark, there is no current. Proceed to step 4. If there is a spark, there is current available at the ignition coil. Therefore, remove the distributor cap and check to see if the ignition points are opening and closing. Crank the engine until the point rubbing block is adjacent to the lobe of the cam; then, by hand, rotate the rotor back and forth to see if the points open and close.

If the points do not open and close, make a temporary point adjustment so that they open wide enough to break the circuit and close tight enough to complete the circuit.

If the points do open and close, check for a small arc each time the points open. If no arc is seen, clean the points with a small point file. If an arc is seen, probably the condenser or ignition coil is defective.

4. If no spark is seen when a jumper is arced between the + terminal of the coil and ground with the ignition switch on, the probable cause is a defective ignition switch, ballast resistor, or wiring. With the ignition switch on, bypass the ignition switch and resistor by "hot-wiring" with a jumper wire between the + terminal of the ignition coil and the positive terminal of the battery. If the engine now starts, have the circuit checked.

Note: Make sure the ignition switch is on before hot-wiring, and make sure the hot-wire is removed before turning off the ignition switch. Some vehicles have an anti-theft circuit which causes the ignition switch to short to ground when the switch is in the off position and the ignition circuit is hot-wired. This will prevent ignition circuit operation.

PROBLEM C

The engine cranks at normal speed but will not start and has a strong smell of gasoline.

Procedure:

1. If a suitable spark is seen at the spark plug when the engine is cranked, turn off the ignition. Remove the carburetor air cleaner, hold the choke butterfly valve open, and look down the primary throats of the carburetor to see if fuel squirts out of the accelerator discharge jets when the throttle linkage is stroked. If no fuel is seen, proceed to problem D.

If fuel squirts from these jets (or jet) the engine is probably "flooded" (too much gasoline resulting in an over-rich mixture). A flooded carburetor will be "soaking wet" with gasoline inside and/or on top. A strong gasoline odour

(A) REMOVING AIR CLEANER

(B) OPENING CHOKE

Fig. 11-12   Checking Fuel at the Carburetor

should also be noticeable under the engine hood.

If the engine is flooded, check to see if gasoline flows out of the carburetor bowl vents when the engine is cranked. If no gasoline flows from the vents during cranking, assume that the engine is merely flooded, replace the air filter, wait 5 to 10 minutes, and attempt to start the engine with the accelerator pedal held to the floor (do not pump it).

If fuel flows from the carburetor bowl vents during cranking, the carburetor needle and seat are most likely being held open by a piece of dirt or a foreign particle. Frequently, tapping the carburetor at its fuel inlet with a hammer or screwdriver handle will dislodge the particle and allow the needle to seat properly. Otherwise, the carburetor will have to be overhauled. If the flow of fuel from the vents ceases after tapping, replace the air cleaner and attempt to start the engine in the same manner as for a flooded carburetor.

PROBLEM D

The engine cranks over at normal speed and has good spark and no gasoline odour, and the fuel gauge indicates fuel in the tank.
Procedure:

1. Remove the air cleaner, hold the choke valve open, and look down the carburetor.

2. If gasoline does not squirt from the accelerator pump nozzles when you stroke the throttle linkage, make sure the linkage to the accelerator pump is properly connected. If it is, there is probably no fuel in the carburetor. Remove the fuel line from the carburetor and check for gasoline flow by cranking the engine. If gasoline does not flow, proceed to step 3.

If fuel does flow, the problem is in the carburetor. If the vehicle is equipped with a fuel filter located in the fuel inlet, remove the filter, reconnect the fuel line, crank the engine for 5 to 10 seconds, and recheck for fuel discharge at the accelerator pump nozzles. If they now squirt fuel, start the engine and replace the fuel filter later.

If no fuel flows after you remove the filter, it is possible that the needle and seat valve have stuck shut. Tap the carburetor at the fuel inlet with a hammer or screwdriver handle to jar them loose, crank the engine, and recheck for fuel at the accelerator pump nozzles. If fuel now squirts from the nozzles, attempt to start the engine in the normal manner. If no fuel flows from the nozzles, the carburetor requires overhauling.

3. If fuel does not flow from the discon-

Fig. 11-13   Checking Fuel Filter

nected fuel line while the engine is cranked, and the vehicle is not out of gasoline and is equipped with an in-line fuel filter (located between the fuel pump and carburetor), remove the filter or its element and crank the engine. If fuel flows, reconnect the fuel line to the carburetor and attempt to start the engine in a normal manner. If fuel does not flow, probably the fuel pump is defective, or the fuel line is broken or plugged.

PROBLEM E

The engine cranks at normal speed but will not start during wet weather.
Procedure:

1. **Turn off ignition.**

2. Using a clean, dry cloth, dry off all the ignition wires. Examine the wires for damaged insulation.

3. Dry off the tops of the spark plugs, the top of the ignition coil, and the distributor-cap towers.

4. Remove the distributor cap and dry off the inside surfaces. Replace cap.

5. Make sure all the wires are securely reattached before trying to start the engine.

PROBLEM F

The engine stops while driving, and can be restarted once or twice but runs for only a short period each time it is restarted.
Procedure:

1. Check the fuel gauge. The engine is probably out of gasoline. If so, add gasoline and crank engine. It may take approximately one minute or more for the fuel pump to deliver fuel to the engine. Do not operate the starter for more than 30 seconds at one time. Allow approximately two minutes for the starter to cool down; then crank the engine again. Repeat this procedure until the engine starts.

2. If the fuel gauge indicates that there is fuel in the tank then follow the procedure as outlined in problem D.

PROBLEM G

The engine stops suddenly while driving and cannot be restarted, yet it cranks over at normal speed.
Procedure:

1. Follow the procedure as outlined for problem B.

PROBLEM H

The engine stalls frequently during the warm-up period in cool, damp weather.
Procedure:

1. On a vehicle equipped with a heat-riser valve located in the exhaust manifold or exhaust pipe, check for freeness of operation. The valve should move back and forth easily.

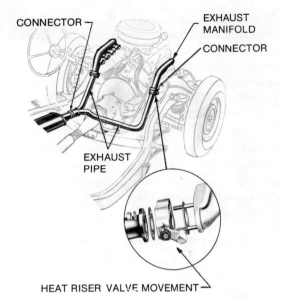

Fig. 11-14   Checking Heat-riser Valve

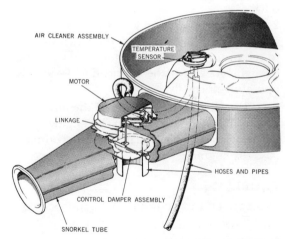

General Motors Products of Canada, Limited

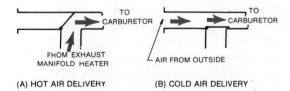

Fig. 11-15   Checking Thermostatically Controlled Air Cleaner

2. On vehicles equipped with a thermostatically controlled air cleaner, check the operation of the air direction valve. Make sure that the hose between the exhaust manifold stove and the air cleaner is in good condition and properly connected. Make sure that the vacuum hoses which operate the control valve are in good condition and properly attached.

3. Additional protection against warm-up stalling in cold weather can be obtained by adding a container of fuel system de-icer fluid to the gasoline tank several times during the winter months.

PROBLEM I

The oil indicator light lights up or flickers on and off while driving.
Procedure:

1. Stop the engine as quickly as safety permits.

2. Check the engine oil level on the dip stick. If the level is low, add oil to fill the crankcase to the proper level. Restart the engine; if the oil light goes out, the lubrication system is operating normally.

3. If the oil level is normal and the indicator light remains on, do not run the engine until the problem has been diagnosed or you may ruin the engine.

PROBLEM J

The temperature indicator light comes on or the temperature gauge registers hot.
Procedure:

1. If the air conditioning unit is being used, shut it off.

2. Regardless of the outside temperature, turn on the heater fan and adjust the heat to the highest possible setting. This adds additional cooling area to the cooling system.

3. If the engine temperature does not decrease within two or three minutes, turn off the engine as quickly as safety permits and open the engine hood.

4. Do not remove the radiator cap until a half-hour after the radiator has stopped steaming, as serious injury from the boiling liquid could result.

5. When the engine has cooled down, add water to bring the cooling system to the proper level. Inspect the cooling system for leaks, and the fan belt for condition and tightness. If the cooling level and the belt are in satisfactory condition, the thermostat could be defective and require replacement.

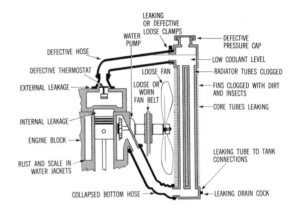

Fig. 11-16   Potential Cooling System Problems

PROBLEM K

The horn sticks and blows continuously.
Procedure:

1. Disconnect the horn wires. (The horn relay has stuck.) It is good policy to be prepared for this problem by learning ahead of time the location of the horn relay control and how to disconnect the horn wires.

PROBLEM L

Brake indicator light lights up.

Procedure:

1. Check to make sure that the emergency brake is completely released.

2. If the light remains lit, one section of the

braking system has failed. The vehicle can still be stopped, but it requires a greater braking distance.

3. Proceed cautiously to an automotive service facility and have the trouble repaired.

PROBLEM M

The brakes fail or pull to one side after driving through water.

Procedure:

1. Reduce speed, and while still moving apply the brakes lightly to dry out the brake mechanism.

PROBLEM N

The power brakes become hard to apply.

Procedure:

1. The vehicle can still be stopped by applying extra pressure to the brake pedal.

2. Check to make sure that all the vacuum hoses between the engine and the power brake unit are attached and in good condition.

3. If the hoses are attached and in good condition, the power unit is defective and requires servicing by a certified automotive mechanic.

PROBLEM O

The power steering becomes hard to steer.

Procedure:

1. The vehicle can still be steered by applying extra effort to the steering wheel.

2. Check the power steering reservoir level, and if it is low, top it up with the proper type of fluid.

3. Check the drive belt for condition and proper tension. Replace or adjust the belt as required.

4. If the drive belt and fluid level are satisfactory, the power steering unit requires repairs by a certified automotive serviceman.

PROBLEM P

The vehicle starts pulling to one side or starts to sway from side to side.

Procedure:

1. Bring the vehicle to a stop as quickly as safety permits.

2. Check all the tires for proper inflation.

3. If a flat tire has developed, never drive the vehicle any further than is necessary to reach a safe place to change the tire.

4. It is good policy to practise the use of the car jack and change a tire in your driveway before it becomes a necessity on the road.

REVIEW QUESTIONS

1. Define the term "preventive maintenance."
2. What factors determine the grade of gasoline you should purchase?
3. List 10 units of an automobile that should be checked each time the vehicle is refueled.
4. List four periodic inspections and state the distance interval when each should be performed.
5. List five checks that should be made first if sudden failure of an engine occurs.
6. How can a "flooded" engine be started?
7. What should a driver do if the oil indicator light lights up or flickers on and off?
8. How is the oil level in the engine checked?
9. What should a driver do if the brake indicator light lights up?
10. What is the most common cause of a vehicle pulling to one side or swaying from side to side?

CONVERSION TABLES

Quantity	Metric Unit	Symbol	Metric to Inch-Pound Unit	Inch-Pound to Metric Unit
Length	millimetre centimetre metre kilometre	mm cm m km	1 mm = 0.0394 in. 1 cm = 0.394 in. 1 m = 3.28 ft. 1 km = 0.62 mile	1 in. = 25.4 mm 1 in. = 2.54 cm 1 ft. = 30.5 cm 1 yd. = 0.914 m 1 mile = 1.61 km
Area	square millimetre square centimetre square metre	mm^2 cm^2 m^2	1 cm^2 = 0.155 sq. in. 1 m^2 = 10.8 sq. ft.	1 sq. in. = 6.45 cm^2 1 sq. ft. = 929 cm^2 1 sq. yd. = 0.836 m^2
Mass	milligram gram kilogram tonne	mg g kg t	 1 g = 0.035 oz. 1 kg = 2.2 lb. 1 t = 2200 lb.	1 oz. = 28.3 g 1 lb. = 454 g 100 lb. = 45.36 kg 1 short ton (2000 lb.) = 0.907 t
Volume	cubic centimetre cubic metre millilitre litre	cm^3 m^3 m ℓ	1 cm^3 = 0.061 cu. in. 1 m^3 = 35.3 cu. ft. 1 mℓ = 0.035 fl. oz. 1 ℓ = 1.76 pts. 1 ℓ = 0.88 qt. 1 ℓ = 0.22 gal. 1 kℓ = 220 gal.	1 cu. in. = 16.387 cm^3 1 cu. ft. = 0.028 m^3 1 cu. yd. = 0.756 m^3 1 fl. oz. = 28.4 mℓ 1 pt. = 0.568 ℓ 1 qt. = 1.136 ℓ 1 gal. = 4.546 ℓ
Temperature	Celsius degree	°C	$°C = \dfrac{5}{9}(°F-32)$	$°F = \dfrac{9 \times °C}{5} + 32$
Force	newton kilonewton	N kN	1 N = 0.225 lb. (f)	1 lb. (f) = 4.45 N
Energy/Work	joule kilojoule megajoule	J kJ MJ	1 J = 0.737 ft. lb. 1 J = 0.948 Btu 1 MJ = 0.278 kW.h	1 ft. lb. = 1.355 J 1 Btu = 1.055 J 1 kW.h = 3.6 MJ

Quantity	Metric Unit	Symbol	Metric to Inch-Pound Unit	Inch-Pound to Metric Unit
Power	kilowatt	kW	1 kW = 1.34 hp 1 W = 0.0226 ft. lb./min.	1 hp (550 ft. lb./s) = 0.746 kW 1 ft. lb./min. = 44.2537 W
Pressure	kilopascal	kPa	1 kPa = 0.145 psi	1 psi = 6.894 kPa 14.7 psi = 101.325 kPa (100 kPa approx) = 1 standard atmosphere
	*kilogram per square centimetre	kg/cm²	1 kg/cm² = 13.780 psi	1 psi = 0.072 kg/cm²
Vacuum	kilopascal	kPa	In SI, vacuum is indicated by numbers below 100 kPa, which is standard atmospheric pressure at sea level. In inch-pound systems, vacuum is measured in inches of vacuum, while pressure above atmospheric pressure is measured in pounds per square inch. 1 in. vac. = 0.46 psi = 3.17 kPa 1 in. vac. = 100 kPa — 3.17 kPa = 96.83 kPa 10 in. vac. = 100 kPa — 31.7 kPa = 68.30 kPa	
Torque	newton metre *kilogram metre *kilogram per centimetre	N.m kg/m kg/cm	1 N.m = 0.74 lb. ft. 1 kg/m = 7.24 lb. ft. 1 kg/cm = 0.86 lb. in.	1 lb. ft. = 1.36 N.m 1 lb. ft. = 0.14 kg/m 1 lb. in. = 1.2 kg/cm
Speed/Velocity	metres per second kilometres per hour	m/s km/h	1 m/s = 3.28 ft./sec. 1 km/h = 0.62 mph	1 ft./s = 0.305 m/s 1 mph = 1.61 km/h

*Not SI units, but included here because they are employed on some of the gauges and indicators currently in use in industry.

INDEX